An Introduction to the Philosophy of Religion

BRIAN DAVIES

Oxford · New York

OXFORD UNIVERSITY PRESS

Oxford University Press, Walton Street, Oxford OX2 6DP

Oxford New York
Athens Auckland Bangkok Bombay
Calcutta Cape Town Dar es Salaam Delhi
Florence Hong Kong Istanbul Karachi
Kuala Lumpur Madras Madrid Melbourne
Mexico City Nairobi Paris Singapore
Taipei Tokyo Toronto

and associated companies in
Berlin Ibadan

Oxford is a trade mark of Oxford University Press

First published 1982 as an Oxford University Press paperback
and simultaneously in a hardback edition
This new edition first published 1993 as an Oxford University Press paperback
and simultaneously in a hardback edition

British Library Cataloguing in Publication Data
Data available

Library of Congress Cataloging in Publication Data
Davies, Brian.
An introduction to the philosophy of religion / Brian Davies p. cm.
Includes bibliographical references and index.
1. Religion—Philosophy. I. Title.
200'.1—dc20 BL51.D363 1993 92-18488
ISBN 0-19-289235-5 Pbk
ISBN 0-19-219253-1

5 7 9 10 8 6

Printed in Great Britain by
Biddles Ltd
Guildford and King's Lynn

For Peter Geach, Elizabeth Anscombe,
Gareth Moore, and James Sadowsky

Acknowledgements

A number of people have been kind enough to comment on material which has found its way into this book. In particular, I must thank Elizabeth Anscombe, Peter Geach, Paul Helm, Herbert McCabe, OP, Hugo Meynell, Alan Ryan, James Sadowsky, SJ, Stephen Salter, Richard Swinburne, Simon Tugwell, OP, K. V. Wilkes, Christopher Williams, and Mark Wynn. None of these people should be taken as agreeing with the content of the book as it stands. But I think that they have helped me to make it a better text than it would have been without their advice. My thanks also go to Jean van Altena for her excellent work as copy-editor of the book.

Blackfriars
Oxford

Contents

Introduction

I⊤ is difficult to say what the philosophy of religion is. One might define it as 'philosophizing about religion'. But people disagree about the nature of philosophy and religion, so this definition has its drawbacks. Philosophy of religion is now a very flourishing branch of philosophy. Thirty years or so ago, specialists in philosophy of religion were a rare breed. But they are now very common, and they publish a lot. Many of them would describe themselves as philosophers of religion. Yet it would be rash to conclude from this that we can easily define 'the philosophy of religion'. It is not, for example, a discipline distinguishable from others as chemistry is from needlework.

In this book I do not attempt the perilous task of defining 'philosophy of religion'. My intention is to offer an introductory look at some of the topics traditionally thought to fall within its scope. The most prominent of these is the existence of God, so much of what follows is devoted to that issue and to matters which arise in connection with it. I also consider the relationship between morality and religion, the concept of miracle, and the notion of life after death.

It is inevitable that my own views will become clear as the book proceeds, for it is hard to discuss any philosophical issue without taking sides, or seeming to do so. But I have tried to write so as to help readers take up some sides for themselves. I have also tried to write on the assumption that readers have little or no philosophical background. This book is therefore a basic introduction for those who are approaching the philosophy of religion for the first time. Its bibliography will, I hope, allow them to take matters further.

A great deal more than I discuss could be brought in under the heading of philosophy of religion. There are, for example, matters arising from the comparative study of religion and from various beliefs peculiar to specific religions. But a complete treatise on the philosophy of religion would be long and complicated, and space is limited in an introduction. In any case, one has to start somewhere.

What follows is a very heavily revised version of a text published by Oxford University Press in 1982. I was asked to provide a second edition of that text, but I have effectively ended up writing a new book, though chunks of the old one remain. I am grateful to Catherine Clarke and Oxford University Press for inviting me to provide this revised edition and for patience in waiting for the finished product. The 1982 text was dedicated to my teachers Dan Williams, Illtyd Trethowan, and Simon Tugwell. The dedication was appropriate at the time, but the new one reflects the help and support which I have received since then.

I

Philosophy and Religious Belief

WHAT should be the role of philosophy with respect to religious belief? The question is hard to answer since people have different ideas as to what constitutes philosophy and religion. A traditional answer, however, is that philosophy can help us to see whether or not religious beliefs are worthy of acceptance.[1] The idea here is that philosophers can single out particular religious beliefs and ask questions like 'Is this belief rationally defensible?' or 'Can this belief be supported by argument or appeal to evidence?' Lying behind such questions is the assumption that religious beliefs are either true or false and that their truth or falsity can be settled or discussed at an intellectual level.

Is this assumption right? Much of what follows is concerned with arguments for the existence of God, so it is worth noting at the outset that, at least with respect to belief in God, many have urged that the assumption is mistaken. Why? One answer which has been given is that belief in God is *neither* true nor false since 'God exists' or 'There is a God' are not meaningful statements and are therefore incapable of being defended or refuted. Another answer given is that, though 'God exists' or 'There is a God' are perfectly meaningful, those who believe in God have no need to show that their belief can be justified at the bar of reason. To start our explorations in the philosophy of religion, let us therefore begin by looking at these positions.

Verification and God

One can begin to understand the first position by noting the work of a famous group of philosophers who, in the 1920s, began to gather in Vienna around a writer called Moritz

Schlick (1882–1936). The group became known as the Vienna Circle, and it included Otto Neurath (1882–1945), Friedrich Waismann (1896–1959), and Rudolf Carnap (1891–1970). These men were influenced by Ludwig Wittgenstein (1889–1951), from whom they claimed to derive a theory of meaning known as the verification principle. From this they drew drastic and far-reaching conclusions.

They held that meaningful statements fall into two groups. First, there are mathematical statements (e.g. 2 + 2 = 4), tautologies (e.g. 'All cats are cats'), and logically necessary statements (e.g. 'Not both P and not-P'). Second, there are factual statements which can be confirmed through the use of the senses, especially through the methods used in sciences like physics, chemistry, and biology. In this way the Vienna Circle tried to locate sense and meaning along with experience. And in doing so, it stood in a well-known philosophical tradition. Effectively, it was agreeing with the Scottish philosopher David Hume (1711–76). 'If', says Hume, 'we take in our hand any volume; of divinity or school metaphysics, for instance, let us ask, *Does it contain any abstract reasoning concerning quantity or number?* No. *Does it contain any experimental reasoning concerning matter of fact and existence?* No. Commit it then to the flames: for it can contain nothing but sophistry and illusion.'[2]

The verification principle became the most distinctive doctrine of logical positivism, which is what the school of thinking represented and influenced by the Vienna Circle came to be called. But the principle was not always stated in the same way. Some early formulations take it as a principle about 'propositions'. Later ones refer to 'statements' and 'sentences'. A distinction was also made between what has been called the 'weak' and the 'strong' version of the verification principle. The weak version became the most popular. It held that (forgetting about mathematical statements, tautologies, and truths of logic) a statement is factual and meaningful only if sense experience can go at least some way to confirming it. But in the early days of logical positivism it was the strong version of the verification principle that was in vogue. Waismann stated it thus: 'Anyone uttering a sentence must know under what conditions he calls it true and under what conditions he calls it false. If he is unable to state these conditions, he does not know what he has said. A statement which cannot be conclusively verified cannot be verified at all. It is simply devoid of any meaning.'[3]

The history of the verification principle is too complicated to follow in detail here. But we can note that all its proponents held that the principle's implications were devastating for belief in God. Take, for example, Carnap. 'In its metaphysical use', he observes, 'the word "God" refers to something beyond experience. The word is deliberately divested of its reference to a physical being or to a spiritual being that is immanent in the physical. And as it is not given a new meaning, it becomes meaningless.'[4] Another illustration of logical positivist methods of dealing with the existence of God can be found in A. J. Ayer's book *Language, Truth and Logic*. 'The term "god" ', says Ayer,

is a metaphysical term. And if 'god' is a metaphysical term, then it cannot even be probable that a god exists. For to say that 'God exists' is to make a metaphysical utterance which cannot be either true or false. And by the same criterion, no sentence which purports to describe the nature of a transcendent god can possess any literal significance.[5]

Note that Ayer is not just denying the existence of God in this passage: he is dismissing the question of God's existence altogether. His position, and that of Carnap, is that, since we cannot get to God by means of empirical research, it is meaningless to say that there is a God. The argument is: (1) If we cannot verify the existence of God empirically, it is meaningless to say that there is a God; (2) We cannot verify the existence of God empirically; (3) So it is meaningless to say that there is a God.

Falsification and God

At this point some thinking related to that just noted ought briefly to be mentioned. Here one can introduce the name of Antony Flew, with whom the emphasis changes from verification to falsification. According to the verification principle, religious statements, including 'There is a God', are meaningless simply because it is not possible to verify them. Flew does not support the principle in this form, but in 'Theology and Falsification'[6] he asks whether certain religious statements might not be suspect because no sense experience counts against them.

Flew begins by relating what he calls a 'parable'.[7] Two explorers come upon a clearing in the jungle. The first explorer maintains that there is an invisible gardener who looks after it. The second denies this suggestion. Various tests (such as keeping watch, using bloodhounds and electric fences) are applied to check whether there is a gardener. All the tests fail to show the gardener's presence, but the first man continues to believe in the gardener's existence. He says, 'But there is a gardener who has no scent and makes no sound, a gardener who comes secretly to look after the garden which he loves.'[8] The second man rejects this move and suggests that there is no difference between the first man's gardener and no gardener at all.

At this point Flew applies his parable to religious statements. Religious believers make claims. They say, for instance, that there is a God who loves human beings. But apparently they are unwilling to allow anything to count against these claims. The claims seem unfalsifiable. Are they, then, genuine claims? Flew does not dogmatically declare that they cannot be, but he evidently has his doubts. 'Sophisticated religious people', he says, 'tend to refuse to allow, not merely that anything actually does occur, but that anything conceivably could occur, which would count against their theological assertions and explanations. But in so far as they do this their supposed explanations are actually bogus, and their seeming assertions are really vacuous.'[9] Flew does not talk in this passage about falsification by sense experience, but it seems reasonable to suppose that this is what he has in mind. The tests which he mentions for checking the gardener's presence could all be called 'sensory'. And from Flew's example of the gardener it should be fairly clear that, in raising the issue of falsification, he has the question of God's existence pretty much in mind. He seems to be suggesting that those who believe in God are unwilling to allow any sense experience to count against their belief, and he seems to be wondering whether this does not render it unintelligible or lacking in content.

Verification, Falsification, and God

What, then, shall we say at this point? Is the statement that there is a God meaningless because it is unverifiable or unfalsifiable?

Writers such as Carnap, Ayer, and Flew surely have one strong point in their favour. This is that we often regard verification and falsification as ways of distinguishing sense from nonsense. If I say that my dog is a brilliant philosopher, you will rightly doubt whether I am talking any sense at all until I point to something about the dog's behaviour that might give some sort of (funny) meaning to my assertion. And you would be justly and similarly sceptical if (a) I say on Tuesday that it will rain on Wednesday, (b) by Thursday it has not rained, and (c) on Thursday I insist that I was right on Tuesday.

Another point which may be made in favour of what Carnap, Ayer, and Flew say might be put in the form of the slogan 'God-talk seems *prima facie* puzzling'. By this I mean that many things said about God just do strike people as obscure or even unintelligible. Nobody with a basic command of English will have problems in making sense of sentences like 'There are elephants in Africa' or 'The British Prime Minister has just called a general election'. But many people will be puzzled by sentences like 'God is transcendent' or 'God is immanent'. It is, of course, true that there are perfectly intelligible statements which few can understand. Such is the case with, for example, various statements accepted by physicists and other scientific specialists. But talk about God is not just employed by some select band of experts. It is usually presented as something of importance to everyone, and it is found on the lips of all sorts of people. And it is a fact that many who are presented with it find themselves simply at sea. They do not appear to be able to make sense of it. One might say that they are lacking imagination, or something like that. But to imagine something is to be able to form a picture of it. And God is not supposed to be picturable.

Yet it is one thing to accept these points and another to agree that the writers so far introduced in this chapter have done anything to establish that there could not be a God. And when we critically examine what they do say, it soon becomes clear that they have not done this.

To begin with, we may challenge a premiss which the writers we have just been noting seem to embrace. They seem to think that we can only ask whether God exists when we have settled the question 'Is God's existence possible?' And that is a view which we may reasonably reject. Why? Because it depends on the unreasonable assumption that a thesis must be shown to be possibly true before we can discuss whether it is actually true. As modern logicians know very well, proving that a thesis is possibly true may be very difficult apart from a study of reasons for believing that the thesis in question is actually true. And proof that a thesis is actually true is proof that the thesis is possibly true. One may therefore consider someone's reasons for believing a thesis without worrying in advance about whether the thesis could possibly be true. And this suggests that one may consider someone's reasons for believing that God exists without worrying in advance about whether or not there could be a God.

In reply to this argument someone may insist that a statement is only meaningful and factual if it is conclusively verifiable or falsifiable by means of sense experience. But that is another unreasonable assumption. For it seems possible to make intelligible and factual universal statements like 'All people spend part of their lives asleep' or 'All cats are mortal'. The first statement here is, as far as we know, true. Yet there is no way in which one could conclusively show that it is true by means of sense experience. For it is always possible that one will one day come across someone who needs no sleep at all. As for the second statement, that too seems true. But it cannot be conclusively falsified. For however old the cats of one's experience may be, they may die one day. Therefore, it is wrong to appeal to conclusive verifiability and falsifiability as criteria of meaningfulness for factual statements.

It might be argued that the weak version of the verification principle serves to establish the impossibility of God's existence once and for all. But this view is open to the initial objection that the weak version of the verification principle does not even satisfy its own criterion of meaningfulness. If one accepts it, then one has to say that a statement is only factual and meaningful if some sense experience or observation statement makes it probable or counts in its favour. But what sense experience or observation statement can count in favour of the claim that a statement is only factual and meaningful if some sense experience or observation statement makes it probable or counts in its favour?

It has been urged that the verification principle is acceptable because it only takes up the ordinary understanding of words like 'factual' and 'meaningful'. Schlick, for example, said that it is 'nothing but a simple statement of the way in which meaning is actually assigned to propositions in everyday life and in science. There never has been any other way, and it would be a grave error to suppose that we have discovered a new conception of meaning which is contrary to common opinion and which we want to introduce into philosophy.'[10] But this remark seems to overlook the fact that many people find meaningful and factual a whole lot of statements which do not seem confirmable only by means of sense experience. Take, for example, religious people and the way they regard as both factual and meaningful statements about God and life after death which, on their own admission, are not confirmable by means of sense experience. And consider the following statement given as an example by Richard Swinburne: 'Some of the toys which to all appearances stay in the toy cupboard while people are asleep and no one is watching, actually get up and dance in the middle of the night and then go back to the cupboard leaving no traces of their activity.'[11] If someone were to say this, talking, let us suppose, about a particular cupboard, we might be utterly incredulous. Swinburne's example is a frivolous one. But it would be stretching things to say that the statement he asks us to consider is meaningless, that it could be neither true nor false. It might be replied that we could not understand a statement unless we knew how it could be shown to be true or false. It might be added that knowing how to show a statement to be true or false means knowing what available sense experience would make it either probable or improbable. But people also seem able to understand statements without being able to say what available sense experience would make it likely or unlikely that they are true. To take another example of Swinburne:

A man can understand the statement 'once upon a time, before there were men or any other rational creatures, the earth was covered by sea', without his having any idea of what geological evidence would count for or against this proposition, or any idea of how to establish what geological evidence would count for or against the proposition.[12]

The truth of this observation is just what someone could well refer to if it were said that Antony Flew's comments about falsifiability make it obvious that statements about God are clearly meaningless. Someone who holds that there is a God might not be able to specify what would count against the truth of the assertion. But it does not follow from this that the assertion is meaningless. I cannot specify what would count against my belief that people with lung cancer are in danger of death. For I am not a medical expert, and I cannot predict the future. But the statement 'People with lung cancer are in danger of death' is hardly meaningless. It is something one says on the basis of past experience. But people who say it need not specify what would count against their assertion in order to suppose that what they say is not meaningless.

So the verification principle in the forms in which we have considered it does not show that there could not be a God. Nor does it seem that God's existence has to be ruled out because it cannot be falsified. Even A. J. Ayer came eventually to admit that this is so. In response to an argument originating from Alonzo Church, he acknowledged that the verification principle cannot be formulated in any satisfactory way. He also accepted that the same applies to criteria of meaning stated in terms of falsification.[13]

Other Moves

Yet might there not be other ways of maintaining that we need not consider whether belief in God can be defended with reference to reason or argument? This question brings us to the second position mentioned at the beginning of this chapter: that though 'God exists' or 'There is a God' are perfectly meaningful statements, those who believe in God have no need to show that their belief can be justified at the bar of reason.

One version of this position is associated with a number of Protestant thinkers, especially Karl Barth (1886–1968), according to whom there are theological objections to natural theology. By 'natural theology' I mean the attempt to show that belief in God's existence can be defended with reference to reason or argument which ought to be acceptable to anyone, not simply those who already believe in God's existence. Advocates of natural theology include such famous philosophers as Anselm of Canterbury (1033–1109), Thomas Aquinas (c.1225–1274), René Descartes (1596–1650), G. W. Leibniz (1646–1716), and John Locke (1632–1704). Barth, however, rejects the whole idea of natural theology. In his view natural theology is irrelevant when it comes to the issue of belief in God.

Why? First, says Barth, human reason is corrupt and cannot reach to a proper knowledge of God. Instead of relying on natural human reason, people should turn to revelation. And they should recognize that God is so utterly different from anything creaturely that their only proper ground for talking about God lies in what God himself has said. More precisely, it lies in what Christ has taught. 'God as our Father, as the

Creator', Barth urges, 'is unknown in so far as He is not made known through Jesus.' He continues:

Jesus' message about God the Father must not be regarded as if Jesus had expressed the familiar truth, that the world must have and really has a creator, and then had ventured to designate this Creator by the familiar human name of 'Father'—not as if on his part he intended what all serious philosophy has named as the highest cause, or as the highest good, as *esse a se* or as the *ens perfectissimum*, as the universal, as the ground of meaning and the abyss of meaning, as the unconditioned, as the limit, the critical negation or the origin; intended it and dedicated it by the name of Father, not altogether unknown to religious language, gave it a Christian interpretation and, as it were baptism. To that we can but say that this entity, the supposed philosophical equivalent of the Creator God, has nothing to do with Jesus' message of God the Father, with or without the name of Father attached.[14]

Many people have urged that 'the God of the philosophers' has little connection with 'the God of religious faith'. And that is roughly Barth's position. According to him, it is also the position of the Bible, which is another reason he gives for taking his view of natural theology.

But Barth's is not the only form of the general view with which we are now concerned. In recent years there have been notable related approaches deriving from the influence of Ludwig Wittgenstein (1889–1951), on the one hand, and the work of certain Calvinist thinkers, on the other. Here, in particular, we may note some arguments of D. Z. Phillips and Alvin Plantinga.

According to Phillips, the project of justifying belief in God by means of reason is misguided both because it springs from a mistaken view of the nature of philosophy and because it does not engage with the true nature of religious belief. In Phillips's view, belief in God is intelligible and acceptable on its own terms, and is not something which stands in need of support by rational or philosophical argument.[15]

With respect to belief in God and the nature of philosophy, Phillips invokes what Wittgenstein says in his *Philosophical Investigations*. In particular, he sets much store by the following comments:

A philosophical problem has the form: 'I don't know my way about.' Philosophy may in no way interfere with the actual use of language; it can in the end only describe it. For it cannot give it any foundation either. It leaves everything as it is.[16]

Phillips also invokes a distinction made by Wittgenstein between 'surface grammar' and 'depth grammar'.[17] Roughly speaking, this is a distinction between what utterances or sentences might *seem* to mean by virtue of their appearance and what they *really* mean. For example, consider the sentence 'I have a pain in my foot'. From a grammatical point of view, this resembles 'I have a key in my pocket'. But we would be quite wrong if we took pain to be some sort of physical object with a precise physical location. Here, then, we can distinguish between what the first sentence seems to mean and what it really means. It might seem to mean that if surgeons were to cut my leg open, they would find a pain-shaped thing. But it actually means something quite different.

Now, says Phillips, the role of philosophy with respect to belief in God is not to ground it in something called 'reason'. Philosophy should analyze or describe the nature of belief in God. Or, as Phillips himself writes:

If the philosopher wants to give an account of religion, he must pay attention to what religious believers do and say . . . The whole conception, then, of religion standing in need of justification is confused . . . Philosophy is neither for nor against religion: 'it leaves everything as it is' . . . It is not the task of the philosopher to decide whether there is a God or not, but to ask what it means to affirm or deny the existence of God.[18]

And, so Phillips goes on to suggest, when philosophers have done this, they will see that, contrary to what surface indications have led many people to suppose, belief in God is not the sort of thing for which 'rational' support or justification is required. If I say 'I have a pain in my foot', it would be wrong for me to defend what I say by urging you to bring in the surgeons and by telling them to look in my foot for a pain. By the same token, says Phillips, 'There is a God' is not the sort of utterance which needs to be defended by 'rational' arguments of the sort employed by supporters of natural theology and the like. For example, Phillips argues, belief in God is not a hypothesis based on grounds. It is not open to falsification, and it is not held tentatively.

The believer's hope is not hope *for* anything, moral improvement, for example . . . It is simply hope, hope in the sense of the ability to live with himself . . . To see the world as God's creation is to see meaning in life. This meaningfulness remains untouched by the evil in the world because it is not arrived at by inference from it.[19]

Nor is it true, adds Phillips, that belief in God is a belief which is based on empirical evidence. God, he says, is not an empirical object which might or might not exist.

One will never understand what is meant by belief in God if one thinks of God as a being who may or may not exist . . . let us assume, for a moment, that the reality of God is akin to the reality of a physical object. It will then make sense to assume that one day we will be able to check whether our belief is true. Let us assume, further, that such a day comes, and that we find that there is a God and that He is as we had always thought Him to be. What kind of a God would we have discovered? Clearly, a God of whom it would still make sense to say that He might not exist. Such a God may, as a matter of fact, never cease to exist . . . A God who is an existent among existents is not the God of religious belief.[20]

According to Phillips, 'God exists' is not an indicative statement. 'Talk of God's existence or reality', he explains, 'cannot be considered as talk about the existence of an object.'[21] Following up on this he writes:

To ask whether God exists is not to ask a theoretical question. If it is to mean anything at all, it is to wonder about praising and praying; it is to wonder whether there is anything in all that. This is why philosophy cannot answer the question 'Does God exist?' with either an affirmative or a negative reply . . . 'There is a God', though it appears to be in the indicative mood, is an expression of faith.[22]

Alvin Plantinga's position seems to have little to do with the philosophy of Wittgenstein, but his approach to justification and belief in God leads him to a conclusion comparable to that of Phillips (though it is also very different in certain important respects). For, in his view (as in that of Thomas Aquinas), those who believe in God are perfectly within their intellectual rights even if they are wholly unable to cite any kind of argument or evidence in favour of the truth of their belief.

According to many people, and as Antony Flew argues, 'If it is to be established that there is a God, then we have to have good grounds for believing that this is indeed so. Until and unless some such grounds are produced we have literally no reason at all for believing; and in that situation the only reasonable posture must be that of either the negative atheist or the agnostic.'[23] According to Plantinga, however, there are no good arguments which force us to accept this position. He does not think that one needs to know about arguments for God in order to be warranted in believing in God.

The position Plantinga adopts is that belief in God can be thought of as 'properly basic'. By this he means that it is rational in the same way and for the same reason as basic perceptual beliefs, memory beliefs, and the like, which do not rest on further, more secure, beliefs. He doubts whether any really convincing arguments can be given for such beliefs, but he does not think that this entails that those who accept them are unreasonable in doing so. And he thinks the same with respect to those who accept without argument that God exists. He suggests that, just as we start to argue with people without trying to defend certain beliefs, we can begin with belief in God and not be required to argue for it with reference to other beliefs which others insist are more rational or believable.

Reason and Belief in God

How should we respond to all this? Should we, for instance, conclude that there is indeed something mistaken in the attempt to ground belief in God in rational discussion or argument? Should we conclude that, even if it is not wholly misguided, the attempt is at least unnecessary?

Take, to begin with, Barth's interpretation of the Bible. This has a lot to be said for it. Biblical writers do not engage in what most people would understand as a rational defence of

belief in God. They seem uninterested in asking whether or
not God exists and why, if he exists, we should believe in his
existence. There is not a single argument for God's existence
anywhere in the Bible, though there are arguments to the
effect that the gods of the heathen are vain delusion. Biblical
authors normally presuppose the existence of God. For them it
does not need arguing. And the same can be said of many,
perhaps most, people who believe in God.

For this reason, so we may add, Phillips also has a case
when he observes that belief in God is not a theoretical or
hypothetical conclusion based on grounds or empirical evidence. The average church-goer would be very surprised at a
sermon beginning 'Today we will consider whether or not it is
reasonable to believe in the existence of God'. And there are
differences between believing in God and believing in a
hypothesis or in something for which one has evidence. In
most cases, hypotheses are entertained tentatively. But those
who believe in God do not normally speak as though it might,
after all, turn out that there is no God. Then again, evidence
for the existence of something often consists of empirical data
produced by empirical objects which, at least in principle, we
can come across directly. Yet God is not usually thought of as
an empirical object to be directly encountered. Under some
philosophical influence, we might fantasize ourselves confirming our belief that such and such is evidence for tigers
being around by capturing tigers or by photographing them.
But nobody suggests that we can capture God or photograph
him.

In other words, both Barth and Phillips have drawn attention to important features of belief in God as it is actually
held by those who believe. And what they have to say about
believers and their belief in God is also correct in other ways.
Barth asserts that God is radically distinct from creatures, that
he is, in Barth's language, 'wholly other'. Phillips says that
God is not a physical object or a being among beings. Both
ways of talking latch on to a major tradition of theological
discourse. In the Bible we find it said that God is incom-
parable. 'To whom will you liken me and make me equal, and

compare me, that we may be alike?'[24] 'You thought that I was
one like yourself. But now I rebuke you, and lay the charge
before you.'[25] In many post-biblical writers we find it said that
God is not a being but the source of being, or Being Itself. We
also find it said that God is a 'necessary being' or a being
whose nature and existence cannot be distinguished.[26]

Can it be, however, that one may reasonably believe in the
existence of God without being able to justify one's belief?
Here again there is much to be said in favour of Phillips's
position and also that of Plantinga. For one thing, someone's
belief that such and such is the case is not to be dismissed
as 'unreasonable' just because the person cannot produce
evidence for the truth of the belief. Children may not be able
to produce evidence for the belief that such and such people
are their parents. But they need not be believing unreasonably
in believing that certain people actually are their parents.
Some philosophers would reply that one is entitled to believe a
proposition only if it is self-evident or incorrigible or evident
to the senses. But, as Elizabeth Anscombe notes, such a
stipulation fails to allow for the fact that 'the greater part of
our knowledge of reality rests upon the belief that we repose
in things we have been taught and told'.[27] It also fails to allow
for the fact that, when we have done with reasoning and the
production of evidence or grounds for beliefs, we are left with
belief that is not based on reasons, evidence, or grounds.[28]

One might reply that authors like Phillips and Plantinga
have no way of ruling out even the wildest of beliefs. If those
who believe in God are rationally entitled to do so without
supporting reasons and the like, why should the same not be
true of all people, regardless of what they believe? But Phillips
and Plantinga need not be especially embarrassed by this
question. Phillips is not denying that people can make mistakes and believe what is false. He is not committed to saying
that anything goes. And Plantinga can observe that the fact
that he does not accept views about belief such as those of
Flew quoted above does not commit him to anything more
than a rejection of the views of Flew. It does not oblige him to
deny that, on the basis of beliefs one is entitled to, one can

dismiss certain other beliefs. An objector might say that, if Plantinga is right, any belief must be deemed to be rational unless we have a criterion to determine what can properly be believed without further evidence or grounds. But Plantinga can reply that one need not have any such criterion to be entitled to say that certain beliefs are false—just as one need not have a criterion of meaningfulness to be entitled to reject as meaningless some such utterance as 'T'was brillig; and the slithy toves did gyre and gymble in the wabe'.[29]

For reasons such as these, then, we may defend Barth, Phillips, and Plantinga. Some have dismissed them in a rather peremptory fashion, but they are by no means so easily disposed of.[30] Students of philosophy of religion should study their writings with care and sympathy. At the same time, however, we may wonder whether what they maintain is justification for holding that we may happily reject or dismiss any attempt to ground belief in God in any kind of reasoning or argument.

To start with, consider once again what Barth says concerning the Bible. As I have suggested, his position may be supported to some extent. But we should not conclude that concern with argument or evidence for God's existence is positively condemned by biblical authors. The fact that these authors do not argue systematically for God's existence does not mean that they are hostile to those who do. And there are sketches of arguments for God's existence even in the Bible. St Paul says that Gentiles are 'without excuse' for failing to recognize that 'what can be known about God is plain to them' since 'from the creation of the world his invisible nature, namely his eternal power and deity, are clearly perceived in the things that have been made'.[31] What exactly St Paul has in mind here is uncertain. But he is clearly not appealing to any special revelation. His line seems to be that anyone should be able to see that there is a God, and that this is clear from the nature of the world around us. It is, perhaps, significant that the First Vatican Council cites St Paul in promulgating its teaching that 'God, the source and end of all things, can be known with certainty from the consideration of created things, by the natural power of human reason', a teaching that was undoubtedly intended as a mandate for proponents of natural theology.[32]

The above reference to revelation brings us to a second objection to Barth. This is that he leaves us with no way of deciding between competing alleged 'revelations'. As a Christian, Barth begins and ends with Christian revelation. But members of other religions are equally firm in holding to what they take to be revelation. So to which of the 'revelations' are we to turn? Barth seems to have no answer to this question, and, for this reason alone, we may well feel inclined to wonder whether there is not something very questionable in what he suggests. There is a long tradition among Christians of holding that the articles of faith (i.e. the teaching of creeds such as the Apostles' Creed) are ultimately unprovable. You can find this view in, for example, Aquinas, according to whom 'to be imperfect as knowledge is of the very essence of faith'.[33] But Aquinas also holds that matters of faith can be supported to some extent by argument and defended from the charge of absurdity in the same way.

A defender of Barth might object to Aquinas's position by repeating Barth's claim that human reason is corrupt. But to say this, and to add that all we can do is rely on revelation, leads to considerable difficulties. If the point being made is that truths of Christianity are above argument, then it cannot even consistently be argued for. People who argued the matter would at once seem to contradict themselves. If truths of Christianity cannot be argued for, then it cannot be argued that there are truths of Christianity which cannot be argued for. Not, at least, if the thesis being argued for counts as a truth of Christianity. More significantly, however, to say that all human reasoning is corrupt is to block the way to any reflection on Christianity—even reflection derived from austerely Christian premises. If our reasoning is totally corrupt, then we cannot even reflect on the true nature of Christian doctrines and indicate their significance for each other. If our reasoning is totally corrupt, we can presumably do little useful work in areas like biblical scholarship and the analysis of the historical factors leading to the advancement of Christian doctrines by Church Councils and the like.

It might still be said that God is 'wholly other' and that this rules out the sort of inquiry to which Barth is opposed. Yet is it so obvious that God is wholly other? The Bible insists that God should not be confused with any creature. But it also talks about him by describing him in terms also used to describe what is not divine. It says, for example, that he acts, that he is good, that he has power, knowledge, and so on. And this is how people speak of God in general. Even those who say such things as that God is 'Being Itself' speak like this. May we not therefore suggest that the nature of belief in God does raise questions about justification or grounds? If it is said, for example, that God is good, why should we use the word 'good' and not the word 'plastic' or 'mammalian'? If it is said that God acts, why is that more accurate than saying that he sleeps or that he lives in a flat in London?

Phillips might reply that belief in God does not raise questions of justification once its nature is properly understood. But, as many of his critics have observed, Phillips seems to misrepresent what it can mean to believe in God, and, in doing so, manages to bypass the fact that, in some of its forms at any rate, belief in God does raise questions like 'How do you know?' or 'What is the evidence for that?' Contrary to what he writes, for example, it surely is the case that 'There is a God' is a statement in the indicative mood, at least for most believers. It states that there is a subject of whom certain attributes can truly be predicated. In that case, however, we can ask what reason there is to suppose that there actually is such a subject. And we can ask this question even if we accept what we have seen Plantinga to be saying. He denies that one must proceed with reference to argument and the like in order to be entitled to believe in God rationally. As we shall find in Chapter 4, however, he does not deny that one can argue successfully for God's existence. He also holds that belief in God is grounded in experience, and can be defended against the arguments of those who have tried to show that it is somehow unreasonable.[34]

The upshot would therefore seem to be that it is by no means improper to consider whether belief in God can be defended by means of argument, reasons, evidence, or the like. The existence of God does not have to be ruled out in advance because of appeal to verification and falsification. Nor do we have to conclude that there is something intrinsically wrong in going beyond the conviction that God exists and asking whether it really latches on to reality.

Yet might it not be said that there are other reasons for refusing to ask this question? In the next chapter we will pursue the issue with reference to a problem often discussed by philosophers of religion, a problem which concerns some of the writers mentioned in this chapter. It centres on the possibility of talking significantly about God in the light of the way people normally speak about him. More precisely, it springs from the fact that talk about God seems to pull in two different directions.

Talking about God

'I LOVE you', says the lady. 'Do you really mean that?', asks her boy-friend. 'No', the lady replies. The boy-friend is speechless, and not without reason. The lady seems to be saying nothing significant. What she gives with one hand, she takes back with the other.

Some people have felt that those who believe in God are rather like the lady just referred to. And, in their view, this means that belief in God raises an insurmountable problem for anyone who supposes that one can reasonably be asked to look at any defence of the view that there actually is a God.

This problem is thought to derive from two facts. The first is that people who speak of God do so by attributing to him certain properties (usually ones implying perfection or excellence) which are normally attributed to things in the world. The second is that God is also often said to be very different from anything that comes within the range of our experience. On the one hand, God is said to be, for example, good or wise. On the other, it is said that God is unique and that our talk of him fails to do him justice.

Here, then, is the problem. If one says that God is very different from anything else, can one really talk significantly about him at all? How can one say that God is good or wise, but not in the sense that ordinary good and wise things are? Is there not a real dilemma here for those who believe in God? Are they not caught between the stools of meaninglessness and misrepresentation?

Causation and Metaphor

One answer which has been given to these questions is that talk about God is perfectly intelligible since it is grounded in

God's activity. The idea here is that God can be said to be thus and so because he has brought it about that there are things which are thus and so.

Suppose we discover a corpse which has clearly been savagely mutilated by someone. We might describe what we find as 'horrifying' or 'outrageous', and we might quickly go on to apply both these terms to the person responsible for what we have found. Our justification for doing so lies in the fact that what has been brought about can fairly be described as 'horrifying' or 'outrageous'.

In other words, we sometimes describe causes in the way that we describe their effects. And, in the light of this fact, some have suggested that we can significantly talk about God by noting his effects and then describing him as we describe them. Thus, for example, it has been argued that we can say that God is good because he is the cause of things that are good, or that God is wise because he is the cause of wisdom as we encounter it in people.

Yet, though it is easy to see the logic of the reasoning present in this line of thinking, there are at least two problems with it. For is it true that causes always literally resemble their effects? And, even if it is, will we not soon be reduced to absurdity if we try to make sense of talk about God by describing him as we describe his effects?

The answer to these questions is 'No' and 'Yes' respectively. It is just not the case that causes always literally resemble their effects. People who are responsible for a state of justice might reasonably (though not necessarily) be truly described as just. And we may readily assume that the parents of a human baby are themselves human. But criminals can give birth to saints. And makers of ice-cream are not themselves made of ice-cream. As for the view that positive discourse about God can be grounded on the fact that he is like what he causes, what of the fact that, if God exists, he has presumably caused a material world containing coloured objects? Are we to say that, since he has done this, God is material and coloured? Few who believe in God would be happy with that conclusion.

It may be said, however, that those who believe in God
should be understood as speaking by means of metaphor,
which brings us to another way sometimes advanced of trying
to make sense of talk about God. We may summarize it as
follows.

When we form positive statements about God, we must
somehow mean what we say. We must mean that God is what
we assert him to be. But he must also be very different from
anything in the universe. We need, then, to speak positively
about him without denying the difference between God and
creatures. We can do this if we think of our talk about God
as metaphorical. When you use a metaphor, you refer to
something by means of words which you can also use in talking
about something very different. One can speak of the 'ship of
State' without implying that the government floats on water.
One can call people 'worms' without being committed to
the assertion that they crawl on the ground. By the same
token, then, one can speak about God by using words which
name or describe things in the universe, and one can do
so metaphorically without being committed to absurd consequences concerning the similarity between God and his
creatures.

Or so the argument goes. And one can defend it up to a
point. It is indeed a fact that vastly different things can be
called by the same name or described in the same way. Poetry
flourishes because of this. But we cannot say that all talk of
God is metaphorical. For with metaphorical language one can
always raise a question about literal truth. One can ask, for
example, whether the State is really a ship or whether one's
friends are really worms. And if we say that all talk of God is
metaphorical, then we should have to deny that God is really
what many would say that he really is.

This may not seem obvious at first. Someone might say,
'God is a mighty fortress'. We then ask, 'Is that really true? Is
God made of stone, for example?' The answer will probably
be: 'Of course not. I am speaking metaphorically.' Here it
would seem that nothing anyone might wish to affirm of God

is being denied. And we might well see some point in asserting that God is a mighty fortress.

But suppose someone now says 'God is alive' or 'God is good'. Again we ask, 'Is that really true? Is he really alive and good? Or are we now using a figure of speech?' If the statements are metaphorical, one ought to be able to reply 'No, it is not really true. God is not really alive and good. We are just using a figure of speech.' But can one reply in such a way? Not if one has anything recognizable as a traditional belief in God, for that surely holds that God is literally alive and good, and that it is not just a figure of speech to call him such. Those who believe in the living and good God do not take themselves as able to assert 'It is not really the case that God is alive and good' as they might take themselves as able to say 'It is not really the case that God is a mighty fortress'.

Negation and Analogy

Defenders of belief in God have not been unaware of the force of the problems raised above, and they have consequently tried to say how one can talk significantly about God without misrepresenting him and without recourse to nothing but metaphor. In particular they have frequently appealed to the importance of negation and analogy.

The appeal to negation is best thought of as an attempt to prevent people from misrepresenting God. Those who make it emphasize the unknowability of God and argue that, though one can talk significantly about God, one can only do so by saying what he is not. A notable advocate of negation is Maimonides (1135–1204), who writes as follows:

There is no necessity at all for you to use positive attributes of God with the view of magnifying Him in your thoughts ... I will give you ... some illustrations, in order that you may better understand the propriety of forming as many negative attributes as possible, and the impropriety of ascribing to God any positive attributes. A person may know for certain that a 'ship' is in existence, but he may not know to what object that name is applied, whether to a substance or to an accident; a second person then learns that a ship is not an accident; a third, that it is not a mineral; a fourth, that it is not a plant growing in the earth; a fifth, that it is not a body whose parts are joined together by nature; a sixth, that it is not a flat object like boards or doors; a seventh, that it is not a sphere; an eighth, that it is not pointed; a ninth, that it is not round shaped; nor equilateral; a tenth, that it is not solid. It is clear that this tenth person has almost arrived at the correct notion of a 'ship' by the foregoing negative attributes . . . In the same manner you will come nearer to the knowledge and comprehension of God by the negative attributes . . . I do not merely declare that he who affirms attributes of God has not sufficient knowledge concerning the Creator . . . but I say that he unconsciously loses his belief in God.[1]

Historically speaking, however, it is analogy that has most interested those who agree that even a unique God can be spoken about significantly. In this connection it is even possible to speak about 'the theory of analogy'. In order to understand what that amounts to, though, one needs to be familiar with some technical terminology.

Suppose I say that Fido and Rover are both dogs. And suppose that what I am talking about are indeed canine animals. I am therefore saying that in some clear respect Fido and Rover have something in common, so that 'dog' means the same thing when applied to each of them. To say that Fido is a dog and that Rover is a dog is to say exactly the same thing of each of them.

But now consider a different example. Suppose I say that something or other is a bat and that something else is also a bat. Let us call what I am talking about A and B. Must 'is a bat' mean exactly the same thing in 'A is a bat' and 'B is a bat'? Not at all. For A may be an object with which cricketers hit balls. And B may be a mammal with wings. The word 'bat' can be applied to two things without meaning the same thing at all.

In more technical language, the difference we have just noted between 'is a dog' and 'is a bat' can be expressed by saying that the word 'dog' in 'Fido is a dog' and 'Rover is a dog' is being used *univocally*, while 'bat' in 'A is a bat' and 'B is a bat' is being used *equivocally*. To apply a word univocally to two things is to say that they are exactly the same in some respect, that the word means the same in both its applications. To apply words equivocally, however, is to use the same words in completely different senses.

Now, according to the theory of analogy, there is a third way of applying the same word to different things, a way which it is important to keep in mind when we are thinking about how one may sensibly talk about God. The idea is that one can use words analogically. The analogical use of words is supposed to lie somewhere between the univocal and the equivocal.

We can see the theory of analogy classically applied to God in the work of Aquinas, who explicitly raises the question 'Are words used univocally or equivocally of God and creatures?' His answer comes in three stages.

First, says Aquinas, God is infinite and incomprehensible, so there is an enormous difference between God and creatures, and the same term cannot be applied to God and to creatures univocally. Take, for example, 'God is wise'. What the attribute word 'signifies in God', Aquinas says, 'is not confined to the meaning of our word but goes beyond it. Hence it is clear that the word 'wise' is not used in the same sense of God and human beings, and the same is true of all other words, so they cannot be used univocally of God and creatures.'[2]

On the other hand, Aquinas observes, words applied to God and creatures cannot always be used equivocally. If we always used words equivocally when talking about God, then, says Aquinas, 'we could never argue from statements about creatures to statements about God'.[3]

Aquinas goes on to conclude that 'words are used of God and creatures in an analogical way'. What does he mean by saying this? He distinguishes between different kinds of analogy, but his basic point is that certain terms can be applied both to God and to creatures, neither univocally nor equivocally, but because of some relation between God and creatures. And the relation which Aquinas has in mind is causal. We can say, for example, that God is good and that some human being is good, because goodness in human beings can be said to exist in God inasmuch as creatures and their properties derive from God as the first cause of all things.

It is important to note that Aquinas does not mean by this that, for example, 'God is good' simply means 'God causes goodness in creatures'. He does not subscribe to the first approach to talk of God noted above. His point is that we can sometimes use the same words in speaking of God and creatures because of certain similarities between God and creatures which, so he thinks, can be inferred because of the fact that creatures derive from or are caused by God. For Aquinas, causes and their most special effects are intimately connected. They are not simply instances of objects or events which we observe to be constantly conjoined, as the philosopher David Hume suggested.[4] The effects in question flow from their causes (rather than from something else) because the causes are things of certain kinds with definite ways of being or working; the cause imposes its character on things.[5] Aquinas therefore concludes that, because creatures come from or are brought about by God, they reveal or reflect something of what he is. And on this basis, says Aquinas, God can (in principle) be named from his creatures, i.e. spoken of by means of words which we use in describing them.[6] For Aquinas, causes can be thought of as exerting themselves or as imposing their character on things. This leads Aquinas to think of the world as something in which we can see something of what God is like. You cannot give what you have not got, and though what you give may not look like you, it will still reflect what you are. By the same token, so Aquinas reasons, God's world reflects what he is, and we might well suppose that he can be spoken of in the way in which we speak of some of his creatures. He might, for example, be said to be living and good.

Negation, Analogy, and God

Does the appeal to negation and analogy serve to allay the doubt that reasons for belief in God are just not worth looking at? Given the way that people talk of God, is the question of his existence a real non-starter? Are writers like Maimonides and Aquinas simply wasting our time?

Talking of God by means of negation has considerable justification once one reflects on the way in which God has been understood within the Judaeo-Christian tradition. He has regularly been thought of as the Creator, as the source of all things other than himself. As Aquinas puts it, 'The word "God" signifies the divine nature: it is used to mean something that is above all that is, and that is the source of all things and is distinct from them all. This is how those that use it mean it to be used.'[7] And, if that is how the word 'God' is used, it seems right to say that we can speak truly in saying what God is not. It is true, for example, to say that God is not anything bodily (i.e. physical or material). If God is the source of the universe, he cannot be something bodily, since anything bodily is part of the universe and cannot therefore account for there being a universe. Only something which is not a body could account for there being a universe of physical objects.

But the position that one can talk significantly about God only by means of negation is still difficult to defend. Here there are at least two points to note.

The first concerns the claim that it is possible to approach some understanding of God simply by saying what God is not. Maimonides evidently thinks that this claim is true. But saying only what something is not gives no indication of what it actually is. And if one can only say what God is not, one cannot understand him at all. We can come to make true statements about things by means of negation. It is, for example, true to say 'The moon is not a piece of cheese'. And sometimes we can guess what something is when someone denies only one thing about it. If a mother who has just given birth is told 'It's not a boy', she will know at once that her baby is a girl. Yet it still remains that, except in rather special cases, if we know only what something is not, we do not know what it is. Suppose I say that there is something in my room, and suppose I reject every suggestion you make as to what is actually there. In that case, you will get no idea at all about

what is in my room. And, going back to the above quotation
from Maimonides, it is simply wrong to say that someone who
has all the negations mentioned in it 'has almost arrived at the
correct notion of a "ship"'. Such a person could equally well
be thinking of a wardrobe or a coffin.

The second point is that people who talk about God do
not normally want to talk about him only in negations. They
usually want to say that some things are definitely true of him.
They make positive affirmations about God. They say, for
example, 'God is the Creator', 'God is powerful', 'God has
knowledge', 'God is everywhere', 'God is eternal', and 'God is
good'. Sometimes, indeed, what looks like a positive assertion
about something may be no such thing. In certain circumstances, 'You are a great help' may mean 'You are no help at
all'. But all the assertions just mentioned not only *look* to be
positive ones about God; those who subscribe to them would
normally understand them *to be* such. As Aquinas drily puts it:
'When people speak of "the living God" they do not simply
want to say . . . that he differs from a lifeless body.'[8]

If a rigid reliance on negation is not without its drawbacks,
however, the theory of analogy is more promising. For there is
a lot to be said for the view that the same word can be literally
applied to different things neither univocally nor equivocally.
This point can be illustrated by quoting a useful passage at the
beginning of Wittgenstein's *Philosophical Investigations*.

Consider for example the proceedings that we call 'games'. I mean
board-games, card-games, ball-games, Olympic games, and so on.
What is common to them all?—Don't say: 'There *must* be something
common, or they would not be called "games"'—but *look and see*
whether there is anything common to them all.—For if you look
at them you will not see something that is common to *all*, but similarities, relationships, and a whole series of them at that. To repeat:
don't think, but look!—Look for example at board-games, with their
multifarious relationships. Now pass to card-games; here you find
many correspondences with the first group, but many common
features drop out, and others appear. When we pass next to ball-
games, much that is common is retained, but much is lost.—Are they
all 'amusing'? Compare chess with noughts and crosses. Or is there

always winning and losing, or competition between players? Think of patience. . . . And we can go through the many, many other groups of games in the same way; can see how similarities crop up and disappear.[9]

What Wittgenstein brings out very clearly is that at least one word can be used significantly in different but related senses without it being true that the word is being used figuratively. And, following the clue offered by his example, we quickly come to see that many words can be used significantly in this way. Take, for instance, 'good'. You can have good food and good books, not to mention good people, good wine, and a good night's sleep. Or again, there is Aquinas's illustration, the word 'healthy'. As Aquinas says, a human being can be healthy, and so can a complexion or a diet. In saying that a human being, a complexion, and a diet are healthy, one is speaking literally, but one is not saying that they are exactly alike. Nor is one saying that they are different as mammalian bats are different from wooden ones.

It seems wrong, then, to hold that the same words literally applied must always bear exactly the same meaning or be used on some occasions in ways that are without sense. And it therefore also seems wrong to insist that nobody can talk significantly about God since words applied to him do not mean exactly what they do when applied to other things. To put it another way, the problem raised at the beginning of this chapter is not obviously insurmountable; just because people do not apply words to God and to creatures either univocally or equivocally, it does not follow that they cannot talk about God significantly and literally. That is what the theory of analogy is basically saying, and in this it is surely right.

Saying what is Said of God

But we are still left with a difficulty. Even if we grant that the univocal/equivocal distinction can be supplemented, we can still ask why particular words are used in talking about God and whether they are capable of being used significantly and literally. We may accept that the word 'game' can be used literally to describe things which do not have a common feature, but we would also agree that not just anything can be called a game. Rescuing a drowning child is not a game; nor is performing a surgical operation. So there is still a general problem for talk about God. Some reason must be given for choosing the terms which are actually applied to him. This point is nicely put by Patrick Sherry who suggests that:

It is not just a matter of saying that there must be some grounds for ascribing perfections to God. We must also insist that if we ascribe the same terms to God and creatures, then there must be a connection between the relevant criteria of evidence and truth. Thus the grounds for ascribing terms like 'love', 'father', 'exist' and 'life' must bear some relationship to the grounds used for our normal everyday application of these terms. Similarly, even if 'God created the world' expresses a unique relationship, its truth conditions must bear some resemblance to our familiar uses of terms like 'make' or 'depends on' (which is not to say that we and must expect to be able to verify the doctrine of Creation empirically here and now).[10]

In other words, it looks as though the terms used in talking about God must be justified in some way if they are not to appear arbitrary and empty of meaning. And the question is, can they be? Aquinas, for example, thought that they could. He held that one can come to a knowledge of God and that one can significantly apply to God words which apply to creatures because there is some positive reason for doing so. But is Aquinas right in adopting this position? Could anybody be right in adopting it?

At this stage in the discussion it is difficult to say, for we have not yet touched on any particular reasons for believing in God or affirming anything of him. For the moment, however, this does not matter. In this chapter we have been asking whether reasons for belief in God are worth looking at in view of some things that are said of him. For all we have seen so far, the answer is 'Yes'.

In the next chapter we shall consider a problem which has led many people to a different conclusion. Before moving on, however, it is worth briefly making a final point. Even from what we have seen already, it should be clear enough that people who believe in God seem committed to thinking of him as something decidedly out of the ordinary. Some would say that he is essentially mysterious. But does this mean that he could not exist? And does it mean that there could never be reasons for belief in God?

Affirmative answers have been offered to both these questions. It has been suggested that if God is really mysterious, then we cannot understand what is being said when he is talked about, in which case it is nonsense to affirm his existence. It has also been said that if God is really mysterious, then it is pointless to try and find reasons for holding that he exists. But these views are not very plausible. One does not have to know exactly what a word means in order to have some understanding of it or use it significantly. I may not know what a volcano is exactly, but I can still talk sensibly about volcanoes. And I can reasonably say that Jones has malaria without being clear as to what exactly I am saying. In other words, I can wield words significantly without being able to define them. As Peter Geach puts it, 'I certainly could not define either "oak-tree" or "elephant"; but this does not destroy my right to assert that no oak-tree is an elephant.'[11] This point does nothing to show that there is a God; but it does suggest that in order to speak meaningfully about God, it is not necessary that one should understand exactly the import of one's statements about him. It may not be possible to define God; one may not be able fully to comprehend him. But this does not mean that one cannot talk significantly about him; nor does it prevent one from asking whether he is there in the first place.

3

God and Evil

MANY of the questions considered in the last two chapters are concerned with the intrinsic possibility of God's existence, with whether there *could* be a God. One outcome of our discussion is that it is advisable to ask whether there is any reason to believe in God, and in Chapter 4 we will begin to do this by turning to one of a series of arguments for God's existence. For the moment, though, I want to consider what many people regard as the clearest indication that there could not be a God. I refer to what is commonly called 'the problem of evil'.

What is the Problem of Evil?

The problem of evil is usually understood as a problem for *classical theism* (sometimes just called *theism*), supporters of which are commonly called *theists*. According to classical theism, God is all-knowing, all-powerful, and all-good. In the world around us, however, we discover a great deal of naturally occurring pain and suffering (natural evil). We also find a great deal of moral evil: morally culpable actions (or refusals to act) which diminish both those who are morally bad and those around them. The problem of evil is commonly seen as the problem of how the existence of God can be reconciled with the pain, suffering, and moral evil which we know to be facts of life. And it has often been said that they cannot be. Thus it has been urged that the problem of evil constitutes grounds for disbelief in God.

The argument here has taken two forms. First, it has been said that evil is evidence against there being a God: that evil shows the existence of God to be *unlikely*. Second, it has been held that evil is proof that there *could not* be a God. The idea here is that theists are caught in a contradiction. They cannot say *both* that there is evil *and* that God exists. Since they can hardly deny that there is evil, it follows that God does not exist. As H. J. McClosky declares:

Evil is a problem for the theist in that a contradiction is involved in the fact of evil, on the one hand, and the belief in the omnipotence and perfection of God on the other.[1]

Notable Responses to the Problem of Evil

One approach to the problem of evil offered by people who believe in God has been to deny the reality of evil and to say that, in spite of appearances, evil is an illusion, an 'error of mortal mind'. This is the view of Christian Science, according to which, in the words of its founder, 'Sin, disease, whatever seems real to material sense, is unreal . . . All inharmony of mortal mind or body is illusion, possessing neither reality nor identity though seeming to be real and identical.'[2]

Another approach focuses on the notion of evil as punishment. The idea here is that evil can be seen as punishment which is justly inflicted by God. There are elements of this view in St Augustine, connected with his theory of the Fall of Adam and Eve. In Albert Camus's novel *The Plague* it is dramatically expressed by the character of Fr. Panneloux, who preaches a sermon which begins with the startling words: 'Calamity has come upon you my brethren, and, my brethren, you deserved it.'

A much more common line of argument, however, is that the existence of some evil is a necessary means to some good. One version of this argument can be found in Richard Swinburne's book *The Existence of God*. According to Swinburne, natural evil provides, among other things, an opportunity for people to grow in knowledge and understanding. He writes:

If men are to have knowledge of the evil which will result from their actions or negligence, laws of nature must operate regularly; and that means that there will be what I may call 'victims of the system' . . . *if* men are to have the opportunity to bring about serious evils for themselves or others by actions or negligence, or to prevent their occurrence, and if all knowledge of the future is obtained by normal induction, that is by induction from patterns of similar events in the past—then there must be serious natural evils occurring to man or animals.[3]

Swinburne considers the possibility of God giving us the necessary knowledge by somehow informing us of the way things are and what we can do about it. He suggests that God might inform people verbally about such matters. But according to Swinburne this would mean that nobody could fail to doubt God's existence and everyone would be forced to accept God and to act as he wished. Furthermore, none of us would be able to choose to acquire knowledge of the world for ourselves. 'I conclude', says Swinburne,

that a world in which God gave to men verbal knowledge of the consequences of their actions would not be a world in which men had a significant choice of destiny, of what to make of themselves, and of the world. God would be far too close for them to be able to work things out for themselves. If God is to give man knowledge while at the same time allowing him a genuine choice of destiny, it must be normal inductive knowledge.[4]

A related view can be found in the work of John Hick, one of the most prominent contemporary writers on the problem of evil. Echoing what he believes to be the position of the early Church Father St Irenaeus (*c*.140–*c*.202), Hick argues that the existence of evil is necessary for the perfect development of human beings. Hick understands evil in the light of God's desire not to coerce people into accepting him. He suggests that people are sin-prone creatures, created as such by God, but able, in a world containing evil, to rise to great heights because they are given the opportunity to become mature in the face of evil. He writes:

Let us suppose that the infinite personal God creates finite persons to share in the life which He imparts to them. If He creates them in his immediate presence, so that they cannot fail to be conscious from the first of the infinite divine being and glory, goodness and love, wisdom, power and knowledge in whose presence they are, they will have no creaturely independence in relation to their Maker. They will not be able to *choose* to worship God, or to turn to Him freely as valuing spirits responding to infinite Value. In order, then, to give them the freedom to come to Him, God . . . causes them to come into a situation in which He is not immediately and overwhelmingly evident to them. Accordingly they come to self-consciousness as parts of a universe which has its own autonomous structures and 'laws' . . . A world without problems, difficulties, perils, and hardships would be morally static. For moral and spiritual growth comes through response to challenges; and in a paradise there would be no challenges.[5]

Notice how much emphasis is placed in this argument on human freedom. Such an emphasis is the main feature of another famous theistic response to the problem of evil: the free-will defence, which tries to show that God's existence is compatible with moral evil. It can be stated as follows.

Much evil can be attributed to human agents. This evil need never have occurred, but if there is to be a world of free human agents, it must be possible for them to bring about moral evil. If they were thwarted in doing so, they would not be really free. Now it is better that there should be a world containing free agents than that there should be a world full of robots or automata. In creating people, therefore, God was faced with an alternative. He could either have created a world lacking moral evil, or he could have created a world where moral evil was a genuine possibility. If he had created the former he could not have created a world containing free agents. In fact, he created the latter, and this means that there is a genuine and unavoidable possibility of moral evil. In creating the world he did create, God was making the better choice, because a world containing free agents is better than a world without them.

For the record, it is worth noting that some writers have tried to extend the free-will defence in order to deal with pain and suffering, which often occur apart from what people do or do not do. According to these writers, we may account for such evil as the result of free choices made by *non-human* creatures. It has been argued, for instance, that we may account for it as the work of fallen angels who are able, through their free decisions, to wreak havoc on the material universe. One can find this view in the writings of St Augustine.[6] It can also be found in C. S. Lewis's *The Problem of Pain* and in Alvin Plantinga's *God, Freedom and Evil*. Lewis says that it seems to him

a reasonable supposition that some mighty created power had already been at work for ill in the universe . . . before ever man came on the scene . . . This hypothesis is not introduced as a general 'explanation of evil'; it only gives a wider application to the principle that evil comes from the abuse of free-will.[7]

According to Plantinga, it is possible that

natural evil is due to the free actions of nonhuman persons; there is a balance of good over evil with respect to the actions of these non-human persons; and it was not within the power of God to create a world that contains a more favourable balance of good over evil with respect to the actions of the nonhuman persons it contains.[8]

Illusion and Punishment

Do the above responses show that it is not unreasonable to believe in God in spite of the evil that apparently exists? In trying to discuss this question, we can start with the first of the views noted above: that evil is an illusion.

Many have been attracted to this suggestion. And they have, as a consequence, often been helped in trying to cope with life. But the suggestion is surely grossly counter-intuitive. Can any rational person seriously hold that, say, the hunger of a starving child is simply an illusion? And even if one could rationally defend this odd conclusion, there is another difficulty. As Peter Geach nicely puts it: 'If my "mortal mind" thinks I am miserable, then I am miserable, and it is not an illusion that I am miserable.'[9] As others have pointed out, even if evil is an illusion, it is a painful one, and it is therefore false that evil is nothing but illusion.

Our first response to the problem of evil is therefore unsuccessful. And the same can be said of the second. For it seems hard to believe that all evil is something deserved. Take, for example, the case of Down's syndrome. Are we to say that newly born babies with this condition have done anything for which it can be regarded as justly inflicted punishment? Questions like this have been pressed very hard, and with good reason. The eighteenth-century Lisbon earthquake killed about 4,000 people, and some tried to make sense of it by calling it 'divine retribution'. Voltaire (1694–1778) replied: 'Did God in this earthquake select the 4,000 least virtuous of the Portuguese?' The question, of course, is to the point. Disease and other misfortunes do not seem to be obviously distributed in accordance with desert. Even the Bible admits as much.[10]

Evil and Consequences

Yet what of the kind of argument represented by Swinburne and Hick? Some would object to it on moral grounds. Take, for example, D. Z. Phillips. He asks: 'What then are we to say of the child dying from cancer?' His reply is: 'If this has been *done* to anyone, it is bad enough, but to be done for a purpose, to be planned from eternity—that is the deepest evil. If God is this kind of agent, He cannot justify His actions, and His evil nature is revealed.'[11] Phillips thinks that it is morally wicked to defend God's goodness by appealing to the fact that evil might be viewed as something he wills as a necessary means to certain goods. And, as Phillips himself observes, this is also the conclusion which Dostoevsky's character Ivan Karamazov reaches in his famous speech to Alyosha in *The Brothers Karamazov*:

And if the sufferings of children go to swell the sum of sufferings which was necessary to pay for truth, then I protest that the truth is not worth such a price . . . I don't want harmony. From love of humanity I don't want it . . . Besides, too high a price is asked for harmony; it's beyond our means to pay so much to enter on it. And so I hasten to give back my entrance ticket, and if I am an honest man I am bound to give it back as soon as possible. It's not God that I don't accept, Alyosha, only I most respectfully return Him the ticket.[12]

Is Phillips wrong in taking the line that he does?[13] It is very hard to see how we are to settle the question, for what is now at stake is a fundamental moral option, something that Wittgenstein calls an 'absolute judgment of value'.[14] Swinburne and Hick are prepared to allow that consequences can morally justify God in bringing about or permitting the evil that exists. Phillips is not. But there seems no way of showing that either side is right or wrong. It is not, for example, as if the parties in this debate disagree about some empirical matter which might finally be settled by further investigation. One side is saying that the whole attempt to justify God in terms of consequences is simply intolerable (Phillips calls it 'a sign of a corrupt mind'[15]). The other side holds that it is not intolerable.

Yet we do, of course, normally accept that someone who permits or actively causes pain and suffering can sometimes be viewed as good. We would, for example, praise someone for cutting off someone's leg in order to save that person's life, even if the operation caused great pain to the patient. At this point, therefore, we may wonder whether the evil which we encounter in the world could possibly be regarded as a necessary means to some good. Can we, for instance, say that pain and suffering could be necessary means to some good?

A problem with Swinburne's and Hick's affirmative answer to this question is that we might well think it possible for God to have brought about a world of free human people without placing them in an environment such as that provided by this world, in which people suffer as they do. One might therefore ask why God did not at the outset place people in a world free from the possibility of pain and suffering. Swinburne thinks it good that people should have the opportunity to wreak havoc or to refrain there from and strive to bring about what is good. And it may well be true that if people are to have this opportunity, then something like our world is necessary. But is it really good that people should have such an opportunity? One might say that without it they cannot be morally good. And it is true that there are virtues which could not be present in a paradise. There could not be courage, for example, for that presupposes danger. Maybe there could also be no prudence or temperateness, for these virtues seem to presuppose the possibility of harm to people. But there seems no reason why people in paradise should not be able to love and do good, even though their failure to do so would not result in anything like the pain and suffering which we come across in this world. Hick maintains that a paradise would be morally static, and one can see what he means. But it also makes sense to say that a paradise containing people would be a very good thing, and that God could bring it about without producing a world containing the pain and suffering found in our world. It makes sense, in fact, to say that a paradise containing people would be better than a world such as ours. What would be lacking would be the need for people to strive to prevent pain and suffering. There would be no struggle to deal with pain and suffering and to overcome it. But that would, surely, be a very good thing—better, indeed, than there being a world in which to be a person is to be involved in a need to struggle to deal with pain and suffering and to overcome them. A paradise would have no martyrs. But who wants martyrs? Even martyrs, presumably, do not want a world in which there are martyrs.

On the other hand, there is an obvious sense in which the occurrence of goodness is inevitably bound up with evil. For much that we can regard as evil is a necessary condition of good. Pain and suffering are not inexplicable. We may not know what, on a given occasion, accounts for an example of pain or suffering. But there will be something which does account for it: something, furthermore, that does so because it is doing well. As Herbert McCabe puts it, 'there can never be a defect inflicted on one thing except by another thing that is, in doing so, perfecting itself'.[16]

In other words, if we are to have a material world of the kind in which we live, in which some things thrive at the expense of others (in which, for example, lions can live because there are other animals on which they can feed), there will inevitably be much that we can think of as evil. In this sense, it may be argued, goodness and evil are bound up with each other. And, so it may be added, the fact that God permits evil or is somehow responsible for it is no proof of his badness. One may think that if a material world like ours cannot exist without a great deal of pain and suffering, then God should never have created such a world. But can it be proved that, in creating a world like ours, God is positively bad? We would not normally call an agent bad just because the agent in question brings about a good which involves the occurrence of what can also be viewed as bad. Some people argue that some pain and suffering is clearly pointless and that this is enough to show either that God does not exist or that it is unlikely that he exists. Hence, for example, William Rowe suggests that the intense suffering of a fawn trapped in a forest fire would be an instance of apparently pointless suffering which could have been prevented by God and which would, if it occurred, be evidence against God's existence. He then goes on to suggest that instances like this seem to abound in nature and that reason therefore suggests that the truth lies with atheism.[17] But the instance cited by Rowe is not obviously a case of pointless suffering. It is a consequence of there being a world which operates according to physical laws rather than a series of miracles. And the same would be true of any instance similar to that cited by Rowe. In any case, how can we be sure that what seems to us pointless really is so? It might even be argued that we ought not to expect to be able to see the point of all suffering. For what falls within the plan of an omnipotent, omniscient God will be something understood only by what is omnipotent and omniscient.[18]

Freedom

For reasons such as these, then, the theist may suggest that pain and suffering do not present an unanswerable case against God's existence. And, with reference to moral evil, those who believe in God may also get some mileage out of the free-will defence. It is a premiss of the defence that a world of free agents is better than a world of automata. Most people would accept this premiss, and it is certainly true that we normally think well of those who allow their fellow human beings a measure of autonomy and freedom. The oppressive parent and the tyrannical lover, the dictator and the bully, tend to be regarded as less than fully admirable. Might it not therefore be said that, if God is really good, he could actually be expected to allow his creatures freedom? And might it not be said that he could actually be expected to allow them to act as they choose, with all the possible implications for the production of evil that this might imply?

It has been suggested that God could have made a world containing only free agents who always acted well and that the non-existence of God follows from the fact that actual free agents have failed to act well. One can find this suggestion in the work of J. L. Mackie. According to him:

If there is no logical impossibility in a man's freely choosing the good on one, or on several occasions, there cannot be a logical impossibility in his freely choosing the good on every occasion. God was not, then, faced with a choice between making innocent automata and making beings who in acting freely, would sometimes go wrong: there was open to him the obviously better possibility of making beings who would act freely but always go right. Clearly his failure to avail himself of this possibility is inconsistent with his being both omnipotent and wholly good.[19]

But, though it seems true that there is no contradiction involved in the notion of people always freely acting well, can God ensure that real people will act well without compromising their freedom? In order to ensure that people always act well, God would presumably have to cause them always to act well. But if God did that, would it not be true that people were not, in fact free?

On at least one view of freedom, the answer will be in the negative. I refer here to what is sometimes called 'libertarianism'. According to this, people's actions are free only if no cause apart from themselves brings it about that they act as they do. But should we accept that a free action cannot be caused by God? One might, at any rate, note that those who believe in God have reason for saying 'No'. For, as Antony Flew puts it, the contrary position conflicts with 'the essential theist doctrine of Divine creation'. And the reason for saying so, as Flew goes on to observe, is that the doctrine of divine creation 'apparently requires that, whether or not the creation had a beginning, all created beings—all creatures, that is—are always utterly dependent upon God as their sustaining cause. God is here the First Cause in a procession which is not temporally sequential.'[20]

There are theists who do not think of creation in these terms. In their view, something can exist and be as it is without being totally dependent on God's causal activity. And for those who think in this way, it will seem natural to suppose that free actions, and other things as well, can exist uncaused by God. In words of John Lucas:

Not everything that happens can be attributed directly to the detailed decision of God. Although He knows how many hairs I have on my head, He has not decided how many there shall be. He distances Himself from the detailed control of the course of events in order, among other things, to give us the freedom of manoeuvre we need both to be moral agents and to go beyond morality into the realm of personal relations.[21]

But the traditional or classical notion of God (what we can identify as classical theism) seems to rule this position out. Traditionally speaking, all things apart from God are there because God makes them to be there, not just in the sense that he lays down the conditions in which they can arise, but also in the sense that he makes them to be for as long as they are there. And on this account, all that is real in creatures is caused by God, including their activity. As Aquinas puts it:

Just as God not only gave being to things when they first began, but is also—as the conserving cause of being—the cause of their being as long as they last . . . so he not only gave things their operative powers when they were first created, but is also always the cause of these in things. Hence if this divine influence stopped, every operation would stop. Every operation, therefore, of anything is traced back to him as its cause.[22]

If we are working with this view, we have to agree that God is causally operative in the existence of all things all the time that they exist. And this must mean that he is causally operative in all the actions of human beings, for these are as real as anything else we care to mention.

In that case, however, must it not follow that there is no such thing as human freedom? If 'X is caused by God' entails that X cannot be a free action, then it does. But theists do not have to accept this entailment, and they have reason for refusing to do so. For how do we proceed when deciding whether or not people have acted freely on a given occasion? We look to see if there is any identifiable thing in the world which has impinged on them to determine their behaviour. But God, by definition, is no such thing. If classical theists are right, he is the cause of there being such things and the cause of them continuing to be. And if that is what God is, then it makes sense to say that his being the cause of human actions need not render such actions unfree.

If Fred kills Bill under the influence of drugs or hypnotism, we say that he has not killed Bill freely. But that is because there is something in the world alongside and outside Fred making him do what he does. This would not be so, however, in the case of God causing an action of Bill. If God is the cause of things in the world existing and continuing to exist, he cannot be part of the world and he cannot act on them from outside as things in the world act on each other. He will, in fact, be the necessary condition of them being and being what they are. Or, as Herbert McCabe puts it: 'The creative causal power of God does not operate on me from outside, as an alternative to me; it is the creative causal power of God that makes me *me*.'[23] And, if that is true, then it makes sense to say that even though my actions are caused by God, they can still be my free actions. As one might also say: 'We are not free in spite of God, but because of God.'[24] This account certainly insists that some human actions are free. But it does so without committing its proponent to the view that free human actions cannot be caused by God, for it is saying that there being such actions depend on God.

One may wonder, however, whether theists who make this move are not now caught in a dilemma that has not been mentioned so far. For suppose it is true that God is the cause of human actions and that this can be so even though some human actions are free. Would it not also be true that God is the cause of moral evil? And would he not be this though able to arrange that there is no moral evil? Most people who believe in God say that his creation and sustenance of creatures is itself grounded in freedom. God does not have to create. But if that is so and if God is the cause of moral evil, should we not conclude that he is proved to be bad on two separate counts? For would he not be bad (a) by being the cause of moral evil and (b) by being the cause of evil which he could have refrained from causing?

Confronted by these questions, a defender of the view that God is good though he causes free human actions might suggest that God is justified in producing moral evil because of some concomitant good. But there does not seem to be any concomitant good when it comes to moral evil. The evil of a lamb's being eaten by a lion might be balanced by the flourishing of the lion. But with moral evil there is no flourishing at all. Those who are guilty of moral evil sometimes do damage to others. And they always damage themselves. For, in being guilty of moral evil, they are failing as moral agents. Good may accidentally arise from someone's being guilty of moral evil, but evil acts in themselves have no good aspect.

There is a fairly traditional theistic response to these observations. According to this, human moral failure cannot be thought of as something for which God is responsible because it is, in a sense, nothing at all. The idea here is that, in being the maker and sustainer of the universe, God can only be responsible for what is real and that human moral failure is somehow unreal.

But that idea is surely very counter-intuitive. What, we may ask, could be more real than human moral failure? The founder of Christian Science said that evil is an illusion. And we have seen why that suggestion is unacceptable. Should we not therefore say that moral evil is perfectly real and that God must cause it if he is the cause of free human actions?

It is worth asking, however, what kind of reality is involved in there being human moral failure. Could it be, for instance, that there are human moral failures in the sense that there are cats? Are human moral failures substances of any sort? Are they things which we can intelligibly take to be created or sustained by God?

The answer would seem to be 'No'. Human moral failures occur when people perform or refrain from performing certain actions. But they are not substances. They are what we have when people (who are substances) fail to aim for a good for which they should aim. But if that is so, it actually does make sense to say that they are, in a way, nothing at all. They are what we have when there is a gap between what is there and what ought to be there. And, if that is so, one might well argue that they cannot be caused by God. For a gap of this sort is not the kind of thing which we can think of as being caused by anything or anyone. It is a matter of absence, of what ought to be there but is not. And, for this reason, the theist may deny that God is the cause of moral evil. If moral evil is an absence of a certain good, it is not something which can be caused by anything, whether divine or human. People may be morally evil, and their evil may be attributed to them. If I am morally evil, then I am at fault. I have gone wrong. But this is not to say that, when people act badly, they cause (bring about) something which we can call moral evil (as someone can be said to be a cause or producer of a substantial thing). By the same token, so we may argue, even though God causes free human actions, it does not follow that he causes something which we can call moral evil. It follows that he has brought it about that there are actions of various kinds. But it does not follow that, if the actions are evil, he has brought about anything which can be considered as an intrinsically evil thing—a blot on the landscape, as it were. All that follows is that he has brought it about that there are people who fail to be as good as they could be. As McCabe, again, writes:

I could not, of course, act unjustly unless I existed and were sustained in being by God. I could not do it unless every positive action I took were sustained in being by God. My desire for riches is a positive thing, and a perfectly good positive thing, created by God—the only thing is that it is a *minor* thing. I should desire other things more than this. My failure to seek my true happiness and fulfilment, of course, since it is a failure, an absence, a non-being, is not created or sustained or brought about by God.[25]

Someone boiling with envy and malice cannot be described just as lacking something. And bad moral qualities can be ascribed to people just like good ones. Fred might be described as just. But he might also be described as unjust. In this sense, so we may say, moral failure is a positive matter. But envy, malice, and comparable drives still involve failure to be as good as one could be. What worries us about them is the fact that they make people less than they should be, that those in their grip are settling for a lesser good.

Looked at from this perspective, the serious question facing someone who says that God causes free human actions is not 'Is God the cause of moral evil?' It is 'Why has God not caused more moral goodness than he has?'. Moral evil may be seen as a matter of what ought to be there but is not. So we need not worry about what causes it. But we may well wonder why there is not more moral goodness than there is or has been. And we may consequently wonder whether God can be good since he has not produced more moral goodness than he has. We may wonder whether God is guilty by neglect.

Some would say that he is (and that he cannot, therefore, be good). But that response assumes that God is under some obligation to produce more goodness than he does. And it seems hard to show that God (whether or not we believe him to exist) should be conceived as under any such obligation. For how would one show this?

One might think in terms of analogies. If I am a teacher and if my pupils end up knowing nothing more than they knew when they came my way, then I might be reproached for failing in my obligation to teach them something. Or, to take another example, nurses are obliged to do certain things, and they may be chided if they do not do them. But it is surely absurd to think of God as having a job in which he contracts to produce a given result. Such a notion of God

would, at any rate, be quite at odds with traditional ways
of conceiving him. And if we think of God as maker and
sustainer of the universe, it is absurd to suggest that there is
any quantity of goodness which he ought to produce. It might
be said that God is obliged to produce the best possible world.
But the best possible world is not something makeable. Talk
of a 'best possible world' is as incoherent as talk of a 'greatest
prime number'. As C. J. F. Williams observes:

> It is a consequence of God's infinite power, wisdom and goodness
> that, for any world we can conceive him creating, it is possible to
> conceive him creating a better world. More than that—for this has
> nothing to do with what we can or cannot conceive—for any world
> which God can create, there is another, better world which he could
> also have created.[26]

The Goodness of God and the Problem of Evil

If what I have said so far is right, the problem of evil does not
rule out the possible existence of God. To the charge that
theism is incompatible with acknowledgement of evil's reality,
one may reply that, for all we know, the evil in the world may
be justified as necessary for certain goods. If it is said that evil
makes it unlikely that God exists, one may respond by saying
that we may well be in no position to determine what might be
produced by an omnipotent, omniscient, good God, and we
can give some reason for saying that the nature of the world as
we find it gives no solid reason to suppose that God is not
good. At this point, however, it is worth pointing out a further
line of defence open to someone who thinks it possible or
likely that there is a God in spite of the existence of evil.
It hinges on the question 'What do you mean by "God is
good"?'

Those who believe that God's existence is impossible or
unlikely because of the reality of evil usually mean 'Given the
reality of evil, it is impossible or unlikely that there is a God
who is morally good'. And many of those who defend belief in
God work on the same assumption. But suppose we now
introduce a new question into the discussion. Suppose we ask

whether the theist is bound to regard God as morally good. Once we do this, a whole new line of defence is open to someone who thinks it reasonable to believe in the existence of God along with the existence of evil. For, clearly, if belief in God is not necessarily belief in the existence of a morally good agent, then the problem of evil cannot even get off the ground in so far as it is taken to be a problem concerning God's moral goodness. As some philosophers would say, it turns into a pseudo-problem. And then, of course, it is not necessarily a reason for ignoring any positive case offered for believing in God. For if the problem of evil depends on thinking of God as a morally good agent and if theists do not have to regard him as such, then the problem is not necessarily a problem for belief in God.

So do we have to say that belief in the existence of God is belief in the existence of a morally good agent? Do we have to suppose that the goodness of God is moral goodness? Here, it seems to me, there are grounds for replying in the negative.

One may, of course, say that if God is good, then he must be morally good, since, if he is not, we cannot mean anything in calling him good. It might also be argued that God must be morally good since moral goodness is the highest form of goodness known to us and cannot, therefore, be lacking in God. But theologians have taught that God is good without holding that his goodness is that of a morally good agent. They have said, for example, that God is good because he somehow contains in himself the perfections of his creatures, all of which reflect him somehow. And it is implausible to hold that moral goodness is the only goodness there is. There are good chairs, good radios, good dinners, good essays, good books, good poems, good maps, good all sorts of things. And to say that moral goodness is the highest form of goodness we know is precisely to beg the question in the context of the present discussion. If we can know that God exists and if God's goodness is not moral goodness, then moral goodness is not the highest form of goodness we know. There is the goodness of God to be reckoned with.

A common objection to this suggestion is to say that God

must be thought of as morally good since God is a person and since persons are good in so far as they are morally good. On this account, God is at least as good as I am when I am good. And, so the argument usually goes, he is actually a lot better. I am sometimes morally bad, but, so many have urged, God always gets it right. He is a perfectly morally good person.[27] Yet a Christian, at any rate, might wonder about the expression 'God is a person'. It does not occur anywhere in the Bible. The Christian God is the Trinity, of Father, Son, and Spirit. And although Christians say that there are three persons in the Trinity, they do not mean that God is three persons in one person. So why should they hold that God is a person?

Perhaps they should say that God is personal and that 'God is a person' says nothing more than that. Even if we accept that point, however, there is surely something odd in the suggestion that to call God good must be to say that he is morally good. For if we are talking of the maker and sustainer of creatures, must it not, rather, be true that God can be neither morally good nor morally bad?

I presume at this point that a morally good agent is someone exemplifying virtues of the sort listed by Aristotle (384–322 BC): the cardinal virtues of prudence, justice, temperateness, and courage. We might also (as, of course, many do) say that an agent is morally good if he or she acts over time in accordance with certain duties or obligations. It has been said that a morally good agent is simply a subject who does no morally bad action. But since that can be true of a dog, something more seems required. To deem an agent to be morally good, we need positive grounds for attributing to that agent virtue or obedience to duty or obligation. And this, of course, means that if something is such that virtue or obedience to duty or obligation cannot intelligibly be attributed to it, we have no reason to think of it as either morally good or morally bad.

So consider now the sense in which the cardinal virtues can intelligibly be ascribed to God. Can we think of him as exemplifying prudence, temperateness, or courage? Not if these virtues are what Aristotle thought them to be, dispositions needed by human beings in order to flourish as human beings. Christians will not find it amiss to speak of God as just. But they cannot mean by this that God gives others what he owes them (commutative justice), for the notion of him being indebted to them makes no sense. As source of everything creaturely, God cannot receive gain by what is creaturely and then return it. If we are entitled to call him just, it can only be because he can be said to act in accordance with his own decrees (this not implying anything about the content of those decrees) or because he gives to his creatures what is good (this not implying that he gives the same to every creature). This, in fact, is the view of God's justice found in the Old Testament. The justice (or righteousness) of God is not there a matter of distributive justice. It is a matter of him acting in accordance with his declared will for Israel.[28]

It might be said that some creatures are such that God ought to give them certain things, e.g. that he ought to reward virtuous people with happiness just because they are virtuous (assuming we draw some distinction between 'being virtuous' and 'being happy'). At this point, however, we come to the issue of God's duties or obligations, and the point to make here is that we have good reason for resisting the suggestion that God has any duties or obligations. Could he, for instance, have duties or obligations to himself? Should he, for example, strive to keep himself healthy? Should he try not to let his talents or abilities go to seed? One might say that God has obligations to others: that he is, for example, obliged to reward good people with happiness. But this suggestion also makes no sense. What can oblige God in relation to his creatures? Could it be that there is a law which says that God has obligations to them? But what law? And where does it come from? Is it something set up by someone independently of God? But how can anyone set up a law independently of God? Is God not the maker of everything apart from himself?

Someone might say that there are duties and obligations binding on God and that this just has to be accepted. But why should we believe this? What, indeed, are we to suppose ourselves to believe in believing this? Perhaps we should be thinking that there are moral laws with which God is presented, just as he is presented with logical laws. And perhaps we should say that, just as God has to accept that a given law of logic holds, so he must accept that there are certain courses of action which he must either refrain from or adopt. But the cases cited here are not parallel. We can speak of God as 'bound' by laws of logic. But this does not mean that he is bound by any command to do what can be done. And it does not mean that he has a duty or obligation to do anything we care to mention. To say that someone has a duty or is obliged to do something is already to suppose that the person in question is bound by some law or other. But why should we suppose that God is bound by some law or other?

One might say that God is bound by moral laws binding on all of us. One might say, for example, that God is bound (or duty bound or obliged) not to murder innocent people. But God, of course, cannot murder innocent people. He cannot be singled out and accused of doing anything which, were Fred to do it, would get him condemned for murder in a court of law. God has no fingerprints. He cannot be proved to have held any gun against someone. Nor can he be seen by anyone to have done so. He can be said to have willed what happens when someone gets murdered (for the person would not have been murdered had God not willed it somehow). But can he be thought to be bound by a moral law forbidding him to will as he does? What would the law be? Perhaps it would run: 'No human being and no god may conspire in the bringing about of the death of an innocent person.' But that law cannot be truly thought to have been obeyed by the God who makes and sustains the universe. For he has most manifestly conspired in the deaths of many innocent people. Had God de-created the universe in 1066, many innocent people who have died since then would not have died. So God conspired in their deaths.

An objector might say that he did so with morally cogent reasons recognized by him as such. It might be argued, for example, that he did so because he knew that this would have resulted in an objectively better state of affairs than some alternative state of affairs. But can it be held that there having occurred all that has happened since 1066 is better than there having been nothing since 1066? One might say that, given 1066 and what followed, there have been more good things than there would have been if history had ended in 1066. But would that mean that a world with 1066 and what followed is objectively better than a world ending at 1066? We can count good things, but can we evaluate between the world ending at 1066 and the world going on until now so as to say that one of them is, in some absolute sense, better than the other? And what is a 'state of affairs'? How many of them can you number around you as you read this book?

Quite apart from such musings, however, the argument is flawed because it presupposes that God has a duty or obligation to do this, that, or the other. One has duties and obligations as part of a definite, describable context. A nurse, for example, has certain duties in the light of such things as hospitals, drugs, sickness, doctors, death, and patients. A parent has obligations against a background of families, children, and society. And so on for other examples. In that case, it makes sense to deny that God has duties and obligations. In the light of what context can he be said to have them? There would seem to be no context at all, and the notion of him having duties and obligations is therefore an idle one. If anything, it should be said that God must be the cause of duties and obligations, for, if God is the Creator, he must be the cause of there being situations in which people have such things (i.e. our good is something deriving from God since he makes us what we are).

Someone might reply that God does have obligations as a parent. Before you produce a child, someone might argue, it is indeed true that you have no obligations to it (because it is not there). But, having produced the child, you do have obligations. And, so the argument might continue, this is how it must be with God. Having fathered me, he is bound to act towards me in certain ways. But this argument would simply miss the point. Let us suppose that God does have obligations towards his creatures. How is he to fulfil them? He can only do so by bringing it about that certain events come to pass. But he can only do that by willing the existence of things. And how can he be obliged to do that?

Reasons for the Existence of God?

A great deal more could be said about the problem of evil. But we now need to move on. Before we abandon the problem of evil altogether, however, it is worth pointing out a further line of defence open to someone who thinks it possible or likely that there is a God in spite of the existence of evil. We can call it the 'Reasonableness of the Existence of God Defence' since it proceeds from the view that it is reasonable to believe in God.

As we have seen, someone who thinks that the existence of evil renders the existence of God impossible or unlikely is arguing as follows:

> Evil exists.
> If evil exists, it is impossible or unlikely that God exists.
> Therefore, it is impossible or unlikely that God exists.

Now this argument is valid, though that is not to say that its premisses and conclusion are true. But suppose one had very good reason for believing that God exists. In that case one would certainly have reason for saying that God's existence is possible. One would also have reason for denying that evil makes it unlikely that God exists, since one would already have good reason to believe that God does exist. One might therefore offer the following argument:

> God exists.
> Evil exists.
> Therefore, both God and evil exist and the existence of evil does not make it impossible or unlikely that God exists.

Now there may be no good reason for believing in the existence of God. But if people thought they had a good reason, they would be justified in using the second of the above arguments in response to the assertion that belief in God can be dismissed in advance because of the problem of evil. Those who want to reject belief in God without reference to reasons for belief in God might find such a move tiresome; but they could only show that it was unreasonable by shifting their ground. In other words, they would now have to start engaging with the believer's reasons for believing in the existence of God.

At this point in our discussion, therefore, perhaps we can join them. To begin with, we shall turn to a line of argument whose philosophical career has been long and various. It centres on the meaning of the word 'God' and is usually referred to as the 'Ontological Argument'.

4

The Ontological Argument

'WHAT'S in a name?', asked Juliet. It could be said that
defenders of the ontological argument think there can be quite
a lot. Before we see why, however, I ought to point out that
there is actually no single argument which alone deserves to be
called 'The Ontological Argument'. For reasons of convention
and convenience I retain the title as a chapter heading. I also
sometimes use the expression 'the ontological argument'. But
'the ontological argument' is best taken as referring to a group
of related arguments.

Ontological Arguments

(a) *Anselm*

The most famous form of the ontological argument is to be
found in St Anselm's *Proslogion*, chapters 2 and 3, where
Anselm offers a *reductio ad absurdum* argument (i.e. an argument whose aim is to show that a proposition is true because
its denial entails a contradiction or some other absurdity).

To begin with, says Anselm, we need to consider what God
is. The answer that Anselm comes up with is that God is
'something than which nothing greater can be conceived'
(*aliquid quo nihil maius cogitari possit*). This, he observes, is
what 'we believe' God to be.[1]

But suppose someone says that there is no God. That
person, says Anselm, 'understands what he hears, and what he
understands is in his intellect (*in intellectu*)'. From this Anselm
concludes that God exists even in the intellect of one denying
his existence. 'Even the Fool [in *Psalms* 13 and 52], then, is
forced to agree that something than which nothing greater

can be conceived exists in the intellect, since he understands this when he hears it, and whatever is understood is in the intellect.'

But does God exist in any other sense? According to Anselm, the answer must be 'Yes'. God, he argues, must exist not only in the intellect but in reality (*in re*). Why? Because, says Anselm, '*Et certe id quo maius cogitari nequit non potest esse in solo intellectu. Si enim vel in solo intellectu est potest cogitari esse et in re quod maius est.*'

What does Anselm mean here? The text can be translated in two ways (people rarely seem to see that there are two possibilities here):

(1) And for sure, that than which a greater cannot be conceived cannot exist only in the intellect. For if it is only in the intellect it can be thought to be in reality as well, which is greater.
(2) And for sure that than which a greater cannot be conceived cannot exist only in the intellect. For if it is only in the intellect, what is greater can be thought to be in reality as well.

Either way, however, it is clear that Anselm is arguing that something can be thought to be greater than something existing only in the intellect and that something than which nothing greater can be conceived therefore does not just exist in the intellect.

That is as far as Anselm gets in *Proslogion* 2. But the argument continues in *Proslogion* 3. Suppose I understand that a certain person exists. Then, so Anselm would say, the person exists in my intellect. And if the person exists outside my intellect, the person exists both in the intellect and outside it. But such a person need not be such that he or she cannot be thought not to exist. I can perfectly well acknowledge the existence of someone without supposing that there is no possibility of that person not existing. By the same token, Anselm seems to assume, even if we know that God exists both in the intellect and outside it, it does not follow that there is no possibility of God not existing.[2] If we think that God is such that there is no possibility of him not existing, we need to know more of him than that he exists both in the intellect and outside it. And the burden of *Proslogion* 3 seems to be to show that we do know this of him.[3]

How? Because, says Anselm, it can be thought that there is something which cannot be thought not to exist and because God must be such a being if he is something than which nothing greater can be conceived. Why? Because, Anselm argues, it can be thought that there exists something that cannot be thought not to exist. And such a thing would be greater than something which can be thought not to exist.

Something can be thought to exist that cannot be thought not to exist, and this is greater than that which can be thought not to exist. Hence, if something than which a greater cannot be conceived can be thought not to exist, then something than which a greater cannot be conceived is not that than which a greater cannot be conceived, which is absurd.

(b) *Descartes, Malcolm, and Plantinga*

So much, then, for Anselm's version of the ontological argument. But the argument also has several other notable forms. In particular, there are the forms defended by Descartes, Norman Malcolm, and Alvin Plantinga.

Descartes's argument comes in the fifth of his *Meditations on First Philosophy*. Here Descartes says that by the word 'God' we mean 'a supremely perfect being'. And this definition of 'God', he continues, allows us to conclude that God really exists.

Why? Because, Descartes argues, existence is 'a certain perfection'. If God is by definition something supremely perfect and if existence is a perfection, it follows that God, by definition, exists and that to deny that this is so is to contradict oneself. Or, in Descartes's words:

Existence can no more be separated from the essence of God than the fact that its three angles equal two right angles can be separated from the essence of a triangle, or than the idea of a mountain can be separated from the idea of a valley. Hence it is just as much a contradiction to think of God (that is, a supremely perfect being) lacking existence (that is, lacking a perfection), as it is to think of a mountain without a valley . . . I am not free to think of God without existence (that is, a supremely perfect being without a supreme perfection) as I am free to imagine a horse with or without wings.[4]

   Malcolm's version of the ontological argument begins by trying to remove certain difficulties.[5] Philosophers often object to the ontological argument by saying that it wrongly treats existence as a perfection which things may have or lack. Malcolm agrees with this criticism, and he allows that Anselm is subject to it. According to Malcolm, Anselm supposes that existence is a perfection in his statement of the ontological argument in *Proslogion* 2. But Malcolm thinks that in *Proslogion* 3 Anselm has an ontological argument that does *not* assume that existence is a perfection. In *Proslogion* 3, says Malcolm, Anselm is saying not that God must exist because existence is a perfection, but that God must exist because the concept of God is the concept of a being *whose existence is necessary*. As Malcolm sees it, *Proslogion* 3 considers God as a being who, if he exists, has the property of *necessary existence*. Since, however, a being who has this property cannot fail to exist, it follows that God actually exists.

If God, a being a being greater than which cannot be conceived, does not exist then He cannot *come* into existence. For if He did He would either have been *caused* to come into existence or have *happened* to come into existence, and in either case He would be a limited being, which by our conception of Him He is not. Since He cannot come into existence, if He does not exist His existence is impossible. If He does exist He cannot have come into existence . . . nor can He cease to exist, for nothing could cause him to cease to exist nor could it just happen that He ceased to exist. So if God exists His existence is necessary. Thus God's existence is either impossible or necessary. It can be the former only if the concept of such a being is self-contradictory or in some way logically absurd. Assuming that this is not so, it follows that He necessarily exists.[6]

   This argument is criticized by Plantinga. But Plantinga also argues that it can be salvaged if restated with the help of the philosophical notion of possible worlds, a notion popularized through the writings of certain modal logicians.[7] Roughly speaking, a possible world is a complete way things could be. For Plantinga, our world is a possible world. So too is a world exactly like ours but in which, for example, Alvin Plantinga is a farmer instead of a philosopher. Working with this notion of possible worlds, Plantinga reformulates Malcolm's argument in the following two propositions.

1. There is a possible world, W, in which there exists a being with maximal greatness.
2. A being has maximal greatness in a world only if it exists in every world.[8]

According to Plantinga, this argument establishes that in every world there is a being with maximal greatness. Unfortunately, however, says Plantinga, the argument does not establish that there is a God in the actual world. It establishes that there is something with maximal greatness. But being maximally great only means existing in every possible world. It does not mean having the attributes traditionally ascribed to God.

As I have said, however, Plantinga thinks that the ontological argument can be defended. And at this point he begins his defence. If he is right in his assessment of Malcolm's argument, it follows that there is a possible world where a being has maximal greatness, which entails that the being exists in every world. But it does not entail that in every world the being is greater or more perfect than other inhabitants of those worlds. Plantinga therefore introduces the notion of 'maximal excellence', which he thinks of as a possible property connected with maximal greatness.

The property *has maximal greatness* entails the property *has maximal excellence in every possible world*.
Maximal excellence entails *omniscience*, *omnipotence*, and *moral perfection*.[9]

Now, says Plantinga, maximal greatness is possibly exemplified. There is a possible world where there is a being who is maximally great. In that case, however (and in view of the understanding of maximal greatness just introduced), in any possible world this being has maximal excellence. And it follows from this that in our world there is a being who has maximal excellence, which is to say that there is actually a God whose existence follows from his essence and who can thus be thought to exist in reality by reasoning that counts as a form of the ontological argument.

How Successful is the Ontological Argument?

Is the ontological argument cogent? Let us consider the question by turning to its various versions.

Anselm and Gaunilo

After the appearance of the *Proslogion* a monk called Gaunilo of Marmoutier wrote a reply to Anselm and virtually accused him of absurdity.[10] According to Gaunilo, if Anselm is correct, then it is not only God's existence that can be established by reasoning akin to Anselm's.

For example: they say that there is in the ocean somewhere an island which, because of the difficulty (or rather the impossibility) of finding that which does not exist, some have called the 'Lost Island'. And the story goes that it is blessed with all manner of priceless riches and delights in abundance, much more even than the Happy Isles, and having no owner or inhabitant, it is superior everywhere in abundance of riches to all those islands that men inhabit. Now, if anyone should tell me that it is like this, I shall easily understand what is said, since nothing is difficult about it. But if he should then go on to say, as though it were a logical consequence of this: You cannot any more doubt that this island that is more excellent than all other lands exists somewhere in reality than you can doubt that it is in your mind; and since it is more excellent to exist not only in the mind alone but also in reality, therefore that it must needs be that it exists. For if it did not exist, any other land existing in reality would be more excellent than it, and so this island, already thought by you to be more excellent than others, will not be more excellent. If, I say, someone wishes thus to persuade me that this island really exists beyond all doubt, I should either think that he was joking, or I should find it hard to decide which of us I ought to judge the bigger fool.[11]

There is one reply that Anselm could offer against this objection.[12] For he never talks about something that is in fact greater than anything else of the same kind. He talks about God as something than which nothing greater can be conceived. Gaunilo concentrates on the notion of an island which is better than all other islands. But Anselm focuses on the notion of God as something that cannot be surpassed in any respect. It might thus be suggested that Anselm and Gaunilo are talking at cross-purposes.

A defender of Gaunilo might, however, accept this point and still try to preserve the thrust of his argument. What if we take it as urging that, if Anselm's argument works, then it is possible to establish the existence, not of the island which is better than all others, but of the island than which no more perfect island can be conceived?

The move has seemed plausible to many, but it need not really be taken as showing that Anselm is mistaken in his argument. For it depends on assuming the coherence of the concept of an island than which no island more perfect can be conceived. Yet, no matter what description of an island is provided, it is always possible that something could be added to it so as to give an account of a better island. As Plantinga puts it:

No matter how great an island is, no matter how many Nubian maidens and dancing girls adorn it, there could always be a greater—one with twice as many, for example. The qualities that make for greatness in islands—number of palm trees, amount and quality of coconuts, for example—most of these qualities have no *intrinsic maximum*. That is, there is no degree of productivity or number of palm trees (or of dancing girls) such that it is impossible that an island display more of that quality. So the idea of a greatest possible island is an inconsistent or incoherent idea; it's not possible that there be such a thing.[13]

Perhaps, then, we might conclude that Anselm's position survives the attack of Gaunilo's island argument. Might it not be refuted on other grounds, however? At this point it is worth referring to Immanuel Kant (1724–1804), for it is commonly claimed that Kant provided absolutely decisive objections to the ontological argument.

Kant and the Ontological Argument

Kant has two main objections to the ontological argument, the first of which he expresses as follows:

> If, in an identical proposition, I reject the predicate while retaining the subject, contradiction results; and I therefore say that the former belongs necessarily to the latter. But if we reject the subject and predicate alike, there is no contradiction; for nothing is then left that can be contradicted. To posit a triangle, and yet to reject its three angles, is self-contradictory; but there is no contradiction in rejecting the triangle together with its three angles. The same holds true of the concept of an absolutely necessary being. If its existence is rejected, we reject the thing itself with all its predicates; and no question of contradiction can then arise. There is nothing outside it that would be contradicted, since the necessity of the thing is not supposed to be derived from anything external; nor is there anything internal that would he contradicted, since in rejecting the thing itself we have at the same time rejected all its internal properties . . . I cannot form the least concept of a thing which, should it be rejected with all its predicates, leaves behind a contradiction.[14]

Is this reasoning acceptable? The text I have quoted is not, perhaps, a terribly clear one. One may wonder what exactly Kant is driving at. But his main point seems clear. Kant is presumably saying that the statement 'God does not exist' is not self-contradictory. Whereas Descartes would say that denying God's existence is like denying that triangles have three sides, Kant is arguing that 'God does not exist' could be true, even if it is, in fact, false. On Kant's view, to define something is to say that if anything matches the definition, then it will be as the definition states. But whether anything does match a given definition is a further question.

Is that right? Considered as a response to Descartes's form of the ontological argument, the answer is surely 'Yes'. Descartes supposes that the concept of God is the concept of something having the perfection of existence. But even if we accept that this is so, it does not follow that there actually is any such thing as Descartes takes God to be. From a given perfection's being part of the concept of a thing, it does not follow that the thing actually exists. Or, to put it another way, one may define a thing how one likes, but it is always a further question whether or not there is anything corresponding to the definition.

One may, wonder, however, whether Kant's argument really engages with what Anselm writes. For is it true that Anselm proposes to define God into existence? Readers will find that most people writing on Anselm assume that he does. But we may, in fact, challenge this assumption. Early in the argument of *Proslogion* 2 Anselm introduces a premiss asserting existence ('Something than which nothing greater can be conceived exists in the intellect'). And his question in *Proslogion* 2 is not whether we can move from a definition of God to the reality of God, but whether we can reasonably suppose that something than which nothing greater can be conceived exists *only in the intellect*.

What of Kant's second objection, however? This is stated by him in the following (famous) passage:

'*Being*' is obviously not a real predicate; that is, it is not a concept of something which could be added to the concept of a thing. It is merely the positing of a thing, or of certain determinations, as existing in themselves. Logically, it is merely the copula of a judgement . . . If, now, we take the subject (God) with all its predicates (among which is omnipotence), and say 'God is' or 'There is God', we attach no new predicate to the concept of God, but only posit the subject in itself with all its predicates, and indeed posit it as being an *object* that stands in relation to my *concept*. The content of both must be one and the same . . . Otherwise stated, the real contains no more than the merely possible. A hundred real thalers do not contain the least coin more than a hundred possible thalers.[15]

Kant seems to be saying that, although the ontological argument holds that 'existing' is a quality, attribute, or characteristic which God must have, when we say that something exists, we are not ascribing to it any quality, attribute, or characteristic. And although this suggestion is often rejected, it seems to me to be correct. Or, to put it another way, '—— exist(s)' can never serve to tell us anything about any object or individual. By 'object' or 'individual' I mean something that can be named. On my account, then, Brian Davies (the writer of the book you are reading) is an object or individual; and to say that existence (or being) is not a predicate is to say that, while there are predicates which do give us information about Brian Davies (predicates truly ascribing properties to him) '—— exist(s)' is not one of them. If 'Brian Davies snores' is true, someone who comes to know this learns something about Brian Davies. 'Brian Davies snores' says something about Brian Davies. This, however, is not the case with 'Brian Davies exists'.

One reason for thinking this lies in the fact that the contrary supposition leads to paradox. If 'exists' ascribes a property to Brian Davies in 'Brian Davies exists', then it looks as though 'Brian Davies does not exist' denies that he has this property. If Brian Davies does not exist, however, how can it be true of him that he lacks a property? Hence the paradox.[16] On the assumption that 'exists' gives a genuine property of individuals, affirmative existential statements (e.g. 'Brian Davies exists') would seem to be necessarily true, and negative existential ones (e.g. 'Brian Davies does not exist') would seem to be necessarily false.

One may feel, however, that this hardly shows that 'exists' does not express a property of individuals. At this point, therefore, let us note that the work done by 'exist' in sentences of the form 'A's exist' can equally well be done by the word 'Someone' or 'Something'. 'Faithful husbands exist' can just as well be rendered by 'Someone is a faithful husband'. Nothing is thereby lost.[17] But 'Someone is a faithful husband' can hardly be taken to be *about* any particular individual. We may assent to it because we know of certain faithful husbands; but the falsity of the proposition would not follow even if all husbands known to us were to become unfaithful.[18] Given that 'Someone' in 'Someone is a faithful husband' is doing the work of 'exist' in 'Faithful husbands exist', it would therefore seem that the work of 'exist' is not to tell us anything about any individual.

That appearances here are not deceptive is best brought out, however, by noting the way in which statements of existence can be viewed as statements of number. The way forward at this point is, I think, indicated by Gottlob Frege (1848–1925) and remarks made by him in *The Foundations of Arithmetic*, where he attacks the suggestion that numbers are properties of objects.

To begin with, Frege draws attention to the difference between propositions like 'The King's carriage is drawn by four horses' and 'The King's carriage is drawn by thoroughbred horses'. Going by surface appearances, one might suppose that 'four' qualifies 'horses' in the first proposition as 'thoroughbred' does in the second. But that, of course, is false. Each horse which draws the King's carriage may be thoroughbred, but each is not four. 'Four' in 'The King's carriage is drawn by four horses' cannot be telling us anything about any individual horse. It is telling us how many horses draw the King's carriage.

So, Frege argues, statements of number are primarily answers to questions of the form 'How many A's are there?'; and when we make them, we assert something not of an object (e.g. some particular horse) but of a concept. 'While looking at one and the same external phenomenon', he writes, 'I can say with equal truth both "It is a (one) copse" and "It is five trees", or both "Here are four companies" and "Here are 500 men".' He continues:

Now what changes here from one judgement to the other is neither any individual object, nor the whole, the agglomeration of them, but rather my terminology. But that itself is only a sign that one concept has been substituted for another. This suggests . . . that the content of a statement of number is an assertion about a concept.[19]

Frege then reinforces his point by means of the example 'Venus has 0 moons'. If number statements are statements about objects, about which object(s) is 'Venus has 0 moons'? Presumably, none. If I say 'Venus has 0 moons', there 'simply does not exist any moon or agglomeration of moons for anything to be asserted of; but what happens is that a property is assigned to the concept "moon of Venus", namely that of including nothing under it'. That is, if 'one' is a property of an object and if numbers greater than one are properties of groups of objects, 'nought' must be ascribable to non-existent objects. But to ascribe a property to a non-existent object is not to ascribe it to anything.

Now, says Frege, 'In this respect, existence is analogous to number. Affirmation of existence is in fact nothing but denial of the number nought.'[20] And if Frege is right about number, that is correct. Indeed, we can strengthen the claim. For statements of existence are more than *analogous* to statements of number; they *are* statements of number. As C. J. F. Williams puts it,

Statements of number are possible answers to questions of the form 'How many A's are there?' and answers to such questions are no less answers for being relatively vague. Nor do they fail to be answers because they are negative. In answering the question 'How many A's are there?' I need not produce one of the Natural Numbers. I may just say 'A lot', which is tantamount to saying 'The number of A's is not small', or 'A few', which is tantamount to saying 'The number of A's is not large'. If I say 'There are some A's', this is tantamount to saying 'The number of A's is not o'. Instead of saying 'There are a lot of A's' I may say 'A's are numerous', and instead of saying 'There are some A's' I may say 'A's exist'. All these may be regarded as statements of number.[21]

Statements of existence, then, are statements of number. They are answers to the question 'How many?', and, considered as such, they do not ascribe properties to objects. And, if that is correct, Kant is right to resist the suggestion that we can argue for God's existence on the assumption that existence is a quality, attribute, or characteristic which God must have. The question, however, is 'Does this criticism engage with the ontological argument?' The answer, I think, is 'Yes and no'.

It clearly engages with the ontological argument as Descartes presents it. Descartes is manifestly passing from a definition of God to the conclusion that God exists by means of the premiss that existence is a perfection which God, by definition, must possess. He even invokes the analogy of a triangle, as Kant does. But, contrary to what is often suggested, we are not obliged to say that Anselm argues in this way. Everything here hinges on the proper translation of his words '*Et certe id quo maius cogitari nequit non potest esse in solo intellectu. Si enim vel in solo intellectu est potest cogitari esse et in re quod maius est.*'

As I noted above, we can translate this passage thus: 'And for sure that than which a greater cannot be conceived cannot exist only in the intellect. For if it is only in the intellect it can be thought to be in reality as well, which is greater.' And if that is the right translation, then Kant's point about existence or being would seem to hold against Anselm, who would seem to be treating 'being in reality' as a perfection or great-making quality, as Descartes does. But Anselm is not making this move if the proper translation of our Latin text is 'And for sure that than which a greater cannot be conceived cannot exist only in the intellect. For if it is only in the intellect, what is greater can be thought to be in reality as well.' If that is what Anselm is saying, his argument is: (1) on the assumption that that than which nothing greater can be conceived is only in a mind, something greater can be conceived; (2) for something greater can be thought to exist in reality as well; (3) the assumption is therefore contradictory: either there is no such thing even in the intellect, or it exists also in reality; (4) but it does exist in the mind of the fool; (5) therefore that than which nothing greater can be conceived exists in reality as well as in a mind. If we want to contest this argument, we should not worry about the premiss 'Existing in reality as well as in the understanding is greater than existing in the understanding alone, i.e. than not existing'. We should concern ourselves with asking whether it is true that we can conceive of something than which nothing greater can be conceived and whether, if that than which nothing greater can be conceived exists only in the mind, something which is greater can be conceived to exist also in reality.

(c) *Malcolm and Plantinga*

Thus we come to the version of the ontological argument defended by Malcolm and Plantinga. From what I have said above, the reader will see that it is arguably wrong of Malcolm to read *Proslogion* 2 as holding that existence is a perfection. He is also arguably wrong in supposing that *Proslogion* 3 is a separate attempt to prove God's existence. But these points of interpretation need not detain us. Malcolm's argument may not be Anselm's, but it is still an argument, and we can ask if it is cogent.

The first thing to be said is that Malcolm seems to be making an acceptable point in saying that, although existence is not a perfection, *necessary existence* can be thought of as being such. In speaking of a thing having 'necessary existence', Malcolm is thinking of something which does not depend for its existence on anything apart from itself; something, further-more, which cannot pass out of existence. It is plausible to hold that such a thing would clearly differ from things (e.g. human beings) which do depend on other things for their existence. It would also differ from things whose existence can be threatened by what happens—by the actions of other things, for instance. And most people would see some point in saying that a thing of this kind would consequently enjoy a certain privilege or perfection.

But having granted this point, we can yet see, I think, that Malcolm's argument fails. One reason for saying so can be seen if we concentrate on its use of the term 'impossible'.

Remember that according to Malcolm: (1) since God cannot come into existence, his existence is impossible if he does not exist; (2) if God does exist, his existence is necessary; (3) God's existence is either impossible or necessary. But 'impossible' here is being used in two senses. First it is being used to mean 'as a matter of fact unable to come about': for when Malcolm first talks about impossibility, he is expressing the view that, if God is in fact the sort of thing that cannot come into existence, then if God does not exist, he cannot in fact exist at all. In the second case, however, 'impossible' is being used to mean 'unable to be thought without contradiction' (i.e. the opposite of 'logically necessary'), for Malcolm explains that if God's existence is impossible, 'the concept of such a being is self-contradictory or in some way logically absurd'. Now Malcolm's conclusion is that God's existence is necessary, i.e. the opposite of impossible. But as Malcolm presents this conclusion, it must mean that the concept of God is the concept of something that is logically necessary. Thus, from 'God's non-existence is as a matter of fact impossible', Malcolm reaches the conclusion that 'God's existence is logically necessary'. But that means that Malcolm is offering a very poor argument indeed. He assumes what he purports to prove, i.e. that there is a God whose non-existence is as a matter of fact impossible.

This point is well brought out by John Hick, who, following Malcolm, distinguishes between (a) something that cannot in fact be brought into existence and (b) something whose non-existence is strictly inconceivable. The first kind of being Hick calls an 'ontologically necessary being'; the second he refers to as a 'logically necessary being'. Then he explains that:

Whether there is an ontologically necessary being . . . is a question of fact, although of uniquely ultimate fact. Given this concept of an ontologically necessary being, it is a matter of logic that if there is such a being, his existence is necessary in the sense that he cannot cease to exist, and that if there is no such being, none can come to exist. This logical necessity and this logical impossibility are, however, dependent upon the hypotheses, respectively, that there is and that there is not an ontologically necessary being; apart from the hypotheses from which they follow they do not entail that there is or that there is not an eternal self-existent being. Hence, there is no substance to the dilemma: The existence of God is either logically necessary or logically absurd.[22]

Another way of seeing why Malcolm's argument will not do is to consider the following argument:

A pixie is a little man with pointed ears.
Therefore there actually is such a thing as a pixie.

Now clearly we would not accept this as an argument for pixies. Why not? Because it seems to move from a definition of 'pixie' to the conclusion that there actually is a pixie. But suppose someone were to reply that if a pixie *is* a little man with pointed ears, then he must *be* in some sense or he would not be there to have pointed ears. That too would be an unjustifiable (if unforgettable) argument. But why? Because it fails to acknowledge that 'is' can be used in at least two different ways. 'Is' can be used in giving a definition, as in 'A novel is a work of fiction'. Or it can be used to explain that there actually is something or other, as in 'There is an abominable snowman after all'. In the first use we are not really saying anything about something that exists: 'A novel is a work of fiction' does not say anything about any particular novel. It explains what the word 'novel' means. In the second use too there is a sense in which we are not saying anything about some particular thing. But nor are we explaining what something (which may or may not exist) is. In 'There is an abominable snowman after all' we are not describing anything; nor are we explaining what we should have found if we discovered one. We are saying that an abominable snowman is what something is. In the above argument from 'A pixie is a little man with pointed ears' to 'There is such a thing as a pixie', there is a move from a premiss containing the first sense of 'is' to a conclusion containing the second. Or, as some philosophers would put it, the argument moves from an 'is' of *definition* to an 'is' of *affirmative predication*. And the argument is unacceptable just because this cannot validly be done. If it could, we could define anything we like into existence.

Returning now to Malcolm, we can see at this point that he is arguing in the same way as the argument about pixies just discussed. He is saying that if God is (definitionally) necessarily existent, then there is something which can truly be said to be necessarily existent. And here lies Malcolm's error. We can certainly agree that if God is definable as a necessary being, then God is by definition a necessary being. And if we can get people to accept our definition, we can easily convict them of self-contradiction if they also say that God is not a necessary being. For then they would be saying both that God is a necessary being and that he is not. But we cannot move from this conclusion to the conclusion that the definition of God as a necessary being entails that there is anything that actually corresponds to the definition of him as necessary. In other words, we cannot infer from 'God is a necessary being' that '——— is God' is truly predicated of anything. It might seem that in that case we would have to end up saying 'The necessary being does not exist', which might be thought to involve the same mistake as that involved in saying 'My mother is not my mother'. But to deny Malcolm's conclusion, all we have to say is: 'Possibly nothing at all is a necessary being', which is certainly not self-contradictory and may even be true.

So Malcolm's version of the ontological argument is unsuccessful. And, if Malcolm is properly representing the argument of Anselm's *Proslogion* 3, the same is true of that argument. But what of Plantinga's argument? It can be briefly stated thus:

1. There is a possible world containing a being with maximal greatness.
2. Any being with maximal greatness has the property of maximal excellence in every possible world.
3. Any being with maximal excellence is omniscient, omnipotent, and morally perfect in every world.
4. Therefore, in our world there is a being who has omniscience, omnipotence, and moral perfection.

Some philosophers would challenge this argument by attacking the whole notion of possible worlds, but the intricacies of this debate cannot be entered into here and, in any case, Plantinga can restate his argument without reference to it. Let us instead concentrate on Plantinga's belief that, from the fact that it is possible for there to be something having the property of maximal greatness and from the fact that our world is a possible world, it follows that in our world there is something omniscient, omnipotent, and morally perfect. Should we accept this inference?

We might say that, without a proof of God's existence, we need not accept that it is possible for there to be something having the property of maximal greatness. In other words, and as Aquinas argued, we might deny that we have a concept of God from which we can proceed to a demonstration of God's existence.[23] But since what is actual is also possible (i.e. since what is the case can be the case), let us agree that our world is a possible world. Let us also agree that a being with maximal greatness is possible and that it is therefore possible that there is a being with maximal excellence in every possible world. Does it really follow that there is actually any being with maximal excellence? One might insist, as many logicians do, that if it is possible that something is necessarily the case, then the something in question is necessarily the case. So one might argue that if there could be a being with maximal excellence in every possible world, then it is necessarily the case that there is a being with maximal excellence in every possible world, including our own.

On the other hand, one might wonder whether it really is possible for there to be something with maximal excellence in every possible world. One might also argue that the fact that maximal excellence is possible does not entail that anything is actually maximally excellent. For one might maintain (a) that what is merely possible just does not have any real existence— not, at least, in the sense in which God is normally thought to have existence, and (b) that a God who exists in all possible worlds does not have any real existence either. To show the existence of God, one might suggest, it seems that one needs more than the possibility of God. From the fact that God is possible, one might argue, it follows only that he is possible, not that he is actual.[24] One might add that knowing that God is possible depends on knowing that he is actual, which would mean that proof of God's existence should proceed not from the concept of God, but from reason to believe that there is something which matches the concept of God.

Conclusion

People encountering the ontological argument for the first time usually feel that it has little to do with belief in God as we find it in practice. They also tend to feel that the argument seems like a trick or an exercise in philosophical conjuring. In this chapter I have defended some versions of the argument, and I have tried to highlight grounds for challenging some of them. But the argument, in some of its forms, is a subtle one, and it is not easily defeated. Readers are now invited to make up their own minds as to whether or not a viable form of the argument can be stated. They may well decide that it cannot. But, even if they do this, they need not conclude that there are no good philosophical grounds for believing in God. For, as we shall see in the next few chapters, it has been held that belief in God's existence can be defended with reference to *non*-ontological arguments.

5

The Cosmological Argument

WE often say that something exists because something else would not be there if the first thing did not exist. A doctor, for example, may argue that a patient has a particular virus because the person is displaying certain symptoms. I now want to turn to a similar argument for the existence of God, commonly called 'the cosmological argument'. This has a long history, and versions of it have been offered by writers from the early Greek period to the present time. Many people who believe in God find it to be the most appealing argument of all.

God and the Beginning of the Universe

There are many things which we know to have come into being. People are a case in point. And these things raise a perfectly natural question. What brought them into being? What got them going? When we are dealing with what has begun to exist, we do not assume that it 'just happened'. We suppose that something produced it, and we ask what that could be.

This familiar way of reasoning brings us to one major version of the cosmological argument. It is particularly associated with a group of writers in the Middle Ages and earlier, a group which belonged to the Islamic kalām tradition of philosophy. So we can call it 'the kalām cosmological argument' (*kalām* is Arabic for 'speech'). But, though the name may sound unfamiliar, the argument is not. It is commonly advanced at a popular level. Whether they know it or not, it is the kalām argument that people are basically offering when they say, as they often do, that they believe in God because 'something must have started it all' or because 'things cannot have got going by themselves'.

The fundamental idea here is that God must exist because the universe must have had a beginning and because only God could have brought this about. Together with this idea goes the belief that everything that has a beginning of existence must have a cause. In the words of one of the kalām argument's most recent defenders:

Since everything that begins to exist has a cause of its existence, and since the universe began to exist, we conclude, therefore, the universe has a cause of its existence . . . Transcending the entire universe there exists a cause which brought the universe into being . . . But even more: we may plausibly argue that the cause of the universe is a personal being . . . If the universe began to exist, and if the universe is caused, then the cause of the universe must be a personal being who freely chooses to create the world . . . the kalām cosmological argument leads to a personal Creator of the universe.[1]

The reader may wonder why it should be thought that if the beginning of the universe was caused to be, 'the cause of the universe must be a personal being'. Defenders of the kalām argument would say, however, that only something like free, intelligent choice can account for the coming to pass of what, like the beginning of the universe, cannot be explained in terms of unfree, non-intelligent, physical processes. The occurrence of such processes depends on the universe being there in the first place. So the cause of the beginning of the universe, if there is one, cannot be an unfree, non-intelligent, physical process. According to defenders of the kalām argument, that leaves only one other kind of cause to be responsible for the universe coming into being. The cause, so the argument runs, must be a personal being.

But is it true that whatever has a beginning of existence must have a cause? That it is true can readily be regarded as something of a philosophical commonplace. Hence, for example, we find Thomas Reid (1710–96) writing:

That neither existence, nor any mode of existence, can begin without an efficient cause, is a principle that appears very early in the mind of man; and it is so universal, and so firmly rooted in human nature, that the most determined scepticism cannot eradicate it.[2]

But some philosophers have argued that there is no way of proving that whatever has a beginning of existence has a cause. Here we might mention David Hume. According to him, the ideas of cause and effect are distinct, and it is possible for something to arise without a cause. As Hume himself expresses the point:

As all distinct ideas are separable from each other, and as the ideas of cause and effect are evidently distinct, 'twill be easy for us to conceive any object to be non-existent this moment, and existent the next, without conjoining to it the distinct idea of a cause or productive principle. The separation, therefore, of the idea of a cause from that of a beginning of existence is plainly possible for the imagination, and consequently the actual separation of these objects is so far possible that it implies no contradiction or absurdity.[3]

Yet, though many have found this to be an attractive argument, it is also open to question. Hume seems to be saying that since we can *imagine* a beginning of existence without any cause, it follows that there *can* be a beginning of existence without any cause. But that is false. As F. C. Copleston observes, 'even if one can imagine first a blank, as it were, and then X existing, it by no means follows necessarily that X can begin to exist without an extrinsic cause'.[4] The same point has been made by Elizabeth Anscombe. In her words:

If I say I can imagine a rabbit coming into being without a parent rabbit, well and good: I imagine a rabbit coming into being, and our observing that there is no parent rabbit about. But what am I to imagine if I imagine a rabbit coming into being without a cause? Well, I just imagine a rabbit coming into being. That this *is* the imagination of a rabbit coming into being without a cause is nothing but, as it were, the *title* of the picture. Indeed I can form an image and give my picture that title. But from my being able to do *that*, nothing whatever follows about what it is possible to suppose 'without contradiction or absurdity' as holding in reality.[5]

In reply to Anscombe, you might say that you can imagine something coming into existence at some time and place and there being no cause of this. But how do you know that the thing in question has come into existence at the time and place at which you picture it as beginning to exist? You have to exclude the possibility of it having previously existed elsewhere and by some means or other come to be where you picture it as beginning to exist. Yet how are you to do that without supposing a cause which justifies you in judging that the thing really came into existence, rather than just reappeared, at one particular place and time? Recognizing that we are dealing with a genuine beginning of existence is something we are capable of because we can identify causes. As Anscombe writes: 'We can observe beginnings of new items because we know how they were produced and out of what . . . We know the times and places of their beginnings without cavil because we understand their origins.'[6] In other words, to know that something began to exist seems already to know that it has been caused. So it seems odd to suppose that there really could be a beginning of existence without a cause. Even Hume seems to have felt this, in spite of what he argues about cause and effect. In a letter written in 1754 he says: 'But allow me to tell you that I never asserted so absurd a Proposition as *that anything might arise without a cause*: I only maintain'd that, our Certainty of the Falsehood of that Proposition proceeded neither from Intuition nor Demonstration; but from another Source.'[7] In a similar vein C. D. Broad (1887–1971) explains that 'whatever I may *say* when I am trying to give Hume a run for his money, I cannot really *believe in* anything beginning to exist without being *caused* (in the old-fashioned sense of *produced* or *generated*) by something else which existed before and up to the moment when the entity in question began to exist'.[8]

So the kalām argument is evidently on to something. We might reasonably suppose that beginnings of existence arise from causal activity. And if the universe began to exist, perhaps we should conclude that the same is true of it. But this, of course, brings us to another question. Did the universe have a beginning?

Some have maintained that scientific evidence suggests that the universe began to exist a finite time ago. According to one author, for instance:

There is no doubt that the models best substantiated today are ones which show the Universe expanding from a 'big bang' some 14,000 million years ago. These models successfully predict not merely the density and rate of recession of the galaxies, but the ratios of the various chemical elements to each other and to radiation in the universe, and above all the background radiation.[9]

One may wonder, however, whether evidence of this kind shows that the universe actually had a beginning. Might we not regard it as evidence only of the date of the 'big bang'? And might we not ask whether the universe might not have existed in some sense before that, or before any stage to which science can reach at the moment?

At this point, certain philosophers will argue that, abstracting from scientific considerations, there are rational arguments which ought to lead us to conclude that the universe really did have a beginning.[10] It has been urged, for example, that if the universe had no beginning, then an infinity of years or generations will have been traversed by now and that this is impossible. Another argument holds that if the universe never began, infinity is being constantly added to as time goes on, which is impossible. Yet another argument hinges on the notion of infinity and the possibility of removing a past event. If the universe had no beginning, then the number of past events is infinite. But, so our third argument runs, the number of members of an infinite set is unaffected by the addition or subtraction of one. There are as many odd numbers as even numbers. And there are as many odd numbers not counting the number 1 as counting it. So, the argument concludes, if the universe had no beginning, a past event could be removed, and we would still be left with the same number of events—which is surely unbelievable.

Not all philosophers have accepted such arguments, however. Some, for instance, have said that if the universe never had a beginning, there will have been no infinity of past events to have been traversed before today. It has also been said that if the universe never had a beginning, then there is no reason to suppose that infinity is being added to in any objectionable sense. Why not? Because, so the argument suggests, if the universe had no beginning, there is no definite number of past moments or events being added to as time goes on, for there is no definite number to which addition is thereby made.

The chief issue at stake in all the arguments for and against the thesis that the universe began is whether or not there can be an infinite set of actual things (e.g. past events). Readers will have to consider how they should react to this problem. They should note, however, that they will surely be saying something odd if they conclude that there might be an infinite set of actual things since it is possible that every event has a predecessor (which is one way of expressing the claim that the universe never had a beginning). 'It is possible that every event has a predecessor' could mean either (a) there might have been more past events than there have been or (b) it might have been the case both that a certain set comprised all the events that occurred and also that an additional event occurred. Now (a) is arguably true. But it does not entail that the universe never began. (b), though, is simply contradictory.[11]

Even if this is so, however, and even if we grant that the beginning of the universe was caused, should it also be agreed that we therefore have a good argument for the existence of God? Could not a cause of the beginning of the universe be something other than God? Must it be 'a personal being', as in the argument outlined above?

If the universe was caused to come into being, it presumably could not have been caused to do so by anything material. For a material object would be part of the universe, and we are now asking about a cause distinct from the universe. For this reason, some philosophers would deny that we should speak of a personal being as accounting for the beginning of the universe. That is because, in their view, to be a personal being is to be something wholly material.

However, it would be widely accepted that, in accounting for what happens, there are only two alternatives available. On the one hand, we can invoke an explanation of a scientific kind, thereby appealing to laws of nature reporting the way in which certain physical effects are brought about by certain physical causes operating involuntarily. On the other hand, we can appeal to personal explanation in terms of the free choice or choices of a rational agent. And if we agree that the universe was caused to be, it is only personal explanation that we are able to invoke. Given that the universe cannot have been caused to be by anything material, and given that the universe was caused to be, the cause of the universe coming to be cannot be thought of except in terms of personal explanation. For this reason, defenders of the kalām argument are justified in saying that the cause of the universe coming to be must be something personal.

But even if we find the kalām argument persuasive, we may still wonder whether it counts as a good argument for the existence of God. For it is usually said that to believe in God is not just to believe that something brought it about that the universe *began* to be. Those who believe in God normally assert that he is responsible for the fact that the universe *continues* to be. Hence, for example, Aquinas, though he believed in God, found no difficulty in holding that, as far as philosophy can show, the universe might never have had a beginning.[12]

So can it be argued that the universe's continued existence should lead us to conclude that God exists? With this question we come to some other notable versions of the cosmological argument, starting with what I shall call 'the argument from contingency'.

The Argument from Contingency

Consider the fact that you are reading this book. That is a happy fact, and we may both be grateful for it. But it is also

something which did not have to be, not just in the sense that
you might never have picked the book up, but also in the
sense that someone who denied that you are reading the book
would not be guilty of self-contradiction. 'X is reading *An
Introduction to the Philosophy of Religion*' is not like 'Some
circles are square'. One may be wrong to assert that it is false,
but one would not be committing a logical error. 'X is reading
An Introduction to the Philosophy of Religion' is not, as we
might put it, true out of logical necessity. It is only contingently
true.

But what if someone says 'The universe exists'? Would it
be contradictory to say 'It's false that the universe exists'?
According to the argument from contingency, it would not.
Proponents of the argument hold that 'The universe exists' is
contingently true, not true of logical necessity. And they
hold this to be the case whether or not the universe had a
beginning. In other words, according to the argument from
contingency, the mere fact that the universe exists is something which, logically, does not have to obtain.

But in that case, so the argument continues, there must be a
reason for the universe being there. If 'The universe exists' is
only contingently true, something must account for the fact
that it is true. There must be a cause of the universe existing.
And, says the argument, the existence of this something cannot be a merely contingent matter. The cause of the universe's
existence must be necessary. It must lie in a being of which we
can say that to deny its existence is to contradict oneself. And,
so the argument from contingency concludes, we can call this
being 'God'. Or, as Leibniz, for example, puts it: 'There must
exist some one Being of metaphysical necessity, that is, to
whose essence existence belongs.'[13]

If the argument from contingency is correct, it would seem
that we can show not only that God exists, but that he *must*
exist, i.e. that his non-existence is strictly impossible. And for
many people this is one of the chief virtues of the argument.
The argument from contingency also insists that where there is
the possibility of something not existing, but where the thing
actually exists, then one will finally account for its existence

only when one arrives at something with which there is no possibility of non-existence. And this, too, for many people, is an attractive assumption. They will say that it allows us to give full rein to our desire that everything should be accounted for completely. They would add that the argument from contingency tidies things up nicely, since it ends with a truth which just cannot be other than it is.

But, even if we are swayed by such considerations, there are problems—ones which readers might already have noticed in their reading of Chapter 4. These concern the two main proposals of the argument from contingency: (1) that 'The universe exists' is contingently true, and (2) that 'God exists' is true of necessity.

Take first 'The universe exists'. If that is true (whether contingently or otherwise), it can only be because to say that something 'exists' is to ascribe to it a genuine property, quality, or characteristic. But, as we saw in Chapter 4, we have reason for denying that this is so. It is not true of things that they 'exist', as if 'existing' were attributable to them as, for example, being bald might be attributable to someone. And if that is the case, it is not true of the universe that it 'exists'. 'The universe exists' is logically on a par with declarations like 'Socrates is scarce' or 'Socrates is numerous'.

Now consider 'God exists'. According to the argument from contingency, this asserts a truth about God, considered as a distinct subject. Not only that. The argument from contingency treats 'God exists' as a necessary truth, as a proposition which cannot consistently be denied. According to the argument from contingency, to deny that God exists would be like affirming that Socrates both is and is not Greek. In that case, however, the argument seems to be suggesting that just as, for example, being three-sided is true of any particular triangle, so existing is true of God. But that is again to presume that to say that something exists is to ascribe to the thing a property, quality, or characteristic. It is to presume, for example, that 'God exists' and 'God is good' are logically on a level. One may deny this, however, just as one may deny that 'The universe exists' tells us anything about the universe. And if that is correct, one would be right to deny that it is true of God that he 'exists' or that 'God exists' is ultimately self-contradictory. According to the argument from contingency, 'God exists' is logically on a level with 'Socrates is bald'. It is supposed to tell us what is true of something. But it does not do that. And if it does not do that, neither does it tell us what is necessarily true of anything (in this case, God).

So perhaps there is indeed something wrong with the argument from contingency. But notice that even if the reasoning of the last few paragraphs is correct, it does not follow that we cannot ask whether or not there is a God (whether God exists). Nor does it follow that we cannot ask this question by reflecting on the universe. To say that 'Socrates is scarce' or 'Socrates is numerous' does not tell us anything about Socrates is not to say that there is no such person as Socrates. And, by the same token, to say that 'God exists' does not tell us anything about God is not to deny that anything is divine. Nor is it to deny that we may rightly conclude that something is divine (if you like, that God exists) by reflecting on the universe. At this point, therefore, we may move on to a final, major version of the cosmological argument, a version which we may call 'the first cause argument'. According to this, we are justified in believing in God since we are justified in raising certain causal questions about the universe as a whole.

The First Cause Argument

Perhaps the most famous version of the first cause argument is to be found in the first three of the so-called Five Ways offered by Aquinas in the *Summa Theologiae*—though here, of course, we have three arguments, not one. We may therefore start by turning to these and asking what they are all about.

(a) *The First Three Ways*

In general, Aquinas's Five Ways employ a simple pattern of argument. Each begins by drawing attention to some general feature of things known to us on the basis of experience. It is then suggested that none of these features can be accounted for in ordinary mundane terms and that we must move to a level of explanation which transcends that with which we are familiar.

Another way of putting it is to say that, according to the Five Ways, questions we can raise with respect to what we encounter raise further questions the answer to which can only be thought of as lying beyond what we encounter.

Take, for example, the First Way, in which the influence of Aristotle is particularly prevalent.[14] Here the argument starts from change in the world.[15] It is clear, says Aquinas, that there is such a thing, and he cites as an instance the change involved in wood becoming hot when subjected to fire.[16] How, then, may we account for it?

According to Aquinas, anything changing is changed by something else. *Omne quod movetur ab alio movetur*. This, he reasons, is because a thing which has changed has become what it was not to begin with, which can only happen if there is something from which the reality attained by the thing as changed somehow derives. Therefore, he concludes, there must be a first cause of things being changed. For there cannot be an endless series of things changed by other things, since if every change in a series of connected changes depends on a prior changer, the whole system of changing things is only derivatively an initiator of change and still requires something to initiate its change. There must be something which causes change in things without itself being changed by anything. There must an unchanged changer.

The pattern of the First Way is repeated in the rest of the Five Ways and therefore in the Second and the Third Ways. According to the Second Way, there are causes and effects in the world. There are, as Aquinas puts it, causes which are related as members of a series. In that case, he adds, there must be a first cause, or something which is not itself caused to be by anything. For causes arranged in series must have a first member.

In the observable world causes are found to be ordered in series; we never observe, nor ever could, something causing itself, for this would mean it preceded itself, and this is not possible. Such a series of causes must however stop somewhere; for in it an earlier member causes an intermediate and the intermediate a last . . . Now if you eliminate a cause you also eliminate its effects, so that you cannot have a last cause, nor an intermediate one, unless you have a first.

According to the Third Way there are things which are generated and perishable (e.g. plants) and things which are ungenerated and imperishable (in Aquinas's language, ungenerated and imperishable things are 'necessary' beings or things which 'must be').[17] But why should this be so? The answer, says Aquinas, must lie in something ungenerated, imperishable and dependent on nothing for being as it is.

Now any necessary being either does or does not owe its necessariness to something else. But just as we must stop somewhere in a series of efficient causes, so also in the series of necessary beings which get their necessity from outside themselves. We must stop somewhere and postulate a *per se* necessary being, the source of others being necessary.[18]

(b) *Some Criticisms*

What should we make of these arguments? Various criticisms have been levelled at them. Let us for the moment note some of these criticisms without comment. We can then consider their value and the value of the first three Ways themselves.

The first concerns Aquinas's principle that nothing changes itself. This principle has been attacked on various grounds. It has been said that we can easily point to things that do change themselves; that we can point, for instance, to people and to animals. It has also been said that Aquinas's principle conflicts with Newton's first law of motion. According to Anthony Kenny, this law 'wrecks the argument of the First Way. For at any given time the rectilinear uniform motion of a body can be explained by the principle of inertia in terms of the body's own previous motion without appeal to any other agent.'[19]

Kenny also offers another criticism of Aquinas's First Way. The Way, says Kenny, depends on the false assumption that something can be made to be actually F only through the

agency of something actually F. But, says Kenny, 'A kingmaker
need not himself be king, and it is not dead men who commit
murders.'[20] 'The falsifications of the principle', Kenny adds,
'are fatal to the argument [sc. of the First Way]. For unless the
principle is true, the conclusion contradicting the possibility of
a self-mover does not follow. If something can be made F by
an agent which is merely potentially F, there seems no reason
why something should not actualize its own potentiality to
F-ness.'[21]

Kenny also advances what he regards as a decisive refutation of the Second Way. Aquinas accepted certain medieval
views about the nature and influence of heavenly bodies, and,
in his view, things like the generation of people involve the
causal activity of the sun. Kenny concentrates on these facts,
suggesting that they can be used to criticize the Second Way.
As he puts it:

Aquinas believed that the sun was very much more than a necessary
condition of human generation. The human father, he explains . . . in
generation is a tool of the sun . . . The series of causes from which the
Second Way starts is a series whose existence is vouched for only by
medieval astrology . . . The First Way starts from an indisputable fact
about the world; the Second starts from an archaic fiction.[22]

Another reason offered for rejecting Aquinas's position
brings us to what is sometimes called 'the problem of infinite
regress'. Aquinas seems to be saying that there is a sense in
which there cannot be an infinite series of causes; that the
buck, so to speak, must stop somewhere. He says that there
cannot be an infinite series of changed changers, caused
causes, or necessary beings each of which owes its necessity to
something else. But people have asked why there cannot be an
infinite series of causes. They have also asked how Aquinas
can avoid contradicting himself. If, for example, nothing
causes itself, how can there be a first cause which does not
itself require a cause other than itself?

It has also been maintained that there is simply no need
to ask the sort of question which Aquinas evidently finds
important. In the first two Ways, he seems to be saying that

we should seek to account for general features of the world such as change, causes, and effects. In the Third Way he seems to be saying that the continued existence of something ungenerated and incorruptible requires a cause. But why? According to some people, features such as these should just be accepted as brute fact. In a famous radio debate with Frederick Copleston, Bertrand Russell (1872–1970) was asked whether he would agree that the universe is 'gratuitous'. The reply was: 'I should say that the universe is just there, and that's all.'[23] Following a similar line of thought, John Hick writes: 'How do we know that the universe is not 'a mere unintelligible brute fact'? Apart from the emotional colouring suggested by the phrase, this is precisely what the sceptic believes it to be; and to exclude this possibility at the outset is merely to beg the question at issue.'[24]

(c) *Are the First Three Ways Cogent?*

Perhaps the first thing to say at this point is that some of the criticisms levelled against the first three Ways are either unfair or inconclusive. Take, for example, Kenny's claim that the Second Way can be rejected because it depends on theories in medieval astrology. This claim is not very plausible. Aquinas may have held odd views about cosmology, but the Second Way is concerned with causes and effects in the world in general. It does not, as such, offer specific causal theories about what in the world causes what. In a sense, it is concerned with causality itself.

It might be replied that, even if we accept this point, it is still true that something not actually F can make something potentially F become actually F. But this argument can also be criticized. It is clearly true, as Kenny says, that kingmakers need not be kings and that dead men do not commit murders. But the First Way does not subscribe to the principle that only what is actually F will make something potentially F actually F. And it would be odd if it did. Apart from the fact that Kenny's counter-examples are so obvious that one could reasonably expect a thinker of Aquinas's stature to have anticipated them, the principle conflicts with medieval views about the temperature of the sun which Aquinas endorses in commenting on the Greek philosopher Aristotle (384– 322 BC).[25] Furthermore, if Aquinas maintained that only what was actually F could make things become F, he would be committed to saying that, for instance, God is hot, cold, pink, and fluffy. For Aquinas holds that God accounts for the changes that occur in the world. But Aquinas would clearly not want to talk of God being hot, cold, pink, or fluffy. For a start, he would say that God is not a body.[26] As is clear from the text of the First Way, what Aquinas wants to say is that only something *actual* will bring about a change to being F in something that is potentially F. The First Way also seems to imply that only something with the power to make something F can ultimately account for something becoming F. But this view is evidently not affected by Kenny's examples. A kingmaker need not be a king, but he must have the power to make kings. Murderers cannot be corpses, yet they must have the power to kill.

But what of Kenny's claim that Newton has disproved the principle that nothing changes or moves itself? And what of the problem of infinite regress? What, too, of the objection that we need not account for change, for causes and effects in the world, and for the fact that the world continues to be?

The reference to Newton does not, in fact, seem to rule out what Aquinas intends to assert. Newton's first law of motion holds that a continuing uniform rectilinear motion of a body does not require explanation in terms of a changer or mover acting on the body. But such motion would not be an example of what Aquinas means by 'change'. For Aquinas, we have change when genuine alteration occurs in a subject. But the uniform rectilinear motion of Newton's first law, if it ever occurred (and we have no reason to believe that it could occur), would be an instance of constancy or lack of change in a subject. Such constancy, of course, might come to an end as a body with uniform rectilinear motion comes, for example, to accelerate or change direction. And that would be an instance of what Aquinas means by 'change'. But he and Newton would then be in agreement. For Newton would also have looked for a cause of this change outside the body itself, and his first law says that such change is produced by an external force.

In reply to this point, someone might observe that it does nothing to meet Kenny's other objection to the principle that nothing changes itself—i.e. the objection based on the fact that people and animals seem to be self-changing. But it is not obvious that apparent self-changers, like people and animals, count as exceptions to what Aquinas has in mind. He does not mean that the world does not contain things which can be thought of as somehow changing themselves. He does not, for example, deny that people can be responsible for change in themselves, or that animals can be so. To stick with the instance of animal change, his position is that, as Christopher Martin puts it,

a dog can only start barking in virtue of some non-barking aspect that it has. But this non-barking aspect cannot be just 'its aspect of non-barking': if the barking cannot cause itself, then neither can the non-barking, as such. It has to be some other actually existing aspect of the dog that causes the barking. So though the dog does initiate its own change in a sense, strictly speaking it is one aspect or part of the dog which initiates a change in another aspect or part. Thus the dog does not initiate its own change in what Aquinas would call the chief or principal sense of this expression: and he claims that this holds good for all material things.[27]

Even if Aquinas is right here, however, one may wonder whether there has to be a first unchanged changer. And one may wonder whether, even if it is true that there are effects brought about by causes, plus ungenerated and imperishable things continuing to exist, there has to be a first cause of these. Why not say, for example, that everything changing has a changer and that the series of things causing change and being changed goes on *ad infinitum*? And why not say something similar for every case of cause and effect and every case (if there are any) of a thing which, without being generated or corruptible, continues to be?

One may, of course, wish to say exactly such things. Hume, for example, seems to want to say them. 'Did I show you the particular causes of each individual in a collection of twenty particles of matter', he writes, 'I should think it very unreasonable, should you afterwards ask me, what was the cause of the whole twenty. This is sufficiently explained in explaining the cause of the parts.'[28] More recently, we find a similar line of thinking presented by Kai Nielsen, who says:

Why could there not be an infinite series of caused causes? An infinite series is not a long or even a very, very long *finite* series. The person arguing for an infinite series is not arguing for something that came from nothing, nor need he be *denying* that *every* event has a cause. He is asserting that we need not assume that there is a *first* cause that started everything. Only if the series were finite would it be impossible for there to be something if there were no first cause or uncaused cause. But if the series were literally infinite, there would be no need for there to be a first cause to get the causal order started, for there would always be a causal order since an infinite series can have no first member.[29]

The idea here seems to be that if each member in a series is supported by another member, the series will somehow be able to stand on its own.

But there are reasons for resisting this idea. For, as James Sadowsky puts it:

It is just as difficult for any supporting member to exist as the member it supports. This brings back the question of how any member can do any causing unless it first exists. B cannot cause A until D brings it into existence. What is true of D is equally true of E and F without end. Since each condition for the existence of A requires the fulfilment of a prior condition, it follows that none of them can ever be fulfilled. In each case what is offered as part of the solution turns out instead to be part of the problem.[30]

As Sadowsky also observes, to suggest otherwise is a bit like saying 'No one may do anything (including asking for permission) without asking for permission'. And Sadowsky's observation can be pertinently pressed by a defender of Aquinas should it be suggested that the possibility of infinite regress is grounds for dismissing the first three Ways.[31]

Take, first, the case of change, and suppose that there is indeed an infinite series of things changing and causing change. It will still be true of the whole series that it is changing, for if parts of a thing are in process of change, the thing itself is in process of change. If we agree that nothing changes itself, it follows that the whole series is changed by something else. And this something else cannot be thought of as itself undergoing change. If it could, it would already be part of the series of things changing and causing change.

A similar line of argument is applicable to the suggestion that there might be an infinite series of causes each of which is an effect of another cause. If that were the case, everything in the series would be an effect, and so would the series as a whole. And that would raise the question 'What is the cause of the series? The answer to this question cannot lie in something which is itself an effect of another cause distinct from itself. Such a thing would already be part of the series of effects. Or it would be a member of a new and different series, which would raise the same problem over again.

Finally, there is the case of what is ungenerable and imperishable. If anything is like that and if it is caused to be as it is, perhaps the cause lies in something else which is also ungenerable and imperishable and also caused to be as it is. But the whole collection of such things would also be caused to be as it is. And we may therefore ask what accounts for the series as a whole. Once again, the answer cannot lie in something within the series. It will have to lie in something which is not caused to be as it is. If it is ungenerable and corruptible, it will not be so because of the agency of something else.

Yet should we seek to account for the changing universe with its causes and effects? As we have seen, some will reply that the universe is 'just there'. And readers content with that reply must conclude that, even if the arguments of Aquinas can be defended from some criticism, they are ultimately unsuccessful. In support of their position, they might even observe that their thinking is in line with at least one famous view of causation, a view usually associated with Hume. As well as maintaining that we can imagine a beginning of existence without a cause, Hume also argues that it is possible to conceive of an effect without conceiving of the cause of that effect, and he concludes that given any supposed effect E which is normally said to be caused by C, we can yet affirm E without implying that C ever existed at all. 'When we look about us towards external objects, and consider the operation of causes' he observes, 'we are never able, in a single instance, to discover any power or necessary connection; any quality, which binds the effect to the cause, and renders the one an infallible consequence of the other.'[32]

On the other hand, we do not normally assume that changes just happen or that things are just there. We seek to account for them in terms of something else. We should not say, for example, that the house just happened to collapse or that trees are just there. We also seek to account for the continued existence of things. As we have seen, Anthony Kenny is critical of Aquinas for accounting for procreation in terms of medieval cosmology. But even in the twentieth century, we know that procreators in the act of procreation depend on all sorts of things for their activity. They need air to breathe. And for that they depend on the earth holding in its place by gravity and the sun's rays keeping it from freezing. And for reasons such as this we might wish, after all, to side with Aquinas and with those who have propounded versions of the cosmological argument similar to his. For, as Peter Geach points out: 'If the world is an object, it again seems natural to ask about it the sort of causal questions which would be legitimate about its parts. If it began to exist, what brought it into existence? In any case, what keeps it from perishing, as some of its parts perish? And what keeps its processes going?'[33]

Someone might observe that the universe keeps going because it is its nature to do so. But it cannot have the nature it has unless it continues to exist, so its continuing to exist can hardly be explained in terms of its nature. As David Braine writes:

The continuance of the very stuff of the Universe, the fact that it goes on existing, is not self-explanatory. It is incoherent to say that the very stuff of the Universe continues to exist by its very nature since it has to continue to exist in order for this nature to exist or to be operative. Hence, nature presupposes existence.[34]

In the end, the questions raised by Geach are perhaps the key ones to consider when passing a verdict on the cosmological argument. The first is certainly crucial to the kalām form of the argument. The others are at the heart of the first cause argument. At this point, therefore, I leave them for the reader to consider, as we now move on to other reasons which have been given for believing in God.

6

The Argument from Design

PEOPLE concerned to offer grounds for belief in God have often resorted to the so-called argument from design, sometimes called the 'Teleological Argument'. So I now want to turn to this argument. Like the ontological and cosmological arguments, it comes in different forms. To begin with, therefore, I shall say something about these forms.

Versions of the Argument from Design

One of the earliest statements of the argument comes in Cicero's *De Natura Deorum*.[1] Here, a figure called Lucilius asks: 'What could be more clear or obvious when we look up to the sky and contemplate the heavens, than that there is some divinity of superior intelligence?' The point Lucilius seems to be making is that the operation of the universe must be somehow controlled or caused by intelligence. And this idea is at the heart of all versions of the argument from design.

But what is it about the operation of the universe that convinces people that the universe bears the mark of divine intelligence? Here we need to distinguish two different notions of design. First, there is design in the sense of *regularity*. Instances of this would be a succession of regular marks on paper, a musical score, the arrangement of flowers in a garden at Versailles, or the repeated and predictable operations of an artefact of some kind (e.g. a clock which chimes every hour). On the other hand, there is design in the sense of purpose. We should be working with this sense of 'design' if we talked about something being 'designed' because it had parts put together for some end or other, as in the case of a radio or television set.

With this distinction in mind, we can now note two lines of argument offered by people who claim to see in the universe evidence of design: the first states that the universe displays design in the sense of purpose, the second that it displays design in the sense of regularity.

Perhaps the most famous form of an argument from design *qua* purpose is that defended by William Paley (1743–1805) in his book *Natural Theology; or Evidences of the Existence and Attributes of the Deity, Collected from the Appearances of Nature*. 'In crossing a heath', says Paley,

suppose I pitched my foot against a *stone*, and were asked how the stone came to be there, I might possibly answer, that, for anything I knew to the contrary, it had lain there for ever; nor would it perhaps be very easy to show the absurdity of this answer. But suppose I found a *watch* upon the ground, and it should be inquired how the watch happened to be in that place, I should hardly think of the answer which I had before given, that, for anything I knew, the watch might have always been there. Yet why should not this answer serve for the watch, as well as for the stone?[2]

Paley's reply is that the parts of a watch are obviously put together to achieve a definite purpose: 'When we come to inspect the watch, we perceive (what we could not discover in the stone) that its several parts are framed and put together for a purpose, e.g. that they are so formed and adjusted as to produce motion, and that motion so regulated as to point out the hour of the day.'[3] And, so Paley goes on to suggest, the universe resembles a watch, and must therefore be accounted for in terms of intelligent and purposive agency. Suppose we introduce the term 'teleological system' and suppose we say that something is a teleological system if it has parts which operate so as to achieve one or more goals. In that case, Paley's view is that watches imply purpose because they are teleological systems. And his argument is that there are systems of this kind in nature, which are not ascribable to people, but which are ascribable to purpose of the kind displayed by people.

One version of an argument from design *qua* regularity is

defended by Richard Swinburne, who calls it a 'teleological argument from the temporal order of the world'. That there is temporal order is, says Swinburne, very evident. This is explained as follows:

Regularities of succession are all pervasive. For simple laws govern almost all successions of events. In books of physics, chemistry, and biology we can learn how almost everything in the world behaves. The laws of their behaviour can be set out by relatively simple formulae which men can understand and by means of which they can successfully predict the future. The orderliness of nature to which I draw attention here is its conformity to formula, to simple, formulable, scientific laws. The orderliness of the universe in this respect is a very striking fact about it. The universe might so naturally have been chaotic, but it is not—it is very orderly.[4]

From all this, Swinburne concludes that some explanation is called for. And his suggestion is that the temporal order of the universe is explicable in terms of something analogous to human intelligence. In Swinburne's view, there are only two kinds of explanation: scientific explanation (in terms of scientific laws) and personal explanation (in terms of the free, conscious choices of a person). According to Swinburne, there can be no scientific explanation of the universe's temporal order, since

in scientific explanation we explain particular phenomena as brought about by prior phenomena in accord with scientific laws; or we explain the operation of scientific laws (and perhaps also particular phenomena) . . . [yet] from the very nature of science it cannot explain the highest level laws of all; for they are that by which it explains all other phenomena.[5]

As Swinburne sees it, therefore, if we are to account for the fact that there are such laws, we will have to appeal to personal explanation. Someone (i.e. God) has brought it about that the universe exhibits a high degree of temporal order. And, so Swinburne adds, the likelihood of this supposition is increased by the fact that God has reason to produce an orderly world. For example, says Swinburne, order is a necessary condition of beauty, and it is good that the world is beautiful rather than ugly.

Kant and the Argument from Design

It is often argued that a decisive refutation of the argument from design can be found in some observations of Kant. All forms of the argument seem to suppose that the universe really contains order independent of our minds. As Kant sees it, however, we would impose order on whatever universe we were in, for only so could we think and reason as we do. According to Kant, we are unable to experience 'things in themselves'. We are presented in experience with an undifferentiated manifold, and we order our experience of things in themselves as our understanding imposes such categories as unity and plurality, cause and effect. Working with this view, some thinkers have suggested that the argument from design fails because, to put it as simply as possible, order is 'mind-imposed' rather than 'God-imposed'.

Kant's account of categories is a complex one which readers should study when seeking to assess the argument from design. But it is not unproblematic, and with an eye on the argument from design, there are at least two points that might here be raised regarding it.

First, it is not clear that Kant's account of the world and human experience is coherent. On Kant's picture there is the world as we experience it plus something behind that, something in relation to which the world as we experience it is a construction or product of our minds. This view involves positing a world of which we can have no experience, in order to contrast it with the world we ordinarily talk about, and many philosophers would regard such a move as pointless. As one writer puts it, 'How can we talk sensibly of the existence of a world independent of order, when to talk at all is to impose order?'[6]

Second, if one accepts Kant's position about the world of our experience and the world beyond it, one should call into question what one would normally not call into question, namely, that we have reason to accept the presuppositions and results of empirical inquiry. In an empirical inquiry we claim to be dealing with things that are in various ways ordered, things that would be so even if nobody were there to experience them. We would not normally say, for instance, that all biological analyses would cease to be true if the human race were suddenly wiped out. But if it is rational to accept the findings and methods of empirical inquiry, then it seems rational to accept the design argument's premiss that order is discovered, not imposed.

Hume and the Argument from Design

Even though they might not feel that Kant has overturned the argument from design, many philosophers would say that the argument has been well and truly refuted by someone else. I refer here to Hume, whose discussion of the argument from design is one of the things for which he is best known. In his *Dialogues concerning Natural Religion* and in *An Enquiry concerning Human Understanding* Hume makes eight basic points against the argument from design. So let us now turn to these.

(a) *Hume's Arguments*

Hume's first point concerns what we can deduce from an effect. 'When we infer any particular cause for an effect', he says, 'we must proportion the one to the other, and can never be allowed to ascribe to any cause any qualities, but what are exactly sufficient to produce the effect.'[7] Now, Hume adds, if design needs to be explained, then explain it; but only by appealing to a design-producing being. To say that this being is God is to go beyond the evidence presented by design.

Hume's second point hinges on the fact that the universe is unique. 'When two *species* of objects have always been observed to be conjoined together', he writes, 'I can *infer*, by custom, the existence of one wherever I *see* the existence of the other; And this I call an argument from experience.'[8] But, Hume continues, this notion of inference cannot be invoked by supporters of the argument from design. Why not? Because, says Hume, the universe is unique, and we therefore have no basis for inferring that there is anything like a human designer lying behind it. 'Will any man tell me with a serious countenance', he asks, 'that an orderly universe must arise from some thought and art, like the human; because we have some experience of it?' His answer is that, if someone were to tell him this, the person's claim could not be backed up. 'To ascertain this reasoning', he explains, 'it were requisite, that we had experience of the origin of worlds; and it is not sufficient surely, that we have seen ships and cities arise from human art and contrivance.'[9]

But suppose we agree that there is a designer whose existence may be inferred from the way things are. Would not such a designer also call for explanation? Hume's next argument is that the answer to this question is 'Yes'. 'If *Reason* be not alike mute with regard to all questions concerning cause and effect', he urges, 'this sentence at least it will venture to pronounce, that a mental world, or universe of ideas requires a cause as much as does a material world or universe of objects.'[10] In fact, says Hume, positing a designer of the world leads to an infinite regression: 'If the material world rests upon a similar ideal world', he says, 'this ideal world must rest upon some other; and so on, without end.'[11] He continues:

Naturalists indeed very justly explain particular effects by more general causes; though these general causes themselves should remain in the end totally inexplicable: But they never surely thought it satisfactory to explain a particular effect by a particular cause, which was no more to be accounted for than the effect itself. An ideal system, arranged of itself, without a precedent design, is not a whit more explicable than a material one, which attains its order in a like manner; nor is there any more difficulty in the latter supposition than in the former.[12]

Hume's fourth point is made in the form of a question. 'And why not become a perfect anthropomorphite?' he asks. 'Why not assert the Deity or Deities to be corporeal, and to have eyes, a nose, mouth, ears, &c.?'[13] As we saw in the case of Paley, some people argue from human artefacts to the existence of a designer whom they deem to be accountable for the universe considered as one great artefact. They do not suppose, however, that this designer is exactly like the people responsible for human artefacts. For example, they normally deny that this designer has a body. But, so Hume argues, they should not do that if they want to be consistent. They should regard the cause of the universe's design as something in every respect like human artificers. Following a somewhat similar line of argument, Hume goes on to suggest that the defender of the argument from design has no reason for denying that there may not be a whole gang of gods working together to produce design in the universe. 'A great number of men', he says, 'join together in building a house or ship, in rearing a city, in framing a commonwealth: Why may not several Deities combine in contriving and framing a world?'[14]

Finally, says Hume, there remain three other objections to the argument from design. The first is that the universe might easily be regarded as a living organism such as a plant, in which case the argument from design fails since it depends on comparing the universe to a machine or artefact of some kind. The next is that the order in the universe might easily be the result of chance. The last objection is that the argument from design fails because the universe shows plenty of signs of disorder.

(b) *Has Hume Refuted the Argument from Design?*

Hume has a strong point in saying that we should not postulate more than is necessary to account for a given effect. We may, of course, sometimes reasonably argue that some cause has characteristics other than those sufficient to produce some effect. If I know that X is made by a human being, I may reasonably suppose that its maker has two legs and a human heart. But I might be wrong. The maker may have one leg and an artificial heart. One might therefore wonder why, if the order in the universe needs explanation, it follows that this explanation will be all that God is said to be. He is often said to be eternal, but does it follow, for instance, that a source of order needs to be eternal?

Hume's point about the uniqueness of the universe also has something to recommend it. That is because in reasoning from effect to cause we often depend on knowledge of previous instances. If you receive a postcard from Paris saying 'Weather here, wish you were nice, Love, Me', you will probably be very puzzled. But if I receive such a card, I shall know that it comes from a certain friend who always writes that on his holiday postcards to me. What is it that enables me to conclude as I do, while you would be merely baffled? It is that I have past experience of my friend and his curious ways, while you (probably) do not. Yet, even though we have experience of human designers and what they produce, nobody supposes that anyone has experience of the origin of universes and of causes which bring them about. And since that is so, we might wonder how one can reason from the universe we inhabit to a designing cause.

What of Hume's other arguments? These, too, have merit. It is true, for example, that designers of our acquaintance are bodily creatures with bodily attributes. It is also true that products which are designed frequently derive from groups of people working together. Since the argument from design is an argument from analogy (since it holds that the universe *resembles* designed things within it and must therefore have a cause *like* theirs), we might therefore wonder how it could possibly justify us in ruling out the idea that evidence of design in the universe is evidence for what is bodily or evidence for the existence of several co-operating designers. And if designers may be thought of as themselves exhibiting order, we might also wonder why we should suppose that appealing to God as a designer of what we find in the universe counts as any kind of explanation for the order we find in the universe. If God is an instance of something orderly, how can he serve to account for the order of orderly things?

Yet this is not to say that Hume has succeeded in refuting the argument from design. Indeed, we now need to note that defenders of the argument have a number of replies which they can make in response to his various criticisms of the argument.

Take first his point about not ascribing to a cause anything other than what is exactly sufficient to produce its effect. Hume seems to think that even if we may causally account

for order in the universe by inferring the existence of something distinct from the universe, the most we can conclude is
that the order is produced by a design-producing being. He
does not think that we are entitled to say that we have any
evidence of God's existence. Yet reason to suppose that order
in the universe has a cause outside the universe is reason to
suppose that the cause of the order in the universe is powerful,
purposive, and incorporeal. It will need to be powerful to
achieve its effect. It will necessarily be incorporeal since it lies
outside the universe. Since it is not a material thing and since
what it produces is order, we may suppose that it is able to act
with intention. For order is naturally explained by reference
to intention unless we have reason to suppose that it has
been brought about by something material, i.e. something the
effects of which are not the result of choice or planning on its
part.

So we are entitled to infer more than an order-producing
being if, as the argument from design holds, we are right to
ascribe order in the universe to a cause outside it. And if it
should be said that more is supposed to be true of God than
that he is powerful, incorporeal, and purposive, a defender of
the argument from design can reply that God is normally said
to be at least this and that the argument from design therefore
provides at least some support for his existence. Suppose I am
wondering whether John has been in my room. I may conclude
that he has because I find a note signed 'John' saying 'I was
here'. If someone then tells me that the note is not evidence of
John's presence because John is six foot tall and the note is not
evidence for someone of that height having been in my room,
I can reasonably reply that it still counts as evidence for John's
presence since he is able to write and since I can recognize his
writing. By the same token, a defender of the argument from
design may say that even if the argument does not establish
that God exists with all the attributes commonly ascribed to
him, the fact that it supports the claim that something with
some traditional divine attributes exists is reason for thinking
of it as latching on to some evidence of God's existence.

But what of Hume's suggestion that the argument from

design fails because the universe is unique? Though, as I have said, it has something to recommend it, this suggestion, too, is open to question. For it is wrong to assume that no question about the origin of something unique can reasonably be raised and answered. Nor is this something which we would normally suppose. Scientists certainly try to account for various things which are unique. The human race and the universe itself are two good examples.

In any case, one may deny that the universe is unique. To say that the universe is unique is not to ascribe to it a property which cannot be ascribed to anything else. It is to say that there is only one universe. And even if there is only one universe, it does not follow that the universe is unique in its properties, that it shares no properties with lesser systems. 'If you were the only girl in the world and I were the only boy', as the once popular song envisaged, there would still be two human beings. And, so we may say, there are lots of things like the universe even if there is only one universe. For the universe shares with its parts properties which can be ascribed to both the universe and its parts. It is, for example, in process of change, as are many of its parts, and it is composed of material elements, as people and machines are. As the version of the argument from design which invokes the notion of regularity holds, the universe is also something exhibiting regularity, as, once again, is the case with people and machines.

This brings us to Hume's third argument: that a designer requires a designer as much as anything else does, and that arguing for a designer lands one in a problem of infinite regress. Does that line of reasoning serve to rule out the argument from design?

It seems to assume that if one explains A by B, but does not offer to explain B, then one has not thereby explained A. And one may doubt whether that assumption should be accepted. As one of the characters in Hume's *Dialogues* says, 'Even in common life, if I assign a cause for any event; is it any objection . . . that I cannot assign the cause of that cause, and answer every new question, which may incessantly be

started?'[15] Even scientific explanations work within a frame-
work in which certain ultimate laws are just claimed to hold.

But there is, perhaps, a better response that can be made to
Hume at this point. For why should we suppose that what is
responsible for order must exhibit an order which stands in
need of a cause distinct from itself? Sources of order are
sometimes things with an order caused by other things. A
factory machine devised to regulate a flow of bottles would
be a case in point. But thoughts are also sources of order
exhibiting order. And we do not need to seek independent
causes which account for the fact that they exhibit order. For
they would not be thoughts if they did not. Hume maintained
that thoughts are a series of ideas which succeed one another
in an orderly way; thus he holds that they have a temporal
order which requires a cause if any order does. But thoughts
are not just ordered by virtue of temporal succession. Each
thought is intrinsically ordered, for thoughts have a logical
structure which philosophers can analyse and try to explicate.
Confronted by Hume's third objection, therefore, defenders of
the argument from design can reply that design in the universe
derives from the mind of God conceiving it. They may then
suggest that it therefore derives from an order which does
not, *qua* order, stand in need of an ordering cause. Like a
human designer's thoughts which lead to something designed,
so, it may be argued, the thoughts of a divine designer are
essentially ordered if they exist at all.

But defenders of the argument from design will not want to
say that God is exactly like human designers, which brings us
to Hume's 'Why not become a perfect anthropomorphite?'
and 'Why not many gods?' arguments. Though one can see the
force of these arguments, they do not succeed in showing that
the argument from design is mistaken. For there are a number
of replies open to someone who wishes to defend some version
of the argument against them.

First, it can be said that the designer of the universe cannot
himself be corporeal without himself being part of the system
of things for which the design argument proposes to account.
Versions of the argument from design are normally concerned

to account for material order in the universe. But they cannot do this by appealing to yet another instance of such order.

Second, it might be pointed out that the argument from design does not have to conclude that the designer of the universe shares all the attributes of the causes whose operations provide the justification for inferring him in the first place. This is because arguments from analogy do not have to assert that since A accounts for B and since C resembles B, something *exactly* like A must also account for C.

Suppose that my office is cleaned by Mrs Mopp. She is fat and cheerful, and she has a limp. I observe her cleaning my office week after week. She always comes in at 10.30 a.m., just before I leave for my coffee-break.

Now suppose I am told on Monday afternoon that Mrs Mopp has resigned. Nobody comes to clean my office at 10.30 on Tuesday, but when I return from my coffee-break I find that my room has been cleaned in the usual way.

What can I infer? That a cleaner has been around, of course. But I do not need to infer that the cleaner was a fat, cheerful woman with a limp. For all I know, the office could have been cleaned by a thin, miserable man with two strong legs.

The point which this example illustrates is applicable both to Hume's 'anthropomorphite' argument and to his question 'Why not many gods?' Human beings imposing order have bodies; but this does not bind us to ascribing a body to everything that can be thought of as responsible for order. It is often the case that order is imposed by groups of human beings; but this does not mean that every instance of order must be produced by a collection of individuals.

In other words, as Richard Swinburne observes, the argument from design may be held to employ a common pattern of scientific reasoning which can be stated as follows:

A's are caused by B's. A*s are similar to A's. Therefore—given that there is no more satisfactory explanation of the existence of A*s—they are produced by B*s similar to B's. B*s are postulated to be similar in all respects to B's except in so far as shown otherwise, viz.

except in so far as the dissimilarities between A's and A*s force us to postulate a difference.[16]

On the basis of this principle Swinburne proceeds to defend his version of the argument from design against Hume's fourth point. He writes:

For the activity of a god to account for the regularities, he must be free, rational, and very powerful. But it is not necessary that he, like men, should only be able to act on a limited part of the universe, a body, and by acting on that control the rest of the universe. And there is good reason to suppose that the god does not operate in this way. For, if his direct control was confined to a part of the universe, scientific laws outside his control must operate to ensure that his actions have effects in the rest of the universe. Hence the postulation of the existence of the god would not explain the operations of those laws: yet to explain the operation of all scientific laws was the point of postulating the existence of the god. The hypothesis that the god is not embodied thus explains more and explains more coherently than the hypothesis that he is embodied.[17]

As a reply to Hume, this seems correct. And, with an eye on the suggestion that there might be many divine designers, it can be supplemented by appeal to the famous principle commonly called 'Occam's razor'. According to this, 'Entities are not to be multiplied beyond necessity'. That, too, is commonly invoked in scientific contexts, and a defender of the argument from design might therefore argue that though there is reason to believe in one designer god, there is no reason to believe in more than one, though there might possibly be more than one. In this connection it is perhaps worth noting that Hume himself seems to accept a version of Occam's razor. 'To multiply causes, without necessity', he says, 'is indeed contrary to true philosophy.'[18]

Let us now pass quickly on to Hume's last three objections to the argument from design: that the universe can be thought of as a living organism, that chance might account for order in the universe, and that the universe contains much disorder. Are these objections decisive? It seems to me that it is certainly possible to doubt that they are.

Even if we press the analogy between the universe and a living organism, we still seem confronted by regularity in the universe. I have said little about this so far, but it does seem true that the universe behaves in regular and predictable ways, as Swinburne much stresses. It is therefore open to defenders of the design argument to draw attention to what Swinburne is talking about and to emphasize the similarity between machines and the universe. For it is characteristic of a machine that it behaves in regular and predictable ways and obeys scientific laws. Defenders of the argument from design might even add that their appeal to a designer helps to explain more than an appeal to the generative power of living organisms in accounting for the order in the universe, an appeal which Hume seems to be making in suggesting that the analogy between the universe and an organism is a problem for the argument from design. For living organisms reproduce regularity because they are already things that display it. Thus it might be said that living organisms cannot explain all the regularity in the universe since they depend on some form of regularity themselves.

Hume's point about chance is that over the course of time there will be periods of order and periods of chaos, so that the universe may once have been in chaos and the present ordered universe may derive from this state. In reply to this point, however, it can be said that Hume is only noting a logical possibility which need not affect the fact that the universe is not now in chaos, which calls for explanation. It might also be said that an explanation of the universe which does not refer to chance grows more credible as time goes by. Thus Swinburne suggests that 'If we say that it is chance that in 1960 matter is behaving in a regular way, our claim becomes less and less plausible as we find that in 1961 and 1962 and so on it continues to behave in a regular way'.[19] In any case, why should it be thought that if something comes about by chance there is no causality or planning afoot? Suppose that the Pope sneezes in Rome at exactly the time that the US President sneezes in Washington. Must we suppose there is a cause of this coincidence of sneezes? Surely not. It is a matter of

chance. But we would not be inclined to suppose that the
Pope's sneezing and the President's sneezing lack causal
explanations.

What of Hume's final point? In one sense it is clearly right:
the universe contains disorder since there are, for example,
pain-producing events of a natural kind (the sort of disorder
which Hume actually has in mind). But this fact need not deter
defenders of the argument from design unless they wish to
hold that every particular thing works to the advantage of
other particular things, which they do not want to do anymore
than anyone else does. They only want to say that there is
order in need of explanation; and disorder *qua* pain-producing
natural events can plausibly be taken as just an illustration
of order. One can, for instance, argue that pain-producing
natural events exhibit order in that their origins can often be
traced and their future occurrence predicted with a fair degree
of success.

Is the Argument from Design Reasonable?

It seems, then, that if they are taken individually, Hume's
arguments against the design argument admit of reply. But
a supporter of Hume might accept this conclusion and still
urge that Hume has knocked a massive hole in the argument.
Consider the following imaginary dialogue:

A. Brown has stabbed Jones to death.
B. Prove that.
A. Brown had a motive.
B. That does not prove that Brown stabbed Jones. Many
   people had a motive for killing Jones.
A. Brown was found at the scene of the crime.
B. That fact is compatible with his innocence.
A. Brown was found standing over Jones holding a
   blood-stained knife.
B. He may have picked it up after the murder was
   committed.
A. Brown says he stabbed Jones.
B. He may be trying to cover up for somebody.

Now B's points here, taken individually, might be all quite correct. But though A may be wrong about Brown, a reasonable person would surely conclude that, when A's points are taken together, they put a question mark over Brown's innocence. Suppose, then, it were said that Hume's arguments, if not all decisive individually, together make it reasonable to reject the argument from design? Evidently, a great deal turns here on the initial strength of the design argument. So let us now consider this by turning to the two forms of the argument distinguished at the outset of this chapter.

The Argument from Purpose

The argument from purpose in nature (which I shall henceforth call 'Paley's argument') is an argument from analogy. It rests on the premiss that certain things in nature really are like human artefacts. So if it is to convince, there must be more than a passing resemblance between human artefacts and things in nature. The trouble is that there are notable dissimilarities between human artefacts and things in nature.

For example, human artefacts, even in cases of automated production, result quite directly from intentional actions. But this is not so in the case of things in nature. Our eyes, for instance, while we were developing in the womb, originated from genetically controlled processes that themselves had natural causes, and so on, back as far as we can determine. These processes might have been the result of design, but if so, the design seems to have been woven into the fabric of nature, so to speak.[20]

Defenders of Paley's argument sometimes say that it is reasonable to think of certain things in nature as if they were machines. They sometimes say that it is reasonable to think of the universe as a machine. But nothing in nature seems to come about as machines do. And we have no reason to think that the origins of the universe resemble the conditions under which machines are produced. In addition to such facts, one might also ponder the question of what it makes sense to ask of a machine and what it makes sense to ask of things

in nature or of the universe as a whole. Confronted by a
machine, we can always ask 'What is it for?' But does it
make sense to ask this question when confronted by natural
phenomena or the universe as a whole? Does it, for instance,
make sense to ask 'What are dogs for?'. Does it make sense
to ask 'What is the universe for?' One might say that dogs
have a role in a structure which contains them. It might be
argued that they serve a purpose when viewed against their
background. But even if that is so, it is hard to see that the
same can be said of the universe. Against what background
might the universe be thought of as serving a purpose?

On the other hand, Paley is surely right about one thing. We
would think of a watch as displaying purpose. Might we not
therefore argue thus: 'Given that there are things in nature
which, like watches, display purpose, we should conclude to
something outside nature lying behind them'?

A common reply is: 'No. We know about watches, and we
know that they are designed by watchmakers. But we have no
comparable knowledge about watch-like things in the universe
which are not produced by people. We know about the origins
of watches, so from any given watch we can safely infer a
watchmaker. But we cannot make any such inference concerning the origins of watch-like things which simply arise in
nature. Since our universe is the only one we know, we have
nothing on which to base an inference concerning the things it
throws up.' Yet this line of reasoning does not really engage
with what Paley actually says. He does not presume that we
are entitled to ascribe to a watch a purpose only on the basis
of our knowledge of watches and watchmakers. He thinks that
our ascription would be justified even if we had never seen a
watch. In his view, watches suggest watchmakers because their
workings are purposive or functional. He thinks that watches
imply purpose since they are teleological systems in the sense
defined above (things with parts which operate so as to achieve
one or more goals). And his argument is that there are systems
of this kind in nature which are not ascribable to people
but which are ascribable to purpose of the kind displayed by
people.

In support of this view, perhaps the first thing to say is that few people know about the processes of watchmaking through personal acquaintance. Our assumption that watches have watchmakers is not, in general, based on what we know of watchmakers and the way they turn out their products. We can, however, say that there are teleological systems in nature the origin of which cannot be ascribed to human beings. For there are various things in nature which are not made or planned by people but which do have parts which function so as to result in something specifiable. The obvious examples are biological. Kidneys, for instance, perform to secrete urine. Eyes exist for sight. And the heart moves as it does so that blood may circulate. With respect to things like these we naturally talk about the jobs they do. And we presume that the characteristic result of their performance comes about because they are performing their functions properly, and not by virtue of chance or external, random constraint. It makes sense to say that kidneys are for the secretion of urine, that eyes are for sight, and that hearts are for the circulation of the blood. In cases like these there is a terminus which is more than accidentally connected with the conditions under which it is realized. In such cases we naturally speak about one thing working thus and so in order that such and such should occur. In this sense there are teleological systems in nature which are not the product of human beings. Human beings depend on them being there.

The question, of course, is whether this has any theistic significance. Does it, for instance, allow us to infer the existence of something analogous to human intention or purpose?

A common reply is that it does not, since teleological systems in nature can be accounted for in terms of natural selection as explained by Charles Darwin (1809–82) and his successors (not to mention his predecessors).[21] The argument here is that there are teleological systems in the natural world because of conditions favouring the development of species which arise due to chance factors at a genetic level. Natural selection is supposed to rule out design, since, according to the theory, the living organisms we find are those which survive the struggle for existence due to useful variations. What accounts for the appearance of design is the disappearance of the unfit. There are no hostile witnesses to testify against design. They have all been killed off.

Even if this theory is true, however, it does not undermine the drift of Paley's argument. Suppose I am a 'creationist'. That is to say, suppose I believe that every member of a given species either is directly created by God or is a descendant of a member of that species. If I come to believe in the evolution of species by natural selection, must I conclude that the species that exist cannot be thought of as designed? By no means. For I can consistently assert that something may arise by mechanical means while also being designed. As Anthony Kenny observes:

If the argument from design ever had any value, it has not been substantially affected by the scientific investigation of living organisms from Descartes through Darwin to the present day. If Descartes is correct in regarding the activities of animals as mechanistically explicable, then a system may operate teleologically while being mechanistic in structure. If Darwin is correct in ascribing the origin of species to natural selection, then the production of a teleological structure may be due in the first instance to factors which are purely mechanistic. But both may be right and yet the ultimate explanation of the phenomena be finalistic. The only argument refuted by Darwin would be one which said: wherever there is adaptation to environment we must see the immediate activity of an intelligent being. But the argument from design did not claim this; and indeed it was an essential step in the argument that lower animals and natural agents did not have minds. The argument was only that the ultimate explanation of such adaptation must be found in intelligence; and if the argument was correct, then any Darwinian success merely inserts an extra step between the phenomena to be explained and their ultimate explanation.[22]

And to Kenny's point one might add another. This is that although natural selection might give us some account of the emergence of teleological systems, it is logically debarred from giving us a full account. As Peter Geach writes:

There can be no origin of species, as opposed to an Empedoclean chaos of varied monstrosities, unless creatures reproduce pretty much after their kind; the elaborate and ostensibly teleological mechanism of this reproduction logically cannot be explained as a product of evolution by natural selection from among chance variations, for unless the mechanism is presupposed there cannot be any evolution.[23]

Geach is saying here that there is much involved in the development of living beings that cannot be explained by the theory of evolution. And, as far as I can gather from the scientists, he is right in this. Natural selection can only occur if creatures bear offspring which closely resemble their parents without resembling them too closely. If offspring are exactly like their parents, natural selection cannot lead to the development of new characteristics. If offspring do not closely resemble their parents, then even if parents have highly adaptive characteristics and bear many more offspring than others, their offspring will not be likely to inherit the characteristics, and the process will stop. So there can be no origin of species unless creatures reproduce pretty much after their kind. And the mechanism of this reproduction is complex and ostensibly teleological.

Yet even if this is so, it still does not follow that nature implies a non-human purposer. Some would say it does, since any teleological system must be accounted for by intelligence or the like. But why should we believe that view? It has a certain plausibility if we take it to mean that wherever there is irreducible purpose, there is a designer. For, as Kenny also says,

It is essential to teleological explanation that it should be in terms of a good to be achieved; yet the good which features in the explanation, at the time of the event to be explained, does not yet exist and indeed may never exist. This is difficult to understand except in the case where the good pre-exists in the conception of the designer: the mind of the designer exists at the appropriate time, even if the good designed does not.[24]

But the point of a process need not be its final stage. In an Aristotelian universe, the cycles of the stars and of generation in living things would have a point (mirroring God's eternal life) even if it never reached a final stage. And must we suppose that there is irreducible purpose which has no designer in the natural world? That is, must we assume that teleological systems in nature are examples of irreducible purpose, or can they be explained as due to some naturalistic, non-purposive factor? Those who say they cannot sometimes reply that, unless we agree with them, we must ascribe the existence of teleological systems in nature to chance. But this assumes that if they are not due to chance, they must be planned. And that is not obviously so. We may presume that a thing must be planned if it does not emerge by chance. But do we contradict ourselves in supposing that something might arise in a perfectly predictable way without anything analogous to forethought? This question leads us straight into the version of the argument from design which focuses on the notion of regularity. So let us now turn to that.

The Argument from Regularity

To begin with, of course, the argument starts with a premiss which few modern people would wish to dispute. The universe does contain a high degree of order, in that scientific laws can be framed and expectations reasonably made about the behaviour of things over a very wide area of space and time. Even when we cannot formulate a law to account for some phenomenon, we tend to assume that there is one. This is not to say that there is a rigid causal nexus such that the state of the universe at any given time necessitates its state at a later time. Nor is it to say that, given certain conditions, then such and such effects must follow. It is not even to say that there is temporal order to be discerned everywhere in the universe. But it is to say what we certainly believe: that, as Swinburne insists, there are very many objects making up the universe and behaving in a generally uniform way.[25]

But should we seek to account for this fact? The regularity version of the argument from design holds that we should account for it with reference to an intelligent cause, i.e. a cause that is intelligent but not part of the universe. This suggestion is open to the reply that, while we may think that order requires explanation of a certain kind, there is no guarantee that there is any such explanation. Our expectations regarding what must account for what might prove unfulfilled in perhaps all cases. On the other hand, it is not always reasonable to speculate on the basis of this possibility. And when we are confronted with orderly arrangements of things, and unless we have positive reason to account for them without reference to intelligence, we simply do seek to account for them with reference to intelligence. Numbers on a set of fifty pages could be set down in a totally random way; but once we discover that they can be regularly translated into something strongly resembling a language, we presume that we are dealing with a code. Bits of machinery could be piled up in a formless and inert heap; but when we come across bits that operate together so as to do something repeatedly and predictably, we presume that they form some kind of artefact. Musical notes could be written down in a totally random way; but if they can be read so as to produce a symphony when played, we call the notes a score.

In other words, unless we have a definite reason for ruling out explanation with reference to intelligent agency, it is reasonable to postulate such agency when confronted by order, i.e. when it is consistent to suppose that the existence of the order is not logically necessary. But if this is so and unless we have a definite reason for ruling out explanation with reference to intelligent agency, then it seems reasonable to postulate intelligent agency when confronted by the order in the universe. For that might never have been there at all, and yet it is there to a high degree. Someone may always observe that the order in the universe is just there and is not the product of intelligence. Order in the universe might be regarded as brute fact in need of no explanation. But granted that we normally attempt to account for order in terms of intelligence when we lack a definite reason for not doing so, such a reply seems arbitrary. A supporter of Hume might say that when we postulate intelligence in accounting for order, we do so only when we are confronted by examples of what we know to be produced by intelligence. But that is just what the present version of the argument from design can be said to do. As we saw earlier, it can be seen as appealing to the fact that the ordered universe taken as a whole is not unique, in that it shares characteristics with its parts of such a kind as to make it reasonable to say that if intelligence can be invoked to account for what is true of these parts, then intelligence can be invoked to account for what is similarly true of the whole. And the intelligence in question will clearly have to be extra-mundane. For it is the whole mundane order that would have to be accounted for by it.[26]

Might it not be said that there is definite reason for ruling out explanation of the universe's order with reference to intelligence? The trouble is that it seems hard to know what kind of reason this could be. When we allow that a certain kind of order is definitely not to be explained with reference to intelligence, we already know that some natural laws, and not intelligence, have brought it about. We rule out intelligence when we think that what we are dealing with could not be otherwise than it is. Thus we can deny intelligent causation of the ridges in the sand which remain when the tide has gone out because we (or, at least, some of us) can definitely account for them with reference to physical laws such as those which govern the movement of wind and waves. But in the case of the order in the universe, it is precisely in physical laws that the order to be accounted for resides. And this order might well be thought of as something which need not have been and, therefore, as something standing in need of explanation. As Ralph Walker puts it:

What is remarkable is that it should be so easy for us to discover laws—not just simple causal laws, but more sophisticated higher order laws that enable us to find unity within widely diverse natural phenomena . . . We prefer simple hypotheses, and mathematically simple ones in particular; how providential, then, that so many fundamental laws of physics and chemistry are expressible as elementary arithmetical relationships. How convenient for us that the periodic table should turn out so neatly, and that gravitational attraction should require no more complex function than the inverse square!

There was no transcendental necessity that things should be so readily comprehensible.[27]

As Walker goes on to allow, one might say that there is nothing remarkable about all this, since if our ways of thinking about the world did not yield results, we would abandon them. But that is to presume that we could stop thinking of the world as we do. And even if we could, there would still remain the fact that there just is enormous regularity of the kind to which Swinburne alludes. Nature keeps on working in such a way as to meet our expectations. Why, then, should this be so?

One answer which has been given to this question is that there is nothing surprising and in need of explanation in the fact that we observe a universe displaying temporal regularity. For if it did not display such regularity, we would not be there to observe it. Yet, though we could only be aware of the universe as orderly if there were quite a degree of order in it, this does not dispose of the fact that there is order, and it does not show that this is not something puzzling and in need of explanation. The point is well brought out by Swinburne, who, with the present objection in mind, introduces what seems to me a devastating analogy.

Suppose that a madman kidnaps a victim and shuts him in a room with a card shuffling machine. The machine shuffles ten packs of cards simultaneously and then draws a card from each pack and exhibits simultaneously the ten cards. The kidnapper tells the victim that he will shortly set the machine to work and it will exhibit the first draw, but that unless the draw consists of an ace of hearts from each pack, the machine will simultaneously set off an explosion which will kill the victim, in consequence of which we will not see which cards the machine drew. The machine is then set to work, and to the amazement and relief of the victim the machine exhibits an ace of hearts drawn from each pack. The victim thinks that this extraordinary fact needs an explanation in terms of the machine having been rigged in some way. But the kidnapper, who now reappears, casts doubt on this suggestion. 'It is hardly surprising', he says, 'that the machine drew only aces of hearts. You could not possibly see anything else. For you would not be here to see anything at all, if any other cards had been drawn.' But of course the victim is right and the kidnapper is wrong. There is something extraordinary in need of explanation in ten aces being drawn. The fact that this peculiar order is a necessary condition of the draw being perceived at all makes what is perceived no less extraordinary and in need of explanation.[28]

In response to what Swinburne says, one might reply that if we are to see at all, then there must be order. For seeing depends on there being order to see. But it still remains that there is order to see in the universe. And, as Swinburne goes on to say, this is what concerns those who defend the argument from design. 'Maybe only if order is there can we know what is there, but that makes what is there no less extraordinary and in need of explanation.'[29]

Still, perhaps one can always refuse to ask why the universe exhibits the order it does. And those who do refuse to ask this question are unlikely to be swayed by any available argument to the contrary. But the position of those who want to ask it is still a plausible one. And this conclusion is strengthened by the fact that if we accept it, we can appeal to what is less in need of explanation than the fact of there being vast temporal regularity. For if we allow that this regularity is not explicable scientifically, we could account for it in terms of something analogous to decision. And the attempt to account for regularity or order in terms of decision is intrinsically more satisfying than the attempt to avoid accounting for it by saying that it is simply there.

The point I have in mind here is usefully brought out by Peter Geach in his book *Providence and Evil*. He reports a story of how a Tsar sought to account for the fact that a soldier always stood on guard in the middle of a lawn in the palace grounds. The Tsar was told that it had always been so, that there was a standing order for it. This explanation did not satisfy him. Finally he discovered that a sentimental Tsaritsa had once put a man on guard there to prevent a snowdrop from being trampled on, and the order had never been countermanded. As Geach observes, 'The Tsaritsa's capricious will was a satisfying explanation beyond which we need not look.'[30] And with respect to the regularity version of the argument from design, it is significant that what its advocates think of as explicable in terms of God is actually something which resembles what we would otherwise seek to explain in terms of intention. Suppose we have many packs of cards some of which prove to be arranged in suits and seniority. We could reasonably infer that the unexamined packs are similarly arranged, and we would account for the grouping observed and inferred not in terms of chance but in terms of intention. By the same token, so one may argue, we have reason for inferring that, given the temporal order of the universe, an order on the basis of which we infer further unobserved order, we again have something for which intentional explanation is legitimate.

Conclusion

I have been arguing in this chapter that there is considerable life in both versions of the argument from design. Readers may well disagree, but at least they now have something with which to disagree. Whether they agree or not, there can be little doubt that discussion of the argument from design will continue for a long time to come. But this is not the place to try to take matters further. Instead we shall turn to a wholly different approach to God's existence from those mentioned so far. Unlike defenders of the cosmological argument and the argument from design, its supporters hold that God is not something whose existence we can believe in by inference. They believe God to be something *experienced*.

7

Experience and God

IT should be clear enough by now how various people have held that argument can be offered to show that it is reasonable to say that there is a God. But it has also been held that the reasonableness of belief in God can be defended, not with reference to argument, but with reference to experience, and it is to this view that I now wish to turn. The question currently at issue is therefore this: Can it be reasonable to believe in God on the basis of experience?

God and Experience

To begin with, we should ask what is meant by saying that it is reasonable to believe in God on the basis of experience. And the answer, perhaps, can be given by means of a contrast.

Sometimes we learn that something exists through inference or deduction from something other than itself. Thus, for example, I might infer that there is a bear in the area because of a trail of destruction which I observe, without actually meeting the bear.

But we often discover that things exist because, as we put it, we have 'first-hand experience' of them. Thus, for example, I might simply walk right into the bear.

According to the position now in question, (a) God can be directly and non-inferentially encountered as an object of experience, and (b) one has reason to say that there is a God if one has encountered him in this way. The idea here is that there is such a thing as a veridical awareness of God which can be taken by those who have it as reason for belief in his existence.

And this line of thinking, we should note, is sometimes developed into an argument based on testimony. What if you have no consciousness of having had any experience of God? Then, so it has been said, you can rely on the testimony of those who say that they have experienced God. I may never have met the Pope, but the testimony of those who have is reason for me to believe that he is real enough. In a similar way, so it has been suggested, the testimony of those who say that they have experience of God (or that they have had it) is reason for anyone to believe in his existence.

Objections to the Above View

A number of reasóns have been given for rejecting the view that God can be reasonably said to exist since there is direct awareness or experience of him. To begin with, I shall simply reproduce without comment those most often advanced.

1. Experience cannot be taken as giving reasonable grounds for belief in God, since the notion of God is an impossible one. There could not be a God and, therefore, there could not be an experience of God.

2. Experience is frequently deceptive. We often say that we are aware of X or that we experience the presence of X, when argument or further experience forces us to conclude that we were mistaken. Thus we note the whole area of mistaken identification (e.g. taking Jones for Smith), misinterpretation of evidence (e.g. regarding apparently converging railway lines as really meeting), and hallucination (seeing objects which are not there to be seen). Any claim based on experience is therefore suspect.

3. People who claim an experience of God may be mistakenly identifying the object of their experience, or they may be hallucinating or insane. Furthermore, people claiming an experience of God may well be influenced by some psychological or social pressure leading them to believe that there is a God. In any case, any proclaimed experience of God must be rejected at the outset (a) because there are no agreed tests for verifying that there has in fact been an experience of God, (b)

because some people report an experience of the absence of God, and (c) because there is no uniformity of testimony on the part of those who claim to experience God.

Are the Objections Decisive?

For the moment let us consider the merits of the above objections individually. Do any of them show that it cannot be reasonable to believe in God on the basis of experience?

The first objection can, perhaps, be fairly quickly dealt with at this stage. More often than not, it reflects the views of people who think that God's existence is intrinsically impossible. I considered some questions relevant to this view in Chapters 1–3, and I argued that they do not show that there could not be a God. Furthermore, it is possible, as I argued in Chapters 5 and 6, to offer a reasonable case for belief in God. So it is at least not evident that there could not be a God, and it is therefore not evident that there could not be a reasonable belief in God based on experience just because there could not be a God. And even if people were to say that they think they have hit on some internal inconsistency in belief in God (or in a belief which could only be true if belief in God is true), others who believe that they have experienced God might simply reply that there must be something wrong with any purported proof that belief in God is inconsistent or somehow demonstrably false. If I have actually encountered something, I have grounds for maintaining that the thing I have encountered is a possibly existing being. By the same token, so it might be argued, the fact that God is an object of experience is reason enough for denying that belief in God is contradictory or that it could not be true for some other reason.

What of the second objection? The main argument against it is that we have no reason to suppose in advance that any claim that something is so is suspect if it is based on experience. On the contrary. It seems right to say that experience can be a source of knowledge. Claims based on experience may be withdrawn by the people who make them, but this does not show that they can never be correct. The argument from the fact of revision cannot be used to deny in some absolute sense the possibility of knowing by experience. Fred may hallucinate when under the influence of drink, and he may emphatically state that there is a goblin in the room. Subsequently he may withdraw his statement. When under the influence again, however, he may withdraw his retraction. The fact that we would normally ignore his second retraction is evidence for our conviction that retraction by itself settles nothing about the truth of what is retracted.

Furthermore, even if it is possible to be mistaken with a claim based on experience, not all such claims need be mistaken. A general argument from illusion or from the possibility of mistaken identification or misinterpretation of evidence cannot always be rationally used in assessing the correctness of all assertions based on experience that something is the case. Context is very important here. It might be reasonable to challenge Fred's assertion about the goblin, but if I am assured by my doctors to be in good health, with normal eyesight, of average sanity and intelligence, it might well be unreasonable for me to doubt that, when I seem to see a train bearing down upon me at a crossing, there really is such a thing. We need to remember what is involved in our notions of mistaken identity, misinterpretation of evidence, and hallucination. Mistakenly to identify X is to have an experience of X and erroneously believe that X is something other than X (e.g. to take Jones for Smith). It must therefore be possible to have an experience of X and correctly believe that it is X (it must be possible to come across Jones and identify him correctly). To misinterpret evidence is to be aware of something and to draw mistaken conclusions about it. It must therefore be possible to be aware of something and to draw correct conclusions about it. To have a hallucination is mistakenly to believe that something is present to one. It must therefore be possible to believe correctly that something is present to one.

In short, there seems good reason to say that some claims can be reasonably upheld on the basis of experience. At a theoretical level, we can argue about the existence of Martians

until we are blue in the face. But thinking one is meeting
them when they land may settle the matter once and for all.
Sometimes one may just have to say that one sees that something is the case. And, of course, if one could not reasonably
do this, then one could not even reasonably say that the
objections made against claims based on experience are worth
taking seriously. For how does one know that there are any
such objections? Only by supposing that at least some things
that seem directly given to one in one's experience are there in
reality. We certainly make mistakes about reality because we
fail to interpret our experience correctly. But if we do not
work on the assumption that what seems to be so is sometimes
so, then it is hard to see how we can establish anything at all
and how we can correct beliefs that are in some way mistaken.
When all suitable qualification has been made, rational inquiry
seems to presuppose that it is generally reasonable to say that
what directly seems to be so is so.

A similar kind of argument to that of the last few paragraphs can be used in reply to the third objection to the view
that belief in God can be reasonably based on experience. We
must surely admit in general terms that if people claim an
experience of God, they may be mistakenly identifying the
object of their experience. Since it seems reasonable to believe
that people sometimes hallucinate and are sometimes insane,
and since it seems reasonable to believe that it is possible to
believe things because of psychological or social pressures,
one must, presumably, also allow that it is possible that a
particular claim to experience of God may spring only from
hallucination, insanity, or the effects of psychological or social
pressures. But several points need to be added.

From 'It is usually or often or sometimes the case that-P' we
cannot deduce that it is always the case that-P. So Fred may be
as mad as a hatter and as drunk as a lord, and it may still be
true that on some particular occasion he got it right and was
reasonable in believing something on the basis of experience.
From 'It is usually or often or sometimes the case that-P' we
cannot even infer that it *might possibly* always be the case. It
might be that most men are below the average height. But it

cannot possibly be that all men are below average height. Furthermore, the truth of a belief is not affected by the factors that bring the belief about. Suppose that Fred says he believes in God on the basis of experience, and suppose that some psychologist or sociologist can produce a plausible account of how Fred got into the state of believing in God. It still does not follow that Fred is wrong or that his experience can never give him grounds for asserting that something is the case.

It is sometimes said that reports of experience of God generally come from people who are in an unusual state or who are psychologically abnormal and that this entitles us to disregard the claim that experience of God is a fact. As Bertrand Russell once put it: 'From a scientific point of view, we can make no distinction between a man who eats little and sees heaven and the man who drinks much and sees snakes.'[1] But even if someone who claims to have experience of God is in an unusual state, or even if the person is psychologically abnormal, might it not be possible that experience of God requires an unusual state or psychological abnormality, just as an aerial view of Paris requires that one be in the unusual state of being abnormally elevated? It might be said that those who are psychologically abnormal display evidence of misperception with respect to matters other than God and that this creates a presumption against any claim they might make to experience God. But that is to assume that what leads to misperception with respect to what is not God must also lead to misperception with respect to God.

If, then, we point to possibilities of hallucination and so forth, perhaps the most we can demand is a bias in favour of disregarding particular claims to experience God. Given clear evidence that Fred normally misinterprets the objects of his experience, that he regularly hallucinates, that he is insane or largely influenced by psychological or social pressures, it might be reasonable to conclude that he is probably mistaken on any given occasion. If people regularly hallucinate, they regularly believe that things exist when they do not. One might therefore argue that it is possible that in the case of any further claim of theirs that something is the case, they are mistaken.

But does this show that no person can reasonably believe in
God on the basis of his or her experience? Since it appeals to
special cases, the answer must be 'No'. The fact that some
people are amazingly prone to get things wrong is not sufficient reason for me to suppose that I am getting things wrong
on some given occasion.

It may be said, however, that there are no agreed tests for
distinguishing experience of God from illusion or mistaken
identification. And it is often urged that if something is said to
be the case, it must be possible to state tests which can be
conducted by several people as a means of confirmation. Some
philosophers would add that these tests must be empirical, and
they would argue that since God is not an empirical entity, it
follows that experience of God should never be claimed to
have occurred.

But these points are not enough to discredit the view that
one can reasonably believe in God on the basis of experience.
First, the truth of a claim that something is the case is independent of any agreed tests used to corroborate it. Second,
there are grounds for denying that any possibly true claim that
something is so must be a statement of empirical fact confirmable in principle empirically. Here I would refer the reader
back to the discussion of Chapter 1.

In addition to these points, there is something further
that needs to be said about the question of agreed tests and
experience of God. For are there really no agreed tests for
picking out a genuine experience of God? Not everyone agrees
about what would count in favour of a claim to have experienced God. But claims to experience things other than God
are frequently disputed. Universal agreement is rare. If, then,
we are to speak about agreed tests being required in order for
one to be reasonable in making a certain claim, we cannot
demand that the agreement involved be universal; not, at
least, without putting a question mark over many assertions
that may well be rationally believed. And once this point is
allowed, it seems far from clear that there are no agreed tests
for distinguishing a genuine experience of God from something else. Those who believe that there actually is experience

of God frequently say something about its effects on the one having the experience, the content of the experience, and the results to be expected in the behaviour of the one having the experience. It is said, for example, that an experience of God is accompanied by a unique sense of humility, of creatureliness, of fear and awe mingled with a strong sense of passivity and dependence. The object of the experience is usually said to be holy, awe-inspiring, loving, and so on. It is commonly accepted that an experience of God will lead people to some kind of conversion or to some kind of change of attitude or increased perspicacity. One may not think that any of these points shows that experience of God is a fact; but at present we are asking whether there are any agreed tests regarding experience of God. And it seems that there are.

We come, then, to the observation that people sometimes report an experience of the absence of God, and that those who claim an experience of God give no uniform testimony concerning the nature and object of their experience. But these observations do not get us very far either. There are people who say that they are struck by the absence of God in their experience. And there are people who never give the notion of God a second thought. But the fact that some people's account of their experience does not square with other people's account of theirs does not, by itself, establish that one of the accounts is wrong or unreasonable. A number of people may have good evidence that a certain animal is to be found in the jungle because they have seen it. Let us suppose that a second group of people go into the jungle to look for the animal in question. They search for a very long time but do not find it. Can we conclude from this that the first group of people did not have reasonable grounds for affirming that the animal was actually there? Obviously not. And if 'uniformity of testimony' means 'absolute agreement', then there is no reason to believe that no claim to have experienced God can be rational because those who claim experience of God do not provide uniformity of testimony concerning the nature and object of their experience. Two astronomers can agree about the existence of a star, and they can be reasonable in holding that it exists even though they see it from different locations and with different instruments. And two doctors can be presented with a virus, and be reasonable in believing in its existence without agreeing about its nature. If A and B claim on the basis of experience that something is the case, but disagree about the nature of the experience and the nature of what is experienced, it does not follow that one of them cannot be right and the other wrong.

What Is Experience of God?

This does not mean that the position we are now considering is without difficulties, however. Take, to begin with, the phrase 'experience of God'. What is it supposed to make us think of? The answer seems to be that it is very hard to say.

One reason for this is that 'experience of God' is an exceedingly odd expression. You can see the oddity of it by asking what would be meant by sentences like 'I had an experience of David Hume' or 'I had an experience of London'. That is not the sort of thing we say. We talk about learning by experience, and we happily make assertions like 'I had a funny experience the other day', 'He is a man of wide experience', or 'I need an experienced secretary'. But 'experience of God' is syntactically peculiar, and this is so even if we deny that 'God' is a proper name like 'Fred' or 'London'. Those who think that 'God' is not a proper name have said that it is a title-term (like 'Caesar') or a general term (what Aquinas calls a *nomen naturae*) like 'man' (in 'Some man is an animal'). But 'I had an experience of Caesar' or 'I had an experience of man' is as odd as 'I had an experience of Hume' and the like. Perhaps this does not matter much, for language is flexible, and we might expect talk about God to differ greatly from other kinds of talk. But there is a *prima facie* difficulty here, and it is compounded by what those who believe in experience of God say in order to give us a grasp of what they are referring to.

One thing said frequently is that experience of God is something like sense experience. You can encounter a donkey;

you can also encounter God. Yet objects of sense experience are material, whereas God is supposed to be incorporeal. Objects of sense experience have definite locations, but God is supposed to be everywhere. Claims to have encountered objects of sense experience can be checked and refuted by means of tests which seem inappropriate in the case of God. If I say that there is a donkey in the sitting room and that I have seen it, you can go and look for yourself. But where is one supposed to look for the presence of God? If I say that there is a dog in the kennel and that I have seen it, your observation of an empty kennel will count against my claim. But what is the equivalent of an empty kennel when it comes to God? The comparison between sense experience and experience of God seems a mystery rather than an explanation. The difference between God and physical objects renders it baffling, rather than illuminating.

Another point often stressed by defenders of the notion of experience of God is that what it amounts to can be understood by noting that it is sharply to be distinguished from inference. But, once again, there are problems with this explanation. For can we draw a rigid distinction between inference and experience? After all, inference can sometimes be spoken of as an experience. But, though an experienced logician is someone who has successfully performed many acts of inference, it does not follow that 'an act of inference' is an 'experience'. However, the everyday experience of anyone can be said to involve inference, if only because we have somehow to interpret our sensations. When I see a black, hairy, barking animal, I call it a dog without hesitation. But simply bumping into dogs will not allow us to recognize them for what they are. Something more complex is involved, something involving the work of reason. That is why new-born babies, who have plenty of sensations, do not know that they are lying in a cot, that nurses are fussing over them, and so on. It is significant that those who distinguish experience of God from inference sometimes slip into the language of inference in developing their position. A good example is H. D. Lewis. In explaining what he means by 'our experience of God' he writes:

We seem to see that in the last resort the world just could not exist by some extraordinary chance or just happen . . . All that we encounter points to a Reality which is complete and self-contained and which is the ultimate ground or condition of all the conditioned limited reality we find ourselves and the world around us to be.[2]

In this connection Lewis refers to 'one leap of thought in which finite and infinite are equally present and which cannot be broken up into steps which we may negotiate one by one'.[3] We have here a sense of contingency, 'not just a feeling . . . but a conviction or insight, a sense that something must be, a cognition in more technical terms'.[4] But this is a way of speaking which is most at home on the lips of people like defenders of the cosmological argument, which is explicitly a matter of inference. It seems to be idling when coming from someone who thinks of God as an object of experience as opposed to inference.

Finally we come to a third way sometimes given of explaining what experience of God is. According to this, it is analogous to experience of people. The basic idea here is that people are essentially non-corporeal, that they are known to each other by a kind of direct apprehension, and that God resembles them in this. He is also essentially non-corporeal, and he can be known by a non-inferential act of awareness. As H. P. Owen, for instance, writes: 'Our direct knowledge of God takes the form of an intellectual intuition which is analogous to our intuition of other human persons in so far as, firstly, it is mediated by signs, and, secondly, it terminates in a spiritual reality.'[5]

But this, once again, is a dubious explanation. For one thing there are reasons for denying that people are essentially non-corporeal. The analogy now at issue trades on views about persons such as those associated with Descartes, according to whom I am essentially an incorporeal substance contingently connected to my body and able to survive without it. We shall return to such views in Chapter 11, but for the moment we can note that they have been subject to serious challenge in both ancient and modern times. They have been much criticized, for example, by writers like Aristotle and Wittgenstein. And for this reason alone we need to be cautious about granting the premiss that the people of whom we are aware in day to day life are analogous to God since they are essentially incorporeal. To say no more than this is not, of course, to do justice to those who think of people as essentially incorporeal: if they are misguided, this should be argued at length, and not just assumed. But it *has* been argued at length and the controversial nature of the view being condemned should at least be acknowledged. In any case, the God/people analogy has other drawbacks which make it unhelpful às a means to understanding what experience of God is. Here one might briefly allude to at least two points.

First, even if people are the disembodied substances of Cartesian thinking, even if they are only in some ways incorporeal, they always, as we encounter them, come with their bodies, and knowing that they are there involves knowing that their bodies exist. God, on the other hand, is supposed to be radically incorporeal. He has no body at all. Once again, therefore, we may wonder how our encounter with people can possibly throw light on what an encounter with God might be.

Second, our dealings with people allow us to count them. We can speak of meeting ten people in a room or five on a bus. We can also speak of meeting just one person. But what entitles us to say that we have met one person rather than ten or five? An obvious answer is that in coming across one person, we come across a physical unit distinguishable in some way from others. In other words, our ability to count the people we meet involves reference to material factors. But although God is nothing material, he is also said to be one. Those who speak of experience of God do not suppose that they are talking about an encounter with five, ten, or twenty deities. But if the analogy between coming across people and coming across God is stressed, that is surely a possibility for which they should allow. In so far as they do not, then the usefulness of the God/people analogy is the more difficult to comprehend.

Recognizing God

So there is a case to be made for saying that the appeal to experience of God is hard to evaluate simply on grounds of its obscurity. But it also has other drawbacks to which we can now turn. These have to do with the question of recognition.

If I know by experience that such and such exists, then I must be able to identify it correctly when I come across it. If, for instance, my experience can tell me that there is a spider in the bath, then I must first be able to recognize a spider when I see one, and I must be able to distinguish it from other things (I must know the difference between spiders and philosophers, for example). By the same token, it would seem that if anyone is in a position to know by experience that God exists (where God is supposed to be an object of experience), then he or she must be able to recognize God and distinguish what is encountered from other possible objects of experience.

Now can anyone be in such a position? All theists agree that in some sense one can, since the end for human beings is union with God, and that would seem to entail a direct knowledge of him. Hence, for example, Aquinas explains that though our knowledge of God is indirect in this life, if 'the created mind were never able to see the essence of God, either it would never attain happiness or its happiness would consist in something other than God'.[6] But Aquinas does not think of seeing God's essence on the model of encountering an object outside oneself, as defenders of the notion of experience of God seem to do. Nor does he think of it as the basis of a case for the reasonableness of belief in God. And that is just as well if we bear in mind what God is said to be in traditional theism. For that seems to suggest that we cannot recognize God as an object of experience.

Consider, for instance, the assertion that God is the creator, the maker of heaven and earth. What recognizable property of an object is being the creator? God is also said to be omnipresent, infinite, omnipotent, and eternal. But how, simply by virtue of an awareness of an object of experience, can anything be recognized to be that? Among other things, God is said to be omniscient. But how can anybody recognize omniscience simply by encountering something omniscient? Maybe one can infer that someone is omniscient; but that is not what we are now considering. At present we are concerned with recognizing a property as something belonging to what one encounters and known by experience rather than inference.

A possible answer to these difficulties lies in the suggestion that some things must be discovered for the first time and that God is such a thing. But though one may be in a position to know that one has met one's first African elephant or whatever, if one knows what one has met, one must be able to recognize it for what it is. And that brings us back to where we were in the last paragraph. Some would reply that knowledge that one has come across God comprises a self-guaranteeing experience of certainty. One can know one has encountered God simply by virtue of the experience. But this line of thinking seems to presuppose that knowledge is a special state of mind to be recognized in the having of it. On the contrary, what determines whether or not I know something is how things stand in relation to the way I take them to be.

Here we need to distinguish between feeling sure and being right. Those who speak about a self-guaranteeing experience of certainty usually mean that we can introspectively distinguish between knowledge and mere belief. With knowledge we are certain, and that is the end of the matter. With belief we are somewhat unsure. But my feelings of certainty cannot be the arbiter of what I really know, for feelings of certainty can occur when one is wrong about that of which one feels certain. One may be convinced that p, and it may well be that p. But one's knowing that p cannot be deduced from the conviction.

In any case, 'I just know' is not a proper answer to 'How do you know?' That question is looking for reasons apart from one's convictions, reasons which entitle one to say that one knows. If I am asked how I know that my pen is on the desk, it is no reply to refer to my conviction that I just know it. I will need to be able to say things like 'I can see it', 'The light is

good', 'I'm not drunk', 'You can pick it up', 'I put it there',
and so on. It is considerations like these that make sense of my
claim to know about the pen. Some will reply that this is false,
since 'knowledge' is hard to define, and here they have a
point. 'Knowledge' is notoriously hard to define. But my not
being able to define X does not preclude my reasonably
maintaining that X is not such and such. And I have excellent
grounds for denying (a) that knowledge is a special state of
mind recognizable in the having of it and (b) that experience
of God occurs since people are convinced that this is what they
have had.

The Sighted, the Dependent, the Ineffable, and the Mystical

At this point, perhaps, enough has been said to indicate some
of the difficulties with the notion of experience of God. But
there still remain four considerations frequently advanced in
its defence, and it would be well to say something briefly about
each before concluding.

(a) *The Arguments*

According to the first, the notion of experience of God
becomes plausible once we recognize that just as some people
are physically sighted (i.e. able to see), so some may be able
to 'see' the reality of God, whereas others are merely blind
to it.

According to the second, there is such a thing as a non-
inferential recognition that everything apart from God is
absolutely and intrinsically dependent, from which it follows
that experience of God can be taken as a fact, since directly to
apprehend the dependence of everything on him is a way of
directly apprehending him.

According to the third, the difficulty of characterizing the
experience of God counts for nothing against its occurrence,
since either the experience is ineffable or its object is or both
are.

According to the fourth, there is something called 'the

experience of the mystics', and this constitutes impressive evidence that God is an object of at least some people's experience.

(b) *Comments*

It is true, of course, that some people see, whereas others are blind. But this does not explain how those who have 'sight' concerning God are in any position to identify the object of their vision. The points aired above about recognizing God are as relevant as ever. Furthermore, it is far from clear that the blind/sighted analogy will perform the job for which it seems designed. According to its proponents, it helps us to see how some might know that something (God) exists, while others lack this knowledge. They also suggest that it would explain why some know what God is, while others do not. But people who are physically blind can know what exists just as well as the sighted. And it is false that the blind are unable to know what it is that the sighted see. Blind people can know what a horse is just as well as people with sight. The blind lack sensations available to the sighted; but, as noted above, we cannot equate knowledge of what things are with the occurrence of sensations in a person. New-born infants with perfect vision are as blind as bats when it comes to knowing what things are.

With respect to the notion of absolute dependence, there are two things to say. The first is that a conviction that everything apart from God is dependent does not by itself warrant the conclusion that it is dependent. Once again, we must distinguish between being sure and being right. Secondly, one may doubt that dependence can be identified as an intrinsic property of things. People in an airplane depend absolutely for their survival on the machine which bears them. But they lose no intrinsic property when they leave it and enter the airport. They undergo no real change, since dependence is a matter of relation between things, not a matter of what things are like in themselves. Whether or not there are creatures who depend on God would not therefore seem to be something to be settled by a direct perception of them as dependent (as one

might directly perceive them to be what they are intrinsically).
Rather, it would seem that it can be settled only by a knowledge that there actually are things which depend on God, a
knowledge that is only derivable from something other than
direct perception of them as dependent. An objector might
note that everything apart from God can have a common
property called 'dependence'. But it is hard to see how anything can count as a property if everything in the world, and
the world as a whole, shares it equally. A property possessed
by everything we can name, even if we exclude God from the
list, is surely no property at all. It might be argued that being
dependent on God is not to have any particular property. In
that case, however, one wonders what it can mean to say that
one can, by experience, recognize that something is dependent
on God.

The last two arguments raise numerous issues which cannot
be adequately dealt with in the space available here. Briefly,
however, there are two points worth making about them. The
first is that if God and the experience of him are strictly
ineffable, the obvious thing to do is to stop talking about
them. The second is that if mystics are evidence for experience
of God, they are also evidence against it, since in classic
instances they often deny that God is in any intelligible sense
an object of human experience.

The drift of the first point here should be obvious: one can
hardly construct an argument out of premises which cannot
be put into words, and an argument for a God of which
nothing can be said is unrecognizable as an argument. If 'we
do not know what' is evidence for 'we do not know what', then
we do not know what we are talking about.

With respect to the second point, I can only report my
findings to the effect that to read what has been said by the
supposedly standard cases of mystical authors is to find oneself
confronted not only by a wealth of divergent reports and
judgements, but also by a repeated insistence that since God is
not a creature, he is just not accessible in the way suggested by
defenders of the notion of experience of God. As one example
among many which could be cited, there is the case of St John

of the Cross (1542–91), a textbook 'mystic' if ever there was
one (others include Meister Eckhart (c.1260–1327), Jan Van
Ruysbroeck (1293–1381), St Catherine of Siena (1347–80),
and St Teresa of Avila (1512–82)). According to him, union
with God is a matter of faith, and 'no supernatural apprehension or knowledge in this mortal life can serve as a proxi-
mate means to the high union of love with God'.[7] 'The Soul',
says St John,

must be voided of all such things as can enter its capacity, so that,
however many supernatural things it may have it will ever remain as it
were detached from them and in darkness. It must be like to a blind
man, leaning upon dark faith, taking it for guide and light, and
leaning upon none of the things that he understands, experiences,
feels and imagines.[8]

Other readers of mystical texts may have different things to
impart concerning their content. And their reading may
convince them that there is such a thing as 'the experience of
the mystics' and that it is good evidence of God's existence.
But if their conviction is to warrant agreement, it will need to
be justified by extensive documentation and research, as well
as by answers to the problems outlined above.

Experiencing-As

Before we move on to other matters, there is one other line of
thought linking the terms 'experience' and 'God' which
deserves a mention. This has been advanced by John Hick,
who takes as his starting point some passages in Wittgenstein's
Philosophical Investigations.[9]

Towards the end of that work, Wittgenstein discusses the
notion of seeing, and he observes that there are different
senses of the word 'see'. One kind of seeing that interests him
is where, after we have looked at something for a while, a new
aspect of it dawns on us, even though what we have been
looking at has not itself changed. The example he cites is the
much reproduced picture which sometimes appears to people
to be a picture of a duck, and sometimes a picture of a rabbit
(Jastrow's 'duck-rabbit').

It is from this picture and others like it that Hick takes his cue. We can, he says, often see things now in one way, now in another, even though what we have been looking at does not really change. What changes is the way we see things. But, Hick adds, *all* perception or seeing or experience of things is really like this. In other words, all experience is a matter of 'seeing-as'. He writes:

It is today hardly a contentious doctrine requiring elaborate argumentation that seeing . . . is not a simple matter of physical objects registering themselves on our retinas and thence in our conscious visual fields . . . We speak of seeing-as when that which is objectively there, in the sense of that which affects the retina, can be consciously perceived in two different ways as having two different characters or natures or meanings or significances . . . We perceive and recognize by means of all the relevant senses co-operating as a single complex means of perception; and I suggest that we use the term 'experiencing-as' to refer to the end product of this in consciousness . . . *All* experiencing is experiencing as . . . To recognize or identify is to experience as in terms of a concept; and our concepts are social products having their life within a particular linguistic environment . . . All conscious experiencing involves recognitions which go beyond what is given to the senses and is thus a matter of experiencing as.[10]

From this conclusion Hick moves to the suggestion that someone who believes in God can be regarded as experiencing everything as something behind which God lies. Believers see the world as a world in which God is present. And since all experience is experience-as, their position is no worse than anyone else's. 'The analogy to be explored', says Hick,

is with two contrasting ways of experiencing the events of our lives and of human history, on the one hand as purely natural events and on the other as mediating the presence and activity of God. For there is a sense in which the religious man and the atheist both live in the same world and another sense in which they live consciously in different worlds. They inhabit the same physical environment and are confronted by the same changes occurring within it. But in its actual concrete character in their respective 'streams of consciousness' it has for each a different nature and quality, a different meaning and significance; for one does and the other does not experience life as a continual interaction with the transcendent God . . . Ordinary secular perceiving shares a common epistemological character with religious experiencing . . . All conscious perceiving goes beyond what the senses report to a significance which has not as such been given to the senses. And the religious experience of life as a sphere in which we have continually to do with God and he with us is likewise an awareness in our experience as a whole of a significance which transcends the scope of the senses . . . We have learned, starting from scratch, to identify rabbits and forks and innumerable other kinds of thing. And so there is thus far in principle no difficulty about the claim that we may learn to use the concept 'act of God', as we have learned to use other concepts, and acquire the capacity to recognize exemplifying instances.[11]

In defence of Hick, it can surely be said that he is right to maintain that, as he puts it, seeing is 'not a simple matter of physical objects registering themselves on our retinas and thence in our conscious visual fields'. We might express this truth by saying that seeing is a matter of finding meaning or significance in things, and meaning and significance are not physical properties. But Hick's account does not show that belief in God can reasonably be based on experience. The major problem here lies in its use of the notion of experiencing-as.

Clearly there is a use for this idea. Sometimes we find that something which undergoes no change first appears to us in one way, then in another. But can we regard all experience as experience-as? Hick says that we can. He holds that just as one can see-as on some occasions, so one can experience-as on all occasions. But if Hick is right, it follows that when we experience something and when we characterize it on the basis of experience, we might be just as entitled to characterize it differently. We experience something as an X, say. And we therefore call it an X. But we could, in principle, experience it as a Y. And we could, in principle, characterize it as a Y.

Surely, however, we must sometimes say that we experience things and that they are exactly as we say they are. If we could not sometimes say this, then how could we ever, as we often wish to do and as it often seems reasonable to do, seriously convict people of mistakenly identifying things? From the fact that people experience something as such and such, it does not follow that they are right in what they say is there. One may often be able to say that something can be experienced either as this or as that; but one cannot always say this. On some occasions 'Here is an X' is either true or false. And on some occasions 'Here is a Y' is either true or false. And this point is presumably one that Hick must ultimately accept himself. For he seems clear enough that all experience really is experience-as. He seems clear, in other words, that his thesis about experience is correct.

So Hick's analysis still leaves us saying that even though people experience things in a certain way, they can be wrong. But this means that Hick's account leaves us with no particular reason for saying that people who claim to experience the world as God's world are not just deluding themselves. They hold that the world is God's world. But are they right? Hick will reply that the world can be experienced as created by God. But I may experience the world as God's world without it following that this is what it is. Something other than the fact that I experience it as such seems to be required.

Where, then, does all this leave us on the question of experience and God? If my arguments have been correct, it seems that although various objections can be made to the view that it is unreasonable to believe in God on the basis of experience, the whole notion of an experience of God either collapses into something that looks like the notion of being convinced by an argument or is just very difficult to understand. Experience of dogs and cats and people is one thing; but experience of what God is supposed to be seems quite different. It is far from clear that its nature can even be elucidated, let alone judged as something to which one could appeal as providing a reasonable ground for belief in God. This conclusion is independent of any reason apart from experience which we may have for believing in God, and, of course, there are evidently people who would disagree with it. Whether readers of this book are to be numbered among them is something they can now go on to consider for themselves.

8

Eternity

THOSE who believe in God have more to say about him than
that he exists. They ascribe certain attributes to him. As we
have seen, they say that God is good, powerful, and so on. It
now seems appropriate to say something more about God's
attributes, but the subject is such a large one that it is hard to
know where to begin or end for the purposes of a book like
this. I have chosen to deal with it in this chapter by turning to
what many believers would take to be a fundamental truth
about God: namely, that God is eternal. God's eternity is
currently a much debated question among philosophers of
religion, which gives us another reason for looking at it. As we
shall see, to consider the proposition 'God is eternal' will also
allow us to look a little at the question of God's activity,
power, and knowledge.

The Meaning of Divine Eternity

What does it mean to call God eternal? Two main answers
have been given. According to the first, 'God is eternal' means
that God is non-temporal or timeless. According to the
second, it simply means that God has no beginning and no
end, that God has always existed and will continue to exist
for ever.

Historically speaking, it is the first of the above notions
of eternity which has been most prevalent. Indeed, one
may call it 'the classical view of divine eternity'. It can be
found in writers like St Anselm, St Augustine, St Thomas
Aquinas, John Calvin (1509–64), Descartes, and Friedrich
Schleiermacher (1768–1834). An especially influential exponent

of it is Boethius (*c*.480–524), whose definition of eternity as timelessness was a starting point for much medieval thinking on eternity. He writes:

Eternity, then, is the complete and perfect possession of unending life, all at once (*tota simul*); this will be clear from a comparison with creatures that exist in time. Whatever lives in time exists in the present and progresses from the past to the future, and there is nothing set in time which can embrace all at once the whole extent of its life . . . Whatever, therefore, suffers the condition of being in time, even though it never had any beginning, never has any ending and its life extends into the infinity of time . . . is still not such that it may properly be called eternal.[1]

The idea here is that God has no beginning or end, no birth and no death, that he differs from us in that his life is not one of limited duration. But to this is added the thought of him not having a life lived in time. The claim, therefore, is that God has nothing that we could recognize as a history or a biography. As Anselm puts it:

You were not, therefore, yesterday, nor will You be tomorrow, but yesterday and today and tomorrow You *are*. Indeed You exist neither yesterday nor today nor tomorrow but are outside all times (*es extra omne tempus*). For yesterday and today and tomorrow are completely in time; however, You, though nothing can be without You, are nevertheless not in place or time but all things are in You. For nothing contains You, but You contain all things.[2]

For a supporter of the second view of eternity (which is something of a modern phenomenon), we can refer, once again, to Richard Swinburne. According to him:

If a creator of the universe exists now, he must have existed at least as long as there have been other logically contingent existing things . . . However, traditionally theists believe not merely that this spirit, God, exists now or has existed as long as created things, but that he is an eternal being. This seems to mean, firstly, that he has always existed—that there was no time at which he did not exist . . . Let us put this point by saying that they believe that he is backwardly eternal. The supposition that a spirit of the above kind is backwardly eternal seems to be a coherent one . . . The doctrine that God is eternal seems to involve, secondly, the doctrine that the above spirit will go on existing for ever . . . I will put this point by saying that he is forwardly eternal. This too seems to be a coherent suggestion.[3]

In Swinburne's judgement, it is incoherent to suppose that God is outside time. But it is coherent to suppose that he has always existed and that he always will exist. On Swinburne's account, there was no time when God did not exist. And there will be no time when he will not exist. And to say that this is so is to say that God is eternal.[4]

Objections to 'God is Timeless'

Most of the controversy about God's eternity has been about the notion of eternity as timelessness. So perhaps we had better plunge into the deep end immediately and consider whether it is reasonable to talk in terms of a timeless God. Many arguments have been advanced to the effect that it is not, and I cannot mention and comment on them all. But we can look at some of the major ones, the first of which holds that to speak of God as timeless is incompatible with believing that God is a person.

(a) *God as an Acting Person*

The argument here is really quite simple. To assert that God is timeless is also to assert that God is wholly changeless or immutable. But can God be changeless or immutable if he is a person? Not according to some writers, who therefore deny that God is timeless. Thus, for example, in *A Treatise on Space and Time*, J. R. Lucas bluntly declares: 'To say that God is outside time, as many theologians do, is to deny, in effect, that God is a person.'[5] Lucas evidently supposes that God *is* a person and that the theologians to whom he refers have somehow got it wrong. And the same conclusion is advanced by Nelson Pike in *God and Timelessness*. In chapter 7 of the book ('God as a Timeless Person'), Pike considers whether God can be called a person if he is also said to be timeless. The conclusion Pike offers is that something timeless cannot really count as a person.

A related line of argument which has been offered turns on the notion of God as something living and acting. For, if God lives and acts, must he not be changeable and, therefore, not timeless? According to Grace Jantzen:

A living God cannot be static: life implies change and hence temporality. This means that the doctrine of immutability cannot be interpreted as absolute changelessness, which would preclude divine responsiveness and must rather be taken as steadfastness of character.[6]

This line of thinking is developed by Nelson Pike and Richard Swinburne, who (between them) argue that a timeless God cannot act and create. According to Swinburne:

If we say that P brings about X, we can always sensibly ask *when* does he bring it about? If we say that P punishes Q, we can always sensibly ask *when* does he punish Q . . . If P at t brings about X, then necessarily X comes into existence (simultaneously with or) subsequently to P's action . . . And so on.[7]

According to Pike, if God creates, then he produces or sustains; but 'the specialized verbs we use when describing a case of deliberate or intentional production . . . seem to carry with them identifiable implications regarding the relative temporal positions of the items produced and the creative activity involved in their production'.[8] According to Pike, temporal implications 'seem to be there in every case; they seem to be part of the "essence" of "produce"'.[9]

But are these arguments decisive? We have already noted grounds for rejecting the first of them. Why should those who believe in God want to insist on the formula 'God is a person'? As noted in Chapter 3, the formula is not a biblical one. Nor does it sit easily with the Christian faith in God as a Trinity. It is also potentially embarrassing for its proponents if they want to say that God is wholly underived. Persons as we understand them are very much part of the universe. And they are very much part of what we would be puzzled about if, with defenders of the cosmological argument, we wonder why there should be a universe. If we are right to wonder along these lines, would we not also be right to ask what accounts for the existence of God—if God is a person? One might, of course, reply that God is not a person as we are persons. But in that case, one might wonder why his being a person should rule out the possibility of his being eternal in the way supposed by the classical view of divine eternity.

Jantzen, Swinburne, and Pike will presumably say that they have explained why God cannot be timeless. But their arguments as noted above are not exactly unanswerable. Jantzen assumes that nothing immutable can have life. But to argue on that assumption is to ignore the possibility (which defenders of God's timelessness regularly accept) that God may be said to live because he brings about effects and does so 'off his own bat', so to speak—i.e. because he is a source of change which is itself unchanged by anything, because he is, as we might put it, the ultimate 'automobile'.[10] With respect to Swinburne, one can agree with part of what he says. If we observe that God has brought about such and such, it would seem natural to ask 'When did he bring it about?' But Swinburne is wrong to suppose that any true answer to this question entails that God is in time or that God changes in himself. And Pike, too, is wrong to suppose that God's creating must involve him in some real change.

Of course, it is true that if, for example, we are told that someone produced something, we can ask 'When?' But we can say when God brought things about without supposing that he changed or occupied time in doing so. For something is brought about by an agent or someone is punished by an agent (to take Swinburne's example) when the something in question is brought about or the person in question is punished. Suppose, then, we say that such and such has been brought about by God. Then we ask 'When?' Suppose the answer is 'At 2 o'clock last Friday'. Does that mean that God must have been undergoing some sort of process at 2 o'clock last Friday? Or does it mean that he must have occupied the time we call '2 o'clock last Friday'? Not at all. It need only mean that at 2 o'clock last Friday such and such came to pass by virtue of God. Whether God changed in bringing it about is a further question, as is the question of whether in bringing it about he did so as something existing in time. Swinburne says that 'If P at t brings about X, then necessarily X comes into existence (simultaneously with or) subsequently to P's action'. But that is by no means obviously true in the sense implied by Swinburne. If 'P' is God, how do we know that his bringing about can be located in time if that is meant to imply that God is himself in time? We may know that things are brought about at different times and that God brings them about—i.e. that they are there because of God. But this does not entitle us to conclude that God cannot bring it about that something be temporally located without himself being temporally located. In general, Swinburne confuses 'God brings it about that X is true at t' with 'God, occupying some moment of time, brings it about at that time that X is true'. And this point is relevant to Pike's position. For what if we have reason for saying that something has been brought about and yet that there is reason for denying that what accounts for what is brought about is located in time? Then we have reason for denying that the notion of bringing about always implies that there is something which, by existing at some time, brings things about. Whether or not we could have reason for denying this is not to be decided, as Pike seems to think, by looking at what seems to be true of familiar cases of bringing about. And if the claim is that God brings about without being in time, what are required are not examples of bringing about when it is not God who is said to bring about.

With respect to all this, an analogy might help. Suppose we ask how people manage to teach. It seems natural to say that they do it by uttering words or by using blackboards and so on (and therefore by undergoing various changes in time). For that is how teaching is effected by people. But teaching cannot be defined as going through certain motions. I can utter true statements until I am blue in the face. I can fill a thousand blackboards with letters and diagrams. But none of these processes will count as teaching unless somebody actually learns something. For this reason it seems necessary to say that if I am interested in knowing whether I have taught somebody something, I am interested not in changes occurring in me, but in changes occurring in somebody else. I cannot teach you except by undergoing change of some kind. But my undergoing these changes does not constitute my teaching you. Unless you actually learn something, they are simply fruitless bits of behaviour on my part. Teaching occurs when learning occurs, when someone changes from a state of ignorance to a state of knowledge concerning some truth. In a similar way, so we may suggest, God's bringing things about need be understood only in terms of things coming about, not in terms of something happening at some time in God. It is a condition and a limitation of my nature that I can only bring about in you the change we call 'learning' by, as a matter of fact, changing myself as something in time. But there is nothing in the notion of teaching that requires such a change in the teacher. There is thus no reason why God should not teach you by bringing about a change in you without in any way changing himself. And, more generally, there is no reason why God should not bring about changes and, in so far as times depend on changes, times without himself changing or being in time.[11]

(b) *Love, Freedom, and the Bible*

But critics of the notion that God is timeless will now wish to press other objections. Three, in particular, are especially popular at the moment. According to the first, the classical view of eternity *leaves us with a God who cannot love*. According to the second, it leaves us with a God *who cannot choose not to create*. According to the third, it *contradicts the Bible*.

The first objection here is much associated with the work of writers known as 'process theologians', including, for example, Charles Hartshorne. But it can also be found in the work of other theologians such as Jürgen Moltmann and the Latin American liberation theologian Jon Sobrino, SJ. According to the classical view of eternity, God is immutable. It therefore follows that he cannot be affected by anything. According to the present objection, however, God must actually suffer if he is truly describable as loving. According to Hartshorne,

for example, when God knows us in our joys, he shares joy
with us, and, when he knows us as suffering, he suffers too.
According to Sobrino (quoting Moltmann):

We must insist that love has to be credible to human beings in an
unredeemed world. That forces us to ask ourselves whether God can
really describe himself as love if historical suffering does not affect
him . . . We must say what Moltmann says: 'We find suffering that is
not wished, suffering that is accepted, and the suffering of love. If
God were incapable of suffering in all those ways, and hence in an
absolute sense, then God would be incapable of loving.'[12]

Yet is all this really true? In its favour we may observe that
when people love, they frequently suffer. Love, indeed, may
lead people to their deaths, for one way of loving is to sacrifice
oneself totally on behalf of those one loves. But why should
one suppose that divine love must be costly for God in a
similar way? God, after all, is commonly held to be perfect.
Yet suffering is a limitation, a restriction on one's freedom. To
say that God suffers might therefore be viewed as a way of
asserting that he is vulnerable, defective, and thwarted. It
might be replied that God must be held to be loving and that
love and limitation always go together. But it does not seem
true that love and limitation always go together. One may
display one's love by limiting oneself. But that is not to say
that love and limitation are inseparable. Indeed, one might
argue that love is capable of its fullest development only where
the lover is not limited by anything. One might also observe
that a subject may be said to love if the subject in question can
be thought of as willing the good of others. And one might
add that even a timeless God can be said to do that if he is also
the creator and sustainer of the universe. For if God is these
things, must it not be true that he is thereby the source of
much that is good in creatures? That this is, in fact, true, has
been a very traditional teaching of religious people. One can
find it, for instance, in Aquinas. As he puts it:

God loves all existing things. For in so far as it is real each is good;
the very existence of each single thing is good, and so also is whatever
it rises to. We have already shown that God's will is the cause of

things, and consequently that in so far as it has reality or any goodness at all each thing must needs be willed by God. God therefore
wills some good to each existing thing, and since loving is no other
than willing good to someone, it is clear that God loves everything.[13]

But perhaps we should reply that if God is timeless, he
cannot truly will anything. This, at any rate, is what the second
objection mentioned above maintains. Why? Because, so the
objection runs, if God is eternal in the classical sense, his will
is unchanging and unchangeable, and he cannot, therefore,
choose to do anything other than create. If God is immutable,
so the argument goes, he can only will what he does will. Since
he has evidently willed to create, the upshot would seem to be
that if God is timeless, he was bound to create and, therefore,
not really free (or not really willing) in creating as he has.

Yet this argument moves too quickly. Up to a point, indeed,
the argument has merit. For if God is eternal in the classical
sense, and if God is the creator, he is changelessly the creator
of whatever it is that he creates. In other words, given that
God has willed to create, creation (on the classical view of
eternity) is somehow inevitable (assuming, of course, that
God's will cannot be thwarted). But given that God is also free
(as our present objection supposes), all that now follows is
that God has freely willed to create what, by virtue of his
changelessness, comes about by virtue of his freely willing
to create. Or, as Aquinas succinctly expresses the point:
'Granted that God wills whatever he does from eternity, the
inference is not that he has to except on the supposition
that he does.'[14] In other words, from the fact that God is
immutable, it does not follow that he is bound to create.
Given that God wills to create, it only follows that he changelessly wills to create.

Yet, so defenders of our third objection to the classical
notion of eternity will now say, all this talk about God's
changelessness is surely of no interest to those who believe in
God as he is depicted in the Bible. According to John Lucas,
for example, 'the whole thrust of the biblical record' implies
that God changes. The Bible:

is an account of God both caring and knowing about the world, even the five sparrows, which at one time had not yet been, and later had been, sold for two farthings, and intervening in the world, doing things, saying things, hearing prayers, and sometimes changing his mind.[15]

'The changelessness of God', says Lucas, 'is not to be naturally read out of the Bible, but rather was read into it in the light of certain philosophical assumptions about the nature of God.'[16] Here Lucas agrees with Richard Swinburne, according to whom:

The God of the Old Testament, in which Judaism, Islam and Christianity have their roots, is a God in continual interaction with men, moved by men as they speak to him . . . If God did not change at all, he would not think now of this, now of that . . . The God of the Old Testament is not pictured as such a being . . . The doctrine of divine timelessness is very little in evidence before Augustine. The Old Testament certainly shows no sign of it . . . The same applies in general for New Testament writers.[17]

How should one react to this line of argument? Initially, perhaps, one might support it by saying that, to some extent, it can be justified, since biblical authors indeed speak of God as a changing individual. As John L. McKenzie shows, 'The philosophical concept of eternity [i.e. the classical concept] is not clearly expressed in either the O.T. or N.T. The Hb. *'olam* and the Gk. *aiōn* both signify primarily an indefinitely extended period of time beyond the lifetime of a single person.'[18] In the article on *aiōn/aiōnios* in Kittel's *Theological Dictionary of the New Testament*, the New Testament position is summed up thus:

The unending eternity of God and the time of the world, which is limited by its creation and conclusion, are contrasted with one another. Eternity is thought of as unending time—for how else can human thought picture it?—and the eternal being of God is represented as pre-existence and post-existence . . . The NT took over the OT and Jewish view of divine eternity along with the ancient formulae. There was new development, however, to the extent that the statements concerning God's eternity were extended to Christ.[19]

Yet defenders of God's timelessness (even those who regard the Bible as authoritative) have not been slow in observing that facts such as these do not disprove what they want to assert. As an example, we may once again refer to Aquinas and see how he reasons on the matter.

To begin with, he agrees with the premiss of Lucas and Swinburne: that the Bible speaks of God as undergoing change or as being temporal. In his discussion of prayer in the *Summa contra Gentiles* he cites Isaiah 38: 1–5 and Jeremiah 18: 7–8 as instances in the Bible where change is ascribed to God.[20] He makes a similar move in his treatment of divine immutability in the *Summa Theologiae*. In Ia, 9, 1, obj. 3, for instance, he notes that 'Drawing near and drawing away are descriptions of movements' and that 'scripture applies them to God' in James 4: 8. And in obj. 4 to Ia, 10, 2 we find: 'Past, present and future do not exist in eternity, which, as we have said, is instantaneously whole. But the Scriptures use verbs in the present, past and future tenses, when talking of God.' In his replies to these objections Aquinas does not dispute the facts to which they draw attention.

On the other hand, he does not regard such facts as forcing us to conclude that God is mutable and temporal. He notes, for example, that although Scripture speaks of God as changing, it also speaks of him as unchanging. He cites Malachi 3: 6 ('I am God, I change not'). He also cites Numbers 23: 19 and 1 Samuel 15: 29. More significantly, he notes that judgement must be exercised in reading Scripture and that this should be borne in mind by anyone invoking its letter as a way of deciding what can truly be said of God.

In Aquinas's view, Scripture is not a dead thing which wears its full significance on its face. He thinks that we must treat it as contemporary and that we need to engage with it using our best available resources, so that there is a kind of dialogue between the words of Scripture and those who read them. This in turn means that, for him, the truths conveyed by Scripture can be other than surface indications might suggest. He thinks that Scripture must be interpreted in the light of what we know.

One thing this means for him is that we need to distinguish between a literal and a non-literal reading of scriptural texts.[21] In his view, a biblical text can be read literally when it tells us what we could not know otherwise and/or when it tells us something not incompatible with what we know to be the case. When, on the other hand, it tells us that, for example, God breathes, we have to interpret in a non-literal sense. Breath, in the literal sense, is what we and other animals produce through our mouths and noses. So bodily creatures alone can be said literally to breathe, and biblical talk about the breath of God must be understood accordingly.

And it is the same, Aquinas thinks, with biblical statements implying a real change in God. According to him, we have reason to deny that God can change, just as we have reason to deny that God has a mouth or a nose. Hence we find that the reply to obj. 1 of Ia, 9, 1 (above) runs:

The scripture is here talking of God in metaphors. For just as the sun is said to enter or depart from a house by touching the house with its rays, so God is said to draw near to us when we receive an influx of his goodness, or draw away from us when we fail him.

The reply to obj. 4 of Ia, 10, 2 is: 'Verbs of different tenses are used of God, not as though he varied from present to future, but because his eternity comprehends all phases of time.' In each case Aquinas wants both to respect the truth of Scripture, to take its words seriously, and also to be faithful to truths we know of God apart from what Scripture says.

In short, he thinks that the Bible (and teaching based on it) contains metaphor or figurative or symbolical language which needs to be read as such. At this point, perhaps, we might agree with him. The Bible evidently does contain metaphor and the like which needs to be read as such. The question, however, is 'Should we treat biblical ascriptions of change to God as metaphorical?' As far as I can see, the only way to answer this question is to consider whether there are positive reasons independent of the Bible for supposing that God is immutable. Aquinas and other defenders of the classical view of eternity think that there are. And we will need to consider what can be said in favour of this conclusion.

(c) *Simultaneity and Now*

Before we do that, however, there are two final objections to
the notion of God as timeless which ought to be noted. One of
them occurs in a well-known article and book by Anthony
Kenny. The other turns on the thought that if God is timeless,
there is a sense in which he cannot really be said to exist. The
objections are connected, since a possible way of responding
to the first might be thought to leave one unable to cope with
the second.

Kenny's objection holds that the classical view of eternity is
incoherent since it entails that past, present, and future are
simultaneous, which, of course, they cannot be. Kenny takes
Aquinas as a standard exponent of divine timelessness. He
then argues as follows:

The whole concept of a timeless eternity seems to be radically incoherent . . . On St Thomas' view, my typing of this paper is simultaneous with the whole of eternity. Again, on this view, the great fire
of Rome is simultaneous with the whole of eternity. Therefore, while
I type these words, Nero fiddles heartlessly on.[22]

Kenny is thinking of the fact that Aquinas sometimes speaks
as though God, in eternity, is related to the course of history
as someone looking out of a tower is related to a line of figures
passing by. The people in the line come before and after each
other. But to the person looking out of the tower, all are
present together. Or, as Aquinas himself writes:

God is wholly outside the order of time, standing, as it were, in the
high citadel of eternity, which is all at one time. The whole course of
time is subject to eternity in one simple glance. So at one glance he
sees everything that is done in the course of time; he sees everything
as it is in itself, not as if it were future relative to his view. It is only
future in the ordering of its causes—though God does see that
ordering of causes. In a wholly eternal way he sees everything that is
the case at any time, just as the human eye sees the sitting down of
Socrates as it is in itself, not in its causes.[23]

It seems to me that, with texts like the one just quoted in
mind, Kenny's argument is successful. If it is supposed that
God's eternity stands to history as an observer stands to what
he or she is observing (i.e. in the relation of simultaneity),

then events which occur at different times would seem to be going on together. If Fred looks out of his tower on Mary, John, and Edith passing by, we can say that Fred is looking out while Mary, John, and Edith pass by (that Fred's looking out is simultaneous with the others passing by). If God in eternity is thought of as an observer and if in a glance he sees Kenny typing and Nero fiddling, we might say that God sees Kenny typing as Nero fiddles (that God's vision is simultaneous with Kenny typing and Nero fiddling and that Kenny's typing is simultaneous with Nero's fiddling). But that cannot be so. For Kenny did not type as Nero fiddled. And Nero did not fiddle as Kenny typed.

But those who wish to assert that God is timeless (including Aquinas) need not be thought of as holding that events in time are simultaneous with eternity. For, as Paul Helm observes, 'the concept of simultaneity is obviously one which implies time'.[24] And defenders of 'God is timeless' might simply deny that God (or God's eternity) is simultaneous with any event at all. They might say, as Helm goes on to say, that 'if God timelessly exists he is neither earlier nor later nor simultaneous with any event of time. He exists time*lessly*'.[25] Indeed, they might wish to say something similar even if it is not God that is in question. For what, say, does 'John is simultaneous with Fred's sneezing at 5.00 p.m. on January 1st 1860' mean? Do we have any use for such sentences? We can, indeed, say things like 'John was breathing while Fred was sneezing'. But expressing the notion of simultaneity in this way leaves us with no need to posit subjects which just *are simultaneous with* events or times.[26]

Yet one may now wonder just what one would be saying if one did say that God is not simultaneous with any event or time—which brings us to the second objection I mentioned at the start of this section. For would one not be denying that God exists *now*? And would this not be equivalent to denying that God exists, *period*? After all, one might argue that if God really is timeless in the terms asserted by Helm, then it must be false that he exists now—just as it must be false that God existed in 1066. But how can it be false that God exists now without it also being false that there is a God at all? One might say that (1) 'It is now true that God exists' does not entail (2) 'It is true that God exists now', and that all the theist needs to endorse is (1). But does this really deal with the problem? 'It is now true that God exists' is equivalent to 'God exists', which is surely either true or false whenever it is propounded. So it looks as though if God does not exist when I say he does, he does not exist. And if God does not exist, how can he be eternal in any sense? One might hold that, though it exists at no time at all, the number 6 exists. One might call it a 'non-actual object'.[27] So perhaps there are things which can exist at no time at all. But God is said to be a living subject. His mode of existence is not usually supposed to be that of a number. So again we may ask what it can mean to say that, although God exists, he does not exist as I speak.

But though this line of reasoning may *seem* to present us with a formidable objection to the notion of God as timeless, it is not, perhaps, all that formidable. For it rests on the assumption that 'God exists now' says something more than 'God exists'. And this assumption is questionable. Suppose I assert 'The tower is being built now'. Does this say any more than 'The tower is being built'? Surely, it does not. We would say 'The tower is being built now' to inform someone who might think that the building of the tower is either over or yet to start. We would want to rule out pastness and futurity of the tower building. And we would do this by inserting 'now', which gives some emphasis in that it is intended positively to exclude pastness and futurity. All the same, what is said by 'The tower is being built now' is just that the tower is being built. If the tower is being built, we can infer that it has not been built and that it is false that it is not being built but will be being built. The thing being emphasized by 'now' is actually derivable from 'The tower is being built'. So 'The tower is being built now' adds nothing to 'The tower is being built'.

By the same token, so we might argue, 'God exists now' adds nothing to 'God exists'. One might say that 'now' has something to do with simultaneity. Suppose I say 'John is doing his homework now'. I am saying that he is doing his homework as I speak. But 'John is doing his homework now' is equivalent to 'John is presently doing his homework' or 'John is actually doing his homework'. And the presentness of an event, we may say, just is the event. 'John is presently doing his homework' is true if 'John is doing his homework' is true. And 'John is actually doing his homework' is true if 'John is doing his homework' is true. The reality of the present, we may say, consists in the absence of qualifying prefix. To say that Reagan's presidency is past is to say that *it has been the case* that Reagan is president. To say that Reagan's presidency is future is to say that *it will be the case* that Reagan is president. But to say that Reagan is president is present is just to say that *Reagan is president*. By the same token, so we may argue, 'God exists now' is equivalent to 'God exists'.

God Everlasting

So perhaps we may conclude that the classical notion of eternity is a defensible one (that it can be defended against some objections, anyway). But what of the other view of eternity, the one which holds that God has always existed and will always exist in time—that God is everlasting? Could that view of God possibly be true?

In so far as it includes the view that God is a changing individual, it could not be true if it is true that God is the first cause of all change, as (so we have seen) one version of the cosmological argument holds. And those who believe that God is a changing individual will have to accept what many will find unbelievable: that a changing individual can be the uncaused cause of a changing universe. For those who believe that God is mutable usually believe that he is the cause of the changing universe and that there is no question of his being caused to be. People who think of God as changeable might say that he is just an ultimate 'brute fact' which stands in need of no cause. Others, however, will wonder why it should be thought that a changeable God can be an ultimate brute fact if the changeable universe cannot be one itself.[28]

Still, perhaps there is no problem in the notion of some-thing living in time along with us and carrying on for ever. Swinburne, for instance, suggests that if it is coherent to suppose that God exists at the present time, then it is 'co-herent to suppose that he exists at any other nameable time; and, if that is coherent, then surely it is coherent to suppose that there exists a being now such that however far back in time you count years you do not reach the beginning of its existence'.[29] He continues: 'We, perhaps, cease to exist at death. But we can surely conceive of a being now existent such that whatever future nameable time you choose, he has not by that time ceased to exist . . . A being who is both backwardly and forwardly eternal we may term an eternal being.'[30] Some philosophers do not like to speak as if times were things to be singled out. And they have very good reason for their aversion. For it is hard to maintain that, as well as being able to individuate subjects of whom we may assert things, we can also individuate times as subjects of which we can predicate attributes or properties, as subjects which can be named.[31] But is it absurd to suppose that something might have been around for ever or that something might continue to be around for ever? Might we not say, for example, that something is divine, that it used to be the case that something is divine, that it was never the case that nothing is divine, that it will never be the case that nothing is divine, and that 'X is divine' is compatible with 'there is not more than one God'? Will this not express the idea that God is everlasting?

There is an argument which would, if we accepted it, oblige us to conclude that there is nothing which has been around for ever, as God, on the present view of 'God is eternal', is supposed to have been around for ever. Those who say that God is everlasting mean us to understand that God had no beginning, in the sense that he has existed for an infinite time past. And, as we saw in Chapter 5, this is a notion which some would deny on the ground that there cannot be an actual infinite (e.g. an actual infinite number of past years or generations). Hence, for example, Paul Helm writes:

The idea that God exists in an infinitely backward extending time runs up against the idea of an actual infinite. For such a prospect requires that an infinite number of events must have elapsed before the present moment could arrive. And since it is impossible for an infinite number of events to have elapsed, and yet the present moment has arrived, the series of events cannot be infinite.[32]

One might reply that the idea of God existing in an infinitely backward extending time does not require an infinite number of events. Perhaps it just requires a finite set of events and one (infinitely long) event. But events are not infinitely long. They are what we report when we say such things as 'John knocked the vase over'. And in any case, even if we can make sense of an infinitely long event, we will be envisaging at least one event of which it can be said that it has existed from infinity (whatever it would mean to say this). And this (would it not?) would seem to require that the one event in question has existed for an infinite number of moments of time past.

But those who believe that an infinite number of moments may have elapsed before the present will not find this argument a refutation of the view that God is everlasting.[33] And if there is, indeed, no problem with the notion of an actual infinite, there may be no problem with the notion that God has always existed. We might ask, however what we would be saying in saying this. For what is asserted of a subject if it is asserted that the subject 'has always existed'? If the subject is God, we are saying, surely, that something is divine and that it always was the case that that thing was divine and that it has never been the case that nothing else was divine. But does this entail that God is everlasting, as opposed to timeless? No, because someone who believes that God is timeless could agree with this proposition (as well as with the more complex one above which resembles it). Indeed, those who believe that God is timeless agree with both these propositions.

Is God Eternal?

Regardless of what we think possible, however, what should we say about the eternity of God as a matter of fact? Are there reasons for supposing that God is eternal on either of the views of eternity just discussed?

Defenders of the classical view have a standard line on this question. They say that God is unchangeable and that he must therefore be timeless.[34] The idea here is that to say that something is changeable is to say that it exists in time, and that to speak of a thing as timeless is to say that it is unchangeable. On this account, being changeable, changing, and being in time go together. To say that something changes is also to say that it exists in time.

Should we agree with this account? In ancient Greek thought it was the exception to allow time without change.[35] And this situation is reflected in post-Newtonian physics, according to which determining simultaneity depends on one's motion or rest. But some have held that there can be time without change. The famous example is Isaac Newton (1642–1727). According to him:

Absolute, true, and mathematical time, of itself, and from its own nature, flows equably without relation to anything external and by another name is called duration: relative, apparent, and common time, is some sensible and external (whether accurate or unequable) measure of duration by the means of motion, which is commonly used instead of true time; such as an hour, a month, a year.[36]

On this account, it would not follow that if God is unchanging or unchangeable, then God is outside time. It would seem to follow that time is what anything exists in, including God.

But does time require change? Aristotle argues that time is essentially connected with change, that time is a measure of change. He does not think that it is identical with change, since many things change, whereas 'time is equally everywhere and with everything', and since change may be fast or slow, whereas 'what is fast and what is slow is defined by time'. But he does maintain that without change there is no time.

When we ourselves do not alter in our mind or do not notice that we
alter, then it does not seem to us that any time has passed . . . If the
now were not different but one and the same, there would be no
time . . . It is manifest, then, that time neither is change nor is apart
from change, and since we are looking for what time is we must start
from this fact, and find what aspect of change it is.[37]

The solution Aristotle arrives at is that time is 'a number of
change in respect of the before and after'.[38] The precise nature
of this theory is a matter of some controversy, but it certainly
seems clear that for Aristotle change is a criterion of time
passing and that we cannot understand what it would be for
time to pass in the absence of change. This seems a highly
plausible conclusion, whatever Newton might have thought
about 'absolute time'. Indeed, because this conclusion seems
so plausible, some have argued that change is unreal—the
famous example being John McTaggart (1866–1925) who,
convinced that time requires change and convinced that
change is unreal, concluded that time is unreal. It might be
replied that each period of time with an end must be followed
by a period of time and that every instant must be followed by
another. It might then be suggested that if all material things
ceased to exist or if all changing things ceased to exist, there
would still be time, and that the same holds if we think of the
beginning of material objects or changing things. But this line
of thinking assumes that times, like people, can be named and
individuated as distinct subjects, which seems a dubious
assumption. And even if we grant it, there would be no way of
noting the passage of time in the absence of change, so the
notion of time before and after the existence of changing
things seems an idle one.

  This argument has been contested on logical grounds, for it
has been urged that time without things changing is logically
conceivable. Thus, for example, Swinburne has written:

Time, like space, is of logical necessity unbounded. After any period
of time which has at some instant an end, there must be another
period of time, and so after every instant. For either there will be
swans somewhere subsequent to a period T, or there will not. In

either case there must be a period subsequent to T, during which there will or will not be swans.[39]

But even assuming that we can individuate 'periods of time' or 'instants' with 'ends', why may swans not cease to exist and there be no time which is the time after which they have ceased to exist? If swans exist after T, perhaps there is a time after T at which swans exist. But if there are no swans after T, we do not have to conclude that there is a time after T. There may just be nothing and no time.

In contesting this suggestion, Swinburne appeals to an argument derived from Sydney Shoemaker. He suggests that 'it seems logically possible that there should be a period of time in which there was nothing existent, preceded and followed by periods of time in which physical objects existed', and that one could have *inductive* evidence for the existence of such periods (i.e. evidence based on samples).

There could be a world, divided into three regions, A, B, C. On A physical objects vanish for a year every three years, after which objects similar to those which disappeared reappear. The objects in B vanish for a year every four years, and those in C for a year every five years, similar objects reappearing in the two regions after the year. These cycles of disappearance will coincide every sixty years. There would then be a period of a year in which there was nothing existent. Observers would have inductive evidence of the existence of such a period.[40]

But this example is of no help to Swinburne either. Suppose objects in A disappear. How do observers know that they have ceased to exist? If they have ceased to exist, why should we suppose that it is *they* which are subsequently sighted, rather than replicas? If they have ceased to exist, why suppose that there is any way of determining the time of their non-existence apart from the fact that objects in B and C continue to change? If people in B and C know that A has 'gone' for one year, what can this mean but that B and C have enjoyed a year? And what can this mean except that there have been changes which constitute the measure of time passing in B and C? And how would one know that there had come a time when A, B, and C ceased to have any members? Swinburne might say that one could infer at some time that there was a previous period when nothing existed, a period sandwiched between two periods when there were things. But to talk of a period here surely makes no sense. How can periods be distinguished except in terms of what goes on (i.e. except in terms of changes)? How can there be a period during which there is nothing at all? One may intelligibly talk of a thing 'disappearing' for a while. But one can only do this if one is able to determine the time of the thing's disappearance with reference to the existence of changing things in relation. If we say, for example, that the magician's rabbit 'disappeared' for ten minutes, we mean that the hands of the clock (and various other things) moved thus and so and that we saw no rabbit.

If we have reason to believe that God is unchangeable, therefore, we have reason to suppose that he is timeless. This means that it will make no sense to speak of God coming into existence or passing out of it. It will also mean that the life of God is one that lacks successive states. One way of expressing this last notion would be to say that if God is timeless, he has no duration. And this is how some writers express their belief in God's timelessness.[41] To say that God lacks duration, however, could be taken to imply that God is a transient being—which is not what traditional defenders of belief in God's timelessness want to assert.

Advantages of 'God is Timeless'

In the light of the above, then, we may perhaps suggest that the classical understanding of 'God is eternal' has much to recommend it. In conclusion, it is also worth noting two further points which can be made in its favour. The first has to do with the traditional belief that God is unlimited. The second is connected with an ancient problem concerning God's knowledge of our actions.

(a) *Eternity and Limitation*

In order to approach the first point, consider how one might go about deciding whether or not something is true of God.

Where would one start? Some would start by appealing simply to what is taken to be teaching which derives from God himself: to 'revelation' located in the words of some 'inspired' person or text. Others would proceed by asking what, on philosophical grounds, must be true of God given that we already have some knowledge concerning him—e.g. that he has created the universe. Yet another way of proceeding would be to start with some widely held belief about God, to consider some other belief about God, and to ask whether the truth of the second belief coheres or conflicts with the first.

To take a non-theological example, suppose we are wondering whether it should be said that Jones keeps his promises. If we already believe that Jones is a normally honest person and if the choice before us is to accept either 'Jones keeps his promises' or 'Jones does not keep his promises', we have reason to endorse 'Jones keeps his promises'. To say that he does not do this is to say something which does not cohere well with 'Jones is a normally honest person'.

Suppose, then, the choice before us is to accept either 'God is eternal in the classical sense' or 'God is merely everlasting'. Can we proceed in something like the way we might with respect to Jones and his promise keeping? The answer, I think, is 'Yes'. And that is because those who believe in God are virtually unanimous in maintaining that God is unlimited. For if we agree that God is unlimited, we have reason for denying that God is changeable, and, in so far as change entails loss, we have reason for saying that God is not temporal.

The reason is simply that change goes with loss. Things which change lose what they once had because of the changes they undergo. For example, it is because I am a changeable individual that the pleasure I had yesterday is now a thing of the past. And it is because I am a changeable individual that I age and lose mental and physical powers that I had at one time. As Yeats observes, 'The innocent and the beautiful/ Have no enemy but time.'

If, then, the believer wants to deny that God is similarly vulnerable, that he is not limited by losing what he once had, whatever that was, an obvious way of doing so would be to embrace the classical view of eternity. For that, as we have seen, clearly denies that there is any successiveness in God. In terms of the classical view of eternity there can be no question of any kind of loss in God. He will simply be and have whatever he is and has. One may, of course, reply that God can be free of certain ravages of time without being wholly immutable. If God has no body, then he cannot, for instance, become physically frail, even though he lives a life of successive states. But he would be losing what he presently experienced in each of his successive states. And loss such as this quite intelligibly suggests limitation of a kind, limitation which those who believe in an unlimited God have reason for refusing to ascribe to him. The argument here is a purely *ad hominem* one. It is of use only against someone who wants to say that God is unlimited. But it seems quite a powerful argument when considered as directed against such a person.[42]

(b) *God's Knowledge of Human Actions*

The second point which may here be mentioned in defence of belief in the classical view of eternity is that subscription to this belief gives one an answer to what many have held to be an insoluble problem for those who believe in God.

The problem is one of reconciling belief in God's omniscience (the belief that God is all-knowing) with belief in the reality of human freedom. As most commonly presented, the problem can be stated in the form of the following argument:

1. If God is omniscient, he knows all that will be true in the future.
2. If someone knows that p, it follows that p.
3. If God knows that some future event will come to pass, the event in question will be such that it cannot but come to pass.
4. If it is true of some future event that it cannot but come to pass, then the event is necessary.
5. If a human action is free, it cannot be necessary.
6. Therefore, if God is omniscient, there can be no future, free human actions.

This argument holds that those who believe in an omniscient God are caught in a contradiction. People who believe in God normally want to say that human beings can perform future, free actions. But, if God is omniscient, must it not be true that there cannot be any such actions?

From 'Fred knows on Monday that John will propose to Mary on Tuesday' we might decline to infer 'John will propose to Mary on Tuesday of necessity'. For we might say that 'Fred knows that p' does not entail 'p is necessary'. After all, I know that I have a red shirt, but my having a red shirt is not necessary. I might never have bought a red shirt.

But if Fred knows on Monday that John will propose to Mary on Tuesday, John on Tuesday cannot bring it about that Fred does not know this on Monday. And it therefore looks as though, if God knows on Monday that John will propose to Mary on Tuesday, John cannot on Tuesday bring it about that God does not know this on Monday. As Richard Sorabji, echoing many other writers, puts it:

If God were not *infallible* in his judgment of what we would do, then we might be able so to act that his prediction turned out *wrong*. But this is not even a possibility, for to call him infallible is to say not merely that he *is* not, but that he *cannot* be wrong, and correspondingly we *cannot* make him wrong . . . The restriction on freedom arises not from God's infallibility alone, but from that coupled with the *irrevocability* of the past. If God's infallible knowledge of our doing exists *in advance*, then we are *too late* so to act that God will have had a different judgement about what we are going to do. His judgement exists *already*, and the past *cannot* be affected.[43]

In response to this argument one might wish to reply as William Lane Craig does. He says that if God knows on Monday that John will freely propose to Mary on Tuesday, that is because of what John freely chooses to do on Tuesday. And if, on Tuesday, John freely chooses to do something other than propose to Mary, God, on Monday, would have known that he would do that.[44] But this reply misses the force of Sorabji's point. God can only know that such and such is the case if it is true that such and such is the case. But God's knowing at some time that such and such will be the case makes it impossible that the such and such should fail to be the case when it comes to be the case. 'What will be will be' does not mean that what will be will necessarily be. But if it is known at time 1 that such and such will be at time 2, then there is nothing to be done at time 2 to ensure that the such and such in question fails to be.

The problem here arises, of course, from the notion that God's knowledge is a matter of foreknowledge. But to believe that God is eternal in the classical sense is to believe that, strictly speaking, God has no foreknowledge. It is to believe that free actions are ones which God just knows (timelessly). Hence, for example, Boethius suggests that God's knowledge is not best compared with human foreknowledge. Rather, it should be thought of as 'knowledge of a never passing instant' in that God sees future things 'present to him just such as in time they will at some future point come to be'. 'With one glance of his mind', says Boethius, God

distinguishes both those things necessarily coming to be and those not necessarily coming to be, just as you, when you see at one and the same time that a man is walking on the ground and that the sun is rising in the sky, although the two things are seen simultaneously, yet you distinguish them, and judge the first to be voluntary, the second necessary.[45]

One might take this suggestion to mean that events which occur at different times really occur at the same time in eternity. And one might therefore find the suggestion incoherent. One might also object to it on the ground that it seems to assert that God can see the future as present, whereas the future really does not exist and is not there to be seen. But Boethius is basically trying to say that when it comes to God, there is no question of foreknowledge or of one state succeeding another. He is saying that with respect to a given human action, there is no question of God knowing that it will occur, then of him waiting for it to occur, then of him knowing that it is occurring, then of him being able to say 'Well, now, that's done'. And for this reason Boethius has an answer to the argument holding that God's knowledge is incompatible with human freedom. In so far as that argument rests on the notion that God's knowledge of human actions is a matter of foreknowledge, it does nothing to show that a timeless God cannot be said to know the free actions of people. For a timeless God could not, strictly speaking, have foreknowledge. What it means to ascribe knowledge to God is a difficult question. But to hold that God is timeless allows one to say that his knowledge of human behaviour is not a matter of foreknowledge and that it is not something which renders human behaviour unfree. To know that such and such is the case does not entail one knowing that the something in question is necessarily the case. By the same token, if God simply knows (rather than foreknows) that people act thus and so, it does not follow that they act as they do of necessity.

Morality and Religion

WE have so far considered a number of questions relevant to the central Judaeo-Christian belief that there is a God. But it is now time to proceed to some other topics to which philosophers of religion have paid attention. The first is that of morality and religion. It is impossible for me to do justice to all the issues which could be raised with reference to this topic, so I shall confine myself to one major question commonly raised by philosophers: namely, 'Is there a relationship between morality and religion?'

Views on the Relationship between Morality and Religion

Let us begin our consideration of this question by noting some of the answers that have been given to it. A number of different ones can be distinguished. Broadly speaking, however, most of them can be categorized under one of four theses. These hold respectively (1) that morality somehow requires religion, (2) that morality is somehow included in religion, (3) that morality is pointless without religion, and (4) that morality and religion are opposed to each other.

(a) *Morality as Requiring Religion*

Those who take the view that morality requires religion usually argue that there is something about morality which should lead us to believe in God. A good example of a writer who thinks in these terms is Kant. As we have seen, he has little time for the ontological argument for God's existence. He also rejects other arguments for belief in God. But he does not conclude that belief in God is irrational. He argues that, since humanity ought to strive for moral perfection and since it cannot be successful in this unless helped by divinity, God must exist to ensure that humanity can achieve that for which it must strive.

According to Kant, morality requires us to aim for the Highest Good. 'The achievement of the Highest Good in the world', he says, 'is the necessary object of a will determined by the moral law ... [which] ... commands us to make the highest possible good in a world the final object of all our conduct.'[1] In Kant's view, however, to will the Highest Good means more than simply willing what is in accord with the moral law. It also means willing a proper return of happiness to those who pursue moral goodness. W. S. Gilbert's Mikado thought that the punishment must fit the crime. Kant thought that there should be reward appropriate to virtue. 'To be in need of happiness and also worthy of it and yet not to partake of it', he maintains, 'could not be in accordance with the complete volition of an omnipotent rational being.'[2]

For Kant, then, willing the Highest Good means willing a correlation between moral rectitude and happiness. But now comes the snag. For in this life it is impossible to ensure what morality requires. We may be rational beings; but we are not omnipotent. So we have a problem on our hands. The Highest Good must be possible; but at one level it seems impossible.

How do we resolve the dilemma? Kant's answer is that we must postulate the existence of God as able to ensure that fidelity to moral requirements is properly rewarded. Why? Because the realization of the Highest Good can only be guaranteed if there is something corresponding to the concept of God, i.e. something able to ensure its realization. Or, as Kant puts it:

The acting rational being in the world is not at the same time the cause of the world and of nature itself. Hence there is not the slightest ground in the moral law for a necessary connection between the morality and proportionate happiness of a being which belongs to the world as one of its parts and as thus dependent on it. Not being nature's cause, his will cannot of its own strength bring nature, as it touches on his happiness, into complete harmony with his practical principles. Nevertheless . . . in the necessary endeavour after the highest good, such a connection is postulated as necessary: we should seek to further the highest good (which therefore must at least be possible). Therefore also the existence is postulated of a cause of the whole of nature, itself distinct from nature, which contains the ground of the exact coincidence of happiness with morality . . . As a consequence the possibility of a highest derived good (the best world) is at the same time the postulate of the reality of the highest original good, namely the existence of God . . . Therefore, it is morally necessary to assume the existence of God.[3]

As Kant sees it, then, the fact that morality demands the realization of the Highest Good and the fact that only God can see to it that the Highest Good comes about lead to the conclusion that there is a God. But this argument is not the only one that has been offered in defence of the view that morality gives us grounds for belief in God. Many writers have argued that one can infer the existence of God from the existence of moral commands or laws. These, it is said, imply the existence of a moral law-giver or a moral commander. Thus H. P. Owen writes: 'It is impossible to think of a command without also thinking of a commander . . . A clear choice faces us. Either we take moral claims to be self-explanatory modes of impersonal existence or we explain them in terms of a personal God.'[4] To arguments like this there has often been added a reference to responsibility and guilt. People often feel morally responsible, and they often feel guilty if they fail to do their moral duty. But, so the argument goes, this situation makes no real sense unless moral laws have a personal explanation. In fact, it is argued, moral laws inspire guilt and responsibility because they have a personal basis in the will of God. Thus John Henry Newman (1801–90) writes: 'If, as is the case, we feel responsibility, are ashamed, are frightened, at transgressing the voice of conscience, this implies that there is One to whom we are responsible, before whom we are ashamed, whose claim upon us we fear.'[5]

In recent years, a variation on this position has been developed by Dom Illtyd Trethowan.[6] He eschews talk about a moral *argument* for God's existence, for he thinks that people come to know of God not through inference, but by means of direct awareness or experience. But he also thinks that knowledge of God must be mediated in some way, that it is not, so to speak, a matter of meeting God face to face. And according to Trethowan, we are directly aware of God in our moral experience. In this, he says, we are confronted by God, since we are confronted by absolute moral obligations and by absolute value. 'The notion of value', he suggests,

is bound up with the notion of obligation. To say that people are worth while, that they have value in themselves, is to say that there is something about them which makes a demand upon us, that we *ought* to make them part of our own project, identify ourselves with them in some sort . . . I propose to say that an awareness of obligation is an awareness of God.[7]

In Trethowan's view, the most reasonable way of accounting for what we are aware of in morality (or in 'moral experience') is to say that its object is absolute, unconditioned, and the source of all creaturely value, especially that of people. 'We have value', he explains, 'because we receive it from a source of value. That is what I mean, for a start, by God. We know him as giving us value. That is why the demand upon us to develop ourselves is an absolute, unconditional, demand.'[8]

(b) *Morality as Included in Religion*

So much, then, for the view that morality requires religion. But what of the view that it is included in religion? The basic idea here is that being moral is part of what being religious means.

One expression of it asserts that a morally obligatory action means 'an action that is willed by God'. On this account, from 'God wills me to do X', one can infer 'I am morally obliged to do X'. But this view can itself be broken up into at least two distinct positions. One can appreciate the difference involved by first considering an example.

Suppose Fred joins an organization in which there is a leader who issues orders. The leader says, 'You ought to do X,' and everybody agrees with him. But Fred replies, 'Yes, I ought to do X, but not because the leader tells me to. He is right in what he says, but the fact that he says it does not make it right.'

Now one version of the view we are at present concerned with is rather like the view of the new member in the above example. It holds that God always wills what is morally obligatory, but the mere fact of God's willing it does not by itself make anything morally obligatory. On this view, the moral value of an action can be deduced from the fact that God wills it, but an action (or a refraining from an action) is not morally obligatory just because God wills it.

According to the other version of the present view, this is not the case. On this version an action (or a refraining from action) is morally obligatory by virtue of being willed by God. On this account, whatever God wills is the morally right' thing to do just because God wills it. People who defend this account sometimes argue that if one thinks that there are moral reasons that oblige one to refuse to do what God wills, then one has not understood what morality is all about. On their view, there is no moral standard against which God's will can be judged. God's will creates moral standards.

(c) *Morality as Pointless without Religion*

Our third view concerning morality and religion does not have any major philosophical advocate so far as I know, though seeds of it might be traced in the writings of Friedrich Nietzsche (1844–1900), especially *The Genealogy of Morals*. But its drift is one that is encountered in non-philosophical contexts, which certainly makes it worth mentioning. It resembles what I once found ascribed to a Trappist monk, who was quoted as saying that if he did not think that heaven existed, he would leave his monastery. It holds that the demands of morality are only worth adhering to if there is a God who will reward one for obeying them and punish one for infringing them.

On this view, therefore, there is no intrinsically moral justification for moral codes or norms. If there is reason for being moral, that can only be because it pays in terms of post-mortem consequences. Notice, however, that it is important not to confuse this conclusion with that of Kant. It may look as though Kant finds morality pointless except on the presumption of a God to ensure that justice prevails. But the appearance would be deceptive. Kant thinks of morality as binding *per se*, and he therefore postulates God. Exponents of the present view work from the opposite direction. They have time for morality only because of what they expect in the light of God's existence.

(d) *Morality as Opposed to Religion*

All the above views hold that there is no real opposition between a moral point of view and a religious one. But according to some people this is mistaken. Both philosophical and theological writers can be invoked to illustrate this way of thinking.

The philosophical writers have been opposed to religion largely on moral grounds. An example is James Rachels. He says that belief in God involves a total, unqualified commitment to obey God's commands and that such a commitment is not appropriate for a moral agent, since 'to be a moral agent is to be an autonomous or self-directed agent . . . The virtuous man is therefore identified with the man of integrity, i.e. the man who acts according to precepts which he can, on reflection, conscientiously approve in his own heart.'[9] Rachels therefore holds that one can disprove God's existence. He argues:

1. If any being is God, he must be a fitting object of worship.
2. No being could possibly be a fitting object of worship since worship requires the abandonment of one's role as an autonomous moral agent.
3. Therefore, there cannot be any being who is God.

Other philosophers have argued differently for the view that morality is opposed to religion. Some have said that religious people can fail to make good citizens.[10] Others have pointed out that much evil has been brought about by religious people and their beliefs. One thinks here of the famous remark of Lucretius (99/94–55/51 BC): *Tantum religio potuit suadere malorum* ('So much evil could religion provoke').[11] A similar sentiment can be found in the writings of Bertrand Russell. 'Religion', says Russell,

prevents our children from having a rational education; religion prevents us from removing the fundamental causes of war; religion prevents us from teaching the ethic of scientific co-operation in place of the old fierce doctrines of sin and punishment. It is possible that mankind is on the threshold of a golden age; but if so, it will be necessary first to slay the dragon that guards the door, and this dragon is religion.[12]

As I said above, theologians have also argued for an opposition between morality and religion. Take, for example, the influential Danish writer Kierkegaard (1813–55). In *Fear and Trembling* he considers the biblical story of Abraham being told by God to sacrifice Isaac (Genesis 22). He says that Abraham was bound to do what God commanded. 'Here', he adds,

there can be no question of ethics in the sense of morality... ordinarily speaking, a temptation is something which tries to stop a man from doing his duty, but in this case it is ethics itself which tries to prevent him from doing God's will. But what then is duty? Duty is quite simply the expression of the will of God.[13]

In this connection Kierkegaard talks about 'a teleological suspension of the ethical', an idea which can also be traced in the work of D. Z. Phillips, according to whom religious belief provides religious believers with their standard for evaluating actions, a standard which is different from, and may be opposed to, a moral standard. 'The religious concept of duty', writes Phillips,

cannot be understood if it is treated as a moral concept. When the believer talks of doing his duty, what he refers to is doing the will of God. In making a decision, what is important for the believer is that it should be in accordance with the will of God. To a Christian, to do one's duty *is* to do the will of God. There is indeed no difficulty in envisaging the 'ethical' as the obstacle to 'duty' in this context.[14]

Morality as Grounds for Belief in God

Let us now begin to consider the views just noted by turning first to the claim that one can move from morality to belief in God. Is the claim an acceptable one?

A problem immediately confronting us in trying to evaluate Kant's position on morality and theism is that it is not quite clear how he means us to understand it. I have said that Kant gives an 'argument' from morality to God, and that is a perfectly proper thing to say in view of the way he writes. But he complicates matters by speaking of God not as something known or proved to exist by virtue of rational argument, but as a postulate of moral reflection (a postulate, as he calls it, of 'practical reason'). Kant's official theory, which he expounds in the *Critique of Pure Reason*, is that reason by itself can do nothing to prove that God exists, that there are no theoretical grounds for theism. If that is so, however, then what is the force of the argument concerning the Highest Good supposed to be?

Historians of philosophy have devoted much time to this question, and a full treatment of Kant's moral argument will have to engage with the results of their research. Taking it at its face value as an argument, though, what Kant offers looks rather impressive in some respects. It is widely accepted by philosophers that 'ought' implies 'can'. If I tell people that they ought to do something, it must surely be true that they can do it. It would be nonsense, for instance, to say to a polio victim, 'You ought to walk to work'. One might therefore be tempted to argue that if the Highest Good ought to be realized, then it can be realized. But since it cannot be realized by human agents, one might feel inclined to say that morality is absurd if God does not exist.

Yet why should we suppose that justice will finally prevail? If God exists, then justice will doubtless triumph in the end; but we surely cannot infer the existence of God from what would happen if God existed.

Kant's reply would presumably be that the Highest Good is possible since we are obliged to aim at it. He might then add that the Highest Good is only possible on the assumption that God exists. But from 'We ought to aim for the Highest Good' it does not follow that anything can bring about the Highest Good. All that follows is that we should try to aim for the Highest Good. If that sounds paradoxical, it is because 'P ought to —— but P cannot ——' sounds absurd when certain tasks are substituted for ——. It seems absurd to say, for example, that someone ought to square circles or that a polio victim ought to walk to work. But it sometimes makes sense to say that someone ought to aim for what he or she cannot in fact achieve. It can, for example, make sense to say that children one knows to be dim ought to aim at learning a foreign language. One may know that they will never master it; so 'John ought to aim to learn French' does not imply 'John can learn French'. But it does imply that John should try to learn French.

To this Kant might say that if the Highest Good cannot be realized, one ought not to aim for it in any sense. But even if we agree with him on that (and many would not), we can now ask why we should not conclude that one just ought not to aim at the Highest Good. The answer one anticipates from Kant is that one certainly ought to aim at the Highest Good. The trouble, however, is that his argument for God now takes on a circular character. It seems to run: 'If God does not exist, it is not the case that one ought to aim at the Highest Good; and one ought to aim at the Highest Good since God exists.' One may well feel uneasy with that line of reasoning. It is valid to argue 'If not-P, then not-Q; but Q, therefore P'. And P, although thus rationally derived from Q, may give the reason why Q holds. But can we suppose that the existence of God follows from the fact that we ought to aim for something which can only exist if there is a God? Why not just say that the something in question is not something to be aimed for?

In any case, there is another problem. This is that we need not agree that only God could ensure the realization of what Kant calls the Highest Good. Given that God is omnipotent and omniscient, he could bring it about. But why must something able to bring it about be omnipotent and omniscient?

As Kant understands it, the realization of the Highest Good requires power and knowledge of a kind which is not found in nature. And that we can happily concede. But why must this power be equivalent to omnipotence? Why must the knowledge be equal to omniscience? As far as I can see, Kant simply does not allow for such questions. He assumes that a sufficient condition for guaranteeing the Highest Good is a necessary condition for doing so. We, on the other hand, might ask why the Highest Good cannot be realized by something more powerful and knowledgeable than human beings but less powerful and knowledgeable than God. Why cannot a top-ranking angel do the job? Why not a pantheon of angels? Why not a pantheon of very clever, Kantian-minded angels?

So Kant's moral argument for God does not work. But what about such arguments as that moral laws imply a moral lawgiver and that the sense of moral responsibility and guilt implies the existence of God to whom we are responsible and before whom we feel guilty?

Anyone who proposes to answer this question must first know whether there is a moral law from which one might argue to a divine lawgiver. And whether there is such a law is a very big question. It takes us straight into some of the most controversial areas of moral philosophy and it cannot be properly discussed in this book. But we can note two major answers that have been given and the implications that these might be said to have.

To begin with, we can note that some philosophers believe in the existence of an objective moral law that is binding on all human beings. This law can be expressed in value judgements which are true independently of anyone's thoughts or attitudes. People can come to know of it, and they can either obey it or disobey it.

According to other philosophers, however, there is no objective moral law. On their view, it is not appropriate to speak of value judgements which are true independently of whatever people may think or feel. On the contrary, so the argument goes, moral judgement is a subjective matter. According to some writers, it is the expression of feeling or the expression of some decision about behaviour. According to others, it is the product of people's desire to survive.

As I say, the rights and wrongs in this area cannot be gone into here. But suppose one adopts the first view. Does it follow that one can then reasonably infer the existence of God? Here it seems that writers like Owen, while not having anything that could be regarded as a demonstrative case, have a plausible line of argument. They certainly hold to our first view about the moral law. They would say that there is an objective moral law. Yet it does seem odd, albeit not self-contradictory, to grant this and to leave matters there.[15] This point is well made by Trethowan. Writing from the viewpoint of one who endorses an objective view of morality, he says: 'The absoluteness of moral obligation, as I see it, is so far from being self-explanatory that if it were not made intelligible by being found in a metaphysical—and in fact, a theistic—context, I should be greatly tempted to hand it over to the anthropologists and the psychologists.'[16] This is not a water-tight argument, but it does raise a problem for someone who believes in an objective and imperious moral law. And if one already has reason for believing in God independently of moral considerations, one might well argue that there is some additional reason for thinking of the moral law with reference to God. For God is normally said to be purposive and intelligent. If one has reason to believe in God, one would thereby have available a model providing a context for talk about a non-human lawgiver.

Yet though it is in general true that claims, demands, and laws derive from a personal source, it is not obviously true that all claims, demands, and laws derive from a personal source. And it is not evident that obedience in morals makes sense only if one is obedient to what is personal. There are claims, demands, and laws which need to be obeyed by anybody studying logic. But even most theists would doubt that truths of logic derive from a personal source. And belief in an objective moral law need not even suggest the existence of God.

Owen seems to think that the moral law is analogous to laws promulgated by human beings. That is why he talks about it with reference to a lawgiver. But others have held that although one can certainly make value judgements that are true independently of people's thoughts and feelings, these judgements gain their ultimate significance in terms of human wants and needs. On this account a moral judgement like 'P ought to do X' means something like 'If P does not want to lose out, then P should do X'. Thus, for example, Peter Geach once wrote: 'One obviously relevant sort of reply to a question "Why shouldn't I?" is an appeal to something the questioner wants, and cannot get if he does so-and-so. I maintain that only such a reply is relevant and rational.'[17] But though this kind of view allows that a moral judgement can be absolutely true, though it is as objectivist a theory of moral judgement as one could desire, and though it accompanies talk about an objective moral law, it does not seem to imply that there is a God any more than the truth of an assertion like 'If you want to get to Paris by 3 o'clock then you need to catch the train at 2 o'clock'. It might be said that if one already has reason to believe in God independently of moral considerations, then the fact that there is a moral law in the present sense is only to be expected. One might argue, for example, that, if there is a God who is intelligent and purposive, then it is only to be expected that he would provide some objective standard against which people can decide whether or not some proposed course of action is likely to benefit them. But simply from the fact that there is such a standard, there seems no particular reason for saying that there must be a God. One might argue that there could not be such a standard if people did not function in particular and predictable ways. And one might add that the fact that they do so function can be used as the premiss of an argument for God's existence. But such an argument would be a version of the argument from design, and it would not depend for its strength on considerations deriving only from the notion of a moral law.

So the first of our views about moral law can be seen as having conflicting interpretations. But the same cannot be said of the second. For if there is no objective, independent moral law, there is no argument from a moral law to the existence of

God as a moral law-giver. And if moral judgements are just expressions of people's feelings or decisions and so on, it is hard to see that they can have any particular weight at all in an argument for God's existence. Not, at any rate, in an argument based on the moral law.

Is Morality Included in Religion?

Let us now consider the claim that morality is included in religion, either because God always wills what is morally obligatory or because 'action willed by God' is what 'morally obligatory action' means.

The first alternative presupposes a number of things. For a start, it presupposes that there are morally obligatory actions for God to will. Some people would deny that this is so, but suppose we let the presupposition pass. It would then seem that the view that morally obligatory actions are always willed by God depends on the truth of two assertions. The first is that there is a God who can be said to will things, who can be said to will morally obligatory actions, and whose will can be known. The second is that God always wills morally obligatory actions.

But is it correct to accept these assertions? I am afraid that we have again come to a question that cannot be debated here, for it raises a host of problems, many of which could occupy a volume by themselves. But one thing does seem fairly clear. Most people who believe in God believe that his will is always directed to what is good. If it is reasonable to believe in God and if it is reasonable to believe this of him, then it is reasonable to believe that God always wills morally obligatory actions. For if there are such actions, they are, by definition, directed towards what is good. And if God's will is always directed to what is good, then he will always will such actions. If this point is accepted, it can be added that there is therefore no obvious absurdity in holding that morality is included in religion. For, as many people see it, religion has to do with doing what God wills. If, then, God always wills what is morally obligatory, then simply by doing what is morally obligatory, one will be doing what God wills.[18]

Granted a fairly standard view of God, then, and granted that there is a God to correspond to it, it would be reasonable to hold that in one sense at least, morality is included in religion. But what of the view that God's will determines what is morally obligatory? Many philosophers would regard it as totally unacceptable for several reasons. The two most often advanced are: (1) the view is morally unacceptable since it entails that if God willed some morally despicable action, the action would thereby become a morally obligatory one; (2) the view assumes that from the fact that God wills some action, it is possible to conclude that the action is morally obligatory. But from 'P wills X' one can never infer 'X is morally obligatory'.

How strong are these objections? A lot depends here on what view we take about certain moral judgements. In the present context, some people would say that even if one knew that God willed X, one might still, depending on what X was, baldly declare that X is totally and unequivocally unacceptable from the moral point of view. These people would therefore say that (1) above is a legitimate conclusion which rules out the suggestion that God's will can be the deciding factor in saying what is and what is not morally obligatory. And in reply to this position I do not really see what can be said. If people assert that, for example, I am absolutely forbidden to kill innocent human beings, and if they add that this holds even if God wills that I kill some innocent human beings, then those people are evidently adopting a very fundamental moral position, one that could conceivably accommodate any argument brought against it.

On the other hand, someone might say that accepting God's will as the ultimate moral criterion is itself a fundamental moral option. And, if it is hard to know how to set about arguing against the people mentioned at the end of the last paragraph, it is hard to know how to set about arguing against the person here. Suppose it is said that one ought always to do what God wills. We may reply that there is no God and that there cannot, therefore, be any obligation to do what he wills. Or we may say that there is no way of knowing what God wills. But unless we can substantiate these claims, it seems that there is little more to be said. We may argue with our opponent; we may suggest that God might possibly will various actions, and we may provide reasons for holding that these actions are immoral. But if the opponent's fundamental premiss is that one is morally bound to do what God wills, I do not see that we are going to get very far. In saying this, I do not just mean that we are unlikely to change our opponent's mind. I mean that we shall not be able to press a charge of error. For in trying to combat our opponent's views, we shall ultimately have to adopt moral positions that are themselves as basic and unsupported as are his or hers. People who say that God's will is the fundamental criterion for determining whether an action is moral are asserting a fundamental premiss in their thinking. And in contesting their thinking, we can only assert our own fundamental premisses. Looked at from this point of view, our position need be no more demonstrably correct than theirs.

I would argue, then, that (1) may or may not be acceptable, depending on our fundamental moral options and on whether it is possible to say that there is a God whose will can be known. But what about (2)?

Anyone familiar with twentieth-century moral philosophy will at once realize that there is a standard defence of (2) likely to be advanced by some philosophers. According to certain writers, there is a difference between statements of fact (such as 'God wills X') and statements of value (such as 'I ought to do X'). These writers would add that statements of value cannot be derived from statements of fact. And they would therefore argue that just because God wills something, nothing whatever follows about what ought to be done.

But even if these writers are correct, it could still be held that God's will can determine what is morally obligatory. The reason for saying this takes us back to what I have just said about (1). For while it is obviously invalid to argue from 'God wills that P should do X' to 'P should do X', people who say that God's will can determine what is morally obligatory may not just be arguing in this way. They may argue:

(a) God wills that P should do X.
(b) One is morally obliged to do what God wills.
(c) Therefore P is morally obliged to do X.

As far as I can see, this is a perfectly valid argument. If it were used with reference to a particular person and action, one might reject it by denying that there is a God whose will can be known. And, if one could show that one was right, then the case against (2) would be made. But if one could not do so, one would have to show that (b) was false. Yet that, as I have already suggested, is not very easy to do. I therefore suggest that (2) is a maintainable position and that, for this reason, and supposing that there is a God whose will can be known, (2) is a possible position for someone to adopt.

Religion and the Point of Morality

What, now, of the view that one only has reason to be moral if there is a God to reward one after death? Should that lead us to link morality and religion?

Those who wish to subscribe to this view are, perhaps, struck by a thought which surely hits most people from time to time. This is the thought that the struggle to be morally good is somehow leading nowhere if death is the end for people. How intolerable, people sometimes say, that we should strive and put ourselves out in the name of morality if we are nothing but perishable bits of a godless universe. If that is the case, why bother to be moral at all?

In this connection too, some have especially appealed to the possibility of total self-sacrifice. There have been atheists who have been prepared to give up everything they have, including their lives, on behalf of others and in the name of morality. But, so the argument goes, such absolute self-sacrifice is fundamentally irrational if there is, indeed, no God.

Yet not everyone has thought in such terms. A good example is Kant. In his view, it is a violation of morality to justify moral behaviour in terms of benefits which might follow for those who are moral. Morality, for Kant, is a matter of duty. And the reason for doing one's duty is simply the fact that it is one's duty. 'The first proposition of morality', he says, 'is that to have moral worth an action must be done from duty.'[19] If that is acceptable, then the argument from rewards cannot even get off the ground. It would not count as an argument from morality at all.

But must we agree that morality is a matter of duty for duty's sake? Why should I accept that I just ought to perform or refrain from a given action? Suppose I declare that all readers of this book ought to subscribe to the Brian Davies vintage port fund, designed to keep me happy every night of the week. Should you protest at this declaration, will it suffice for me to reply by saying 'You just ought'?

If you say 'Yes', you may send your contribution to me at Blackfriars, Oxford, OX1 3LY. And please send enough to buy a *good* vintage port. But you might, understandably, want to say 'No'. For when people ask why they should or should not act thus and so, it makes sense to appeal to what they somehow need. And 'need' here can be explained in terms of what contributes to the fulfilment of people *qua* people. What that amounts to may be something about which parties in a debate might differ, and many would say that the notion of human fulfilment lacks content. But is it, for instance, wrong to observe that people in general have reason to be just, since one can only flourish properly as a member of society in which it can be presumed that contracts will be honoured and people treated equally? To take just two other examples, is it wrong to say that one has reason to cultivate the classical virtues of courage and temperance, since lack of them will quickly impede one from getting on with even the most ordinary day to day affairs? As Geach, again, remarks, 'Courage is constantly needed in the ordinary course of the world . . . People would often not be born but for the courage of their mothers . . . Nobody who was thoroughly cowardly would play physically demanding games, or climb a mountain, or ride a horse or a bicycle.'[20] As for temperance, try to down ten plates of spaghetti and a crate of beer, and then try to convince yourself that you had no need to do otherwise.

These remarks are nothing but a sketch of an approach to ethics which needs to be developed at length. But they indicate how it can be held that there are reasons for moral behaviour which are more than an appeal to duty for the sake of duty. Notice, however, that they are not reasons which presuppose the existence of God. In so far as they are cogent, therefore, there are grounds for rejecting our third view of the relationship between morality and religion. For this insists that if God does not exist to reward us, we have no reason to be moral. But maybe we have reason to be moral regardless of God's existence.[21]

Is Morality Opposed to Religion?

I have so far argued both for and against various versions of the view that morality is included in religion. Now it remains to consider the assertion that morality is opposed to religion. In noting forms that this assertion has taken, I earlier referred to the view of James Rachels, according to whom, (a) one can disprove God's existence on moral grounds, and (b) someone who believes in God cannot be an autonomous moral agent. So let us turn immediately to Rachels's position.

Perhaps the first thing to be said about it is that considered as a disproof of God's existence, it is very weak indeed. For Rachels seems to suppose that if there is a being worthy of worship, then there could not be autonomous moral agents. But there is an obvious reply to this supposition. For it is surely possible that there be a being worthy of worship who does nothing to interfere with people who wish to remain autonomous moral agents. And it is also possible that a being worthy of worship will require that people always act as autonomous moral agents. This point is well brought out in a case against Rachels offered by Philip L. Quinn in his book *Divine Commands and Moral Requirements*. As he observes:

An autonomous moral agent can admit the existence of God if he is prepared to deny that any putative divine command which is inconsistent with his hard-core reflective moral judgements really is a divine command. He can resolve the supposed role-conflict by allowing that genuine divine commands ought to be obeyed unconditionally but also maintaining that no directive which he does not accept on moral grounds is a genuine divine command. For the following propositions are logically compatible:

God exists.

God sometimes commands agents to do certain things.

God never commands anything an autonomous and well-informed human moral agent would, on reflection, disapprove.[22]

Yet might it not be argued that if a being is worthy of worship, then the worshipper is bound to do what the being wills? And does this not mean that being a worshipper is incompatible with being an autonomous moral agent? Rachels evidently supposes that the answer to these questions is affirmative. But it is not such at all. For worshippers can consistently say that what they worship is a being who always wills them to behave as autonomous moral agents. And if a worshipper were to say this, then Rachels's case would clearly collapse. It would also collapse if someone who believes in and worships God were simply to say that God knows all moral truths and always directs people in accordance with them. Such a believer would be giving unqualified allegiance to God's commands, but it does not follow that this entails abandoning one's autonomy as a moral agent. Rachels says that autonomous moral agents act in accordance with precepts which they can, on reflection, conscientiously approve in their own hearts.[23] But what is to stop such people acting in accordance with a belief that God can always be relied upon to command in accordance with what is morally proper?

Yet what of the general thesis that morality and religion should be thought of as opposed to each other? Does it actually have any clear sense? There is a case for denying that it does. One reason for saying so is that the word 'morality' clearly has different associations for different people. What one person regards as morality, another may dismiss as immorality, or as plain triviality. And it often seems impossible to say in such disputes that either party is in some objective sense right. General statements about what morality is should be regarded with suspicion, for the boundaries dividing the moral and the non-moral may be very fuzzy indeed. For this reason, one ought to be suspicious about the general and very sweeping statement that religion and morality are necessarily opposed to each other.

A second reason for rejecting this statement brings us to a related point regarding the term 'religion'. If I say that religion and morality are opposed to each other, I assume that there is a fairly easily identifiable thing called 'religion'. But this assumption is very questionable indeed. In Henry Fielding's novel *Tom Jones*, Mr Thwackum declares: 'When I mention religion I mean the Christian religion; and not only the Christian religion but the Protestant religion; and not only the Protestant religion, but the Church of England.' Yet few philosophers or theologians would be happy to accept this definition since it seems to exclude so much. Many writers, in fact, would go so far as to say that 'religion' just cannot be defined. 'It is', says Ninian Smart, 'partly a matter of convention as to what is counted under the head of religion and what is not.'[24] Here Smart is in agreement with what William P. Alston writes on 'Religion' in *The Encyclopedia of Philosophy*. Alston notes various attempts to define 'religion', and suggests that none of them states necessary and sufficient conditions for something to be a religion. He concludes that the most that can be done is to note various characteristics of religion.

When enough of these characteristics are present to a sufficient degree, we have a religion. It seems that, given the actual use of the term 'religion', this is as precise as we can be. If we tried to say something like 'for a religion to exist, there must be the first two plus any three others', or 'for a religion to exist, any four of these characteristics must be present', we would be introducing a degree of precision not to be found in the concept of religion actually in use ... The best way to explain the concept of religion is to elaborate in detail the relevant features of an ideally clear case of religion and then indicate the respects in which less clear cases can differ from this, without hoping to find any sharp line dividing religion from non-religion.[25]

The implication of such reflections is that it is misleading to say that religion and morality are necessarily opposed to each other. This means that we can call into question statements like that of Russell noted earlier. A great deal that he considered harmful may well have been done by people in the name of religion. But many religious people would accept this fact while objecting to the very things to which Russell objected. Indeed, they would argue that many of the key values for which Russell stood are an essential part of religious aspiration. Thus, and returning to the precise points made by Russell in his remark quoted earlier, there are, for example, Christians who argue strongly in favour of pluralistic and open education, for pacifism and for scientific co-operation. And all this on theological grounds. Russell might reply that religion should still be seen as a source of evil which should be eradicated in order to make way for a kind of Utopia. But, as Mary Midgley observes, 'whatever may have been its plausibility in the eighteenth century, when it first took the centre of the stage', this view 'is just a distraction today'.[26] Moral atrocity seems to abound even where the influence of religion is non-existent, and, as Midgley goes on to suggest, what it might be held to require from thinkers is 'an atrociously difficult psychological inquiry' rather than 'a ritual warfare about the existence of God' and the like.[27]

But it ought to be added that there are evidently religious believers whose religious beliefs entail for them moral judgements sharply at odds with those adopted by many moral thinkers. And sometimes it may be quite impossible to resolve the resulting conflict. Take, for instance, the conflict between many secular moralists and those theologians who hold certain views about topics like divorce because they think that they have access to divinely inspired words of Christ. These secular moralists and theologians often seem to share a great deal of common ground regarding criteria for making various moral judgements; but they can evidently reach a deadlock in the long run because one group thinks that sound moral teaching has been revealed by God, while the other does not. And until they can come to agree on matters like revelation, no solution to their final disagreement seems possible.

This kind of thing may, of course, lead one to ask whether religion does not, after all, demand some kind of view opposed to anything that can be regarded as a moral one. But this is not a question to answer in general terms; and indeed, I doubt whether it is very clear to begin with. As should be evident from the diversity of views referred to in this chapter, anyone concerned with the relationship between morality and religion will need to proceed slowly and with reference to various understandings of both morality and religion.

Miracle

A WORD that often creeps into the active vocabulary of religious people is 'miracle'. Many would say that miracles occur or that they have occurred. It is also sometimes suggested that they provide evidence for various things, notably the existence of God, or the truth of some particular religion or the teaching of certain religious leaders. The topic of miracle has occasioned much philosophical and theological debate, and it therefore seems appropriate at this point to say something about it.

What is a Miracle?

What are we discussing when we talk about miracles? The answer is not all that obvious, for those who refer to miracles have offered various understandings of what it is they are talking about.

(a) Definitions of 'Miracle'

A widespread view of miracles sees them as breaks in the natural order of events in the material world. Sometimes these breaks are referred to as 'violations of natural laws', and it is often said that they are brought about by God or by some extremely powerful being who can interfere with the normal course of nature's operation. A classic definition of 'miracle' in these terms comes from David Hume, who wrote on miracles in Chapter X ('Of Miracles') of his *Enquiry concerning Human Understanding*. 'A miracle', says Hume, 'may be accurately defined, *a transgression of a law of nature by a particular volition of the Deity or by the interposition of some invisible agent*.'[1]

Similar definitions can be found in recent works by Richard Swinburne and John Mackie. According to Swinburne, a miracle is 'a violation of a law of nature by a god, that is, a very powerful rational being who is not a material object (viz., is invisible and intangible)'.[2] According to Mackie, a miracle is 'a violation of a law of nature' brought about by 'divine or supernatural intervention'. 'The laws of nature', Mackie adds, 'describe the ways in which the world—including, of course, human beings—works when left to itself, when not interfered with. A miracle occurs when the world is not left to itself, when something distinct from the natural order as a whole intrudes into it.'[3]

A related (though different) account of 'miracle' is offered by Aquinas. 'Those things must properly be called miraculous', he writes in the *Summa Contra Gentiles*, 'which are done by divine power apart from the order generally followed in things'. Aquinas distinguishes between three kinds of miracle. There are, he says: (1) 'events in which something is done by God which nature could never do', (2) 'events in which God does something which nature can do, but not in this order', and (3) events which occur 'when God does what is usually done by the working of nature, but without the operation of the principles of nature'.[4] As an example of (1) Aquinas cites the case of the sun going back on its course or standing still.[5] As an example of (2) he instances the case of someone living after death, seeing after being blind, or walking after being paralysed. The idea here seems to be that some miracles are states or events which could exist in nature, but which would not exist in this order unless produced miraculously. Finally, and by way of illustrating what he means by (3), Aquinas gives the example of someone being instantaneously cured of a disease, which doctors might have been able to cure given sufficient time. He seems to be saying that some miracles involve quite ordinary or common states or processes, but ones brought about without the causes which usually bring them about.

Here, then, is a fairly strong understanding of miracles: as events which cannot be explained in terms intelligible to the natural scientist or observer of the regular processes of nature. But it has also been suggested that a miracle need only be an extraordinary coincidence of a beneficial nature interpreted religiously. One can find this understanding at work in a well-known article by R. F. Holland.[6] Suppose a child escapes death because a series of explicable physical events cause a train-driver to hit the brakes on a train bearing down on the child. Holland suggests that the delivery involved here can be regarded as miraculous from the religious point of view. In certain circumstances, he says, 'a coincidence can be taken religiously as a sign and called a miracle'. But, Holland adds, 'it cannot without confusion be taken as a sign of divine interference with the natural order'.[7]

(b) *Comments on the Definitions*

Should we accept any of the above understandings of 'miracle'? For one reason, at any rate, the answer would seem to be 'No'. That is because, as I have presented them, and with the possible exception of what Holland writes, they lack what religious people seem to regard as an important element. Those who believe that miracles have actually occurred normally hold that they are events of some religious significance.[8] The idea here is that miracles reveal something about God or that they teach us some religious truth. As Swinburne says: 'If a god intervened in the natural order to make a feather land here rather than there for no deep ultimate purpose, or to upset a child's box of toys just for spite, these events would not naturally be described as miracles.'[9] We may put this by saying that not just any purported divine intervention and not just any purported violation of a natural law would be deemed to be miraculous by those who believe in miracles.

But what of the notion of divine intervention? And what of the notion of a violation of a natural law? Are these not essential to the notion of a miracle? Here there are a number of points to be made, the first of which concerns the notion of God intervening.

It is very common to find people speaking of miracles as

divine interventions. As we have seen, Mackie speaks in such terms. For him, the world has certain ways of working when left to itself, and miracles are instances of God stepping in. But should we suppose that God is literally able to intervene? To say that something has intervened on a given occasion would normally be taken to imply that the thing has moved in where it was not to be found in the first place. The notion of intervention involves the idea of absence followed by presence. In this sense, I can be said to intervene in a fight when I enter the fight myself, having formerly not been part of it. Does it make sense, however, to speak of God moving in where he has not been present before? And does it make sense to think of miracles as cases of God moving in?

It makes sense to speak and think in such a way if we take God to be a kind of observer in relation to the world, and if we think of the world as able to carry on independently of him. On such a view, sometimes referred to as 'Deism', there is no intrinsic problem with the notion of God intervening (though classical deists were not, in fact, supporters of belief in miracles as divine interventions).[10] But matters are different if, along with orthodox Christianity, we hold that the world is always totally dependent on God for its existence. If that is the case, then God is always present to his creatures as their sustainer and preserver. He is 'omnipresent', or 'ubiquitous', and it therefore makes sense to deny that he can, strictly speaking, intervene. Thus it makes sense to deny that miracles should be thought of as cases of divine intervention. As Alvin Plantinga, commenting on Mackie's definition of 'miracle', puts it, 'on the theistic conception the world is never 'left to itself' but is always (at the least) conserved in being by God'.[11] Hence, for example, it is no part of Aquinas's concept of 'miracle' that miracles are cases of divine intervention. In his thinking, God, as creator and sustainer, is always present to everything. And for this reason, he maintains, God is as present in what is not miraculous as he is in the miraculous. Miracles, for Aquinas, do not occur because of an extra 'wonder-ingredient' (i.e. God). They occur when something is *not* present (i.e. a created cause or a collection of created causes). For this reason, he argues, miracles can only be brought about by God.

On the other hand, the notion of a violation of a natural law is, surely, in some sense part of what we might call 'the traditional notion of the miraculous'.[12] As we have seen, R. F. Holland finds it in order for events which have perfectly ordinary explanations to be called 'miracles'. And there seems no overriding reason for dismissing this use of 'miracle' unequivocally. But it is not the use of 'miracle' which has been in the forefront throughout the many centuries in which people have spoken of and debated about miracles. Much more prevalent has been the view that miracles are events which strictly admit of nothing that we could possibly call a scientific explanation. Generally speaking, the assumption has been that things in the world have certain properties and ways of working which cannot produce events of the kind that have been called miracles. Generally speaking, the assumption has been that miracles are events which do not accord with what writers like Swinburne and Mackie mean by 'laws of nature': i.e. theories stating how certain things in the world regularly operate in certain conditions, theories which may reasonably be used in predicting how certain things in the world will operate in certain conditions in the future. It is because miracles have been regularly understood in this sense that they have been thought of as brought about by God or by some other agent not part of the material world.

It ought, perhaps, to be noted that some writers have denied that what I am calling the traditional understanding of the miraculous is properly traditional. For, it has been argued, my 'traditional understanding of the miraculous' is not to be found in the Bible. Hence, for example, we find the following observations in a book by Samuel M. Thompson:

The notion of *miracle* as something which happens in nature and is contrary to the laws of nature is a curiously confused concept. In the first place, no such conception can be found in the Biblical sources of the Hebrew-Christian tradition, for those sources did not have the conception of natural law. To call an event a *miracle* is to call it a 'marvel', and to say that it evokes wonder and awe. It is to say that the event is inexplicable apart from its supernatural significance. Even if direct intervention by God occurs in nature only ignorance can make it appear capricious. Whatever it is, it has its explanation and it fits the rational order of being. If we cannot account for it in terms of the natural order it is because the natural order is not the whole of the rational order of being. We have to assume that complete knowledge would show us the complete harmony of divine and natural causation in every event.[13]

But, considered as an interpretation of the Bible, this view is somewhat implausible. What, for example, of Psalm 148, with its talk of created things which God has established by an ordinance which will not pass away?

It is correct to say that in English translations of the Bible, 'miracle' is sometimes used to refer only to an event which the author regards as somehow significant or as somehow pointing beyond itself. It is also correct to say that biblical authors never speak of 'natural laws' and that some of them (e.g. the author of the fourth Gospel) do not regard the significance of miracles as exhausted by saying that they are events which are contrary to what modern authors mean by 'natural laws'. According to R. H. Fuller, the Bible 'knows nothing of nature as a closed system of law. Indeed the very word "nature" is unbiblical.'[14] But it is surely going too far to suggest that, in the sense of 'natural law' noted above, biblical authors have no notion of natural law and that they have no notion of miracles as violations of natural laws. As authors like Swinburne and Mackie understand it, and as Swinburne writes himself, the following events, if they occurred, would be violations of natural laws:

Levitation, resurrection from the dead in full health of a man whose heart has not been beating for twenty four hours and who was dead also by other currently used criteria; water turning into wine without the assistance of chemical apparatus or catalysts; a man getting better from polio in a minute.[15]

Yet this is exactly the sort of event typically referred to in the Bible (or, at least, the New Testament) as miraculous. And though biblical authors do not indulge in the sort of qualification present in the list just given, readers of their texts ought to be able to see that they often seem to presuppose something like it when they talk of the miraculous. In many cases, at any rate, they presume that miracles cannot be brought about by the physical powers of objects in the world. Such a presupposition seems evident, for example, in the remark ascribed to the man in St John's Gospel who is said to have had his sight restored by Jesus. 'Never since the world began has it been heard that any one opened the eyes of a man born blind. If this man were not from God he could do nothing.'[16]

Is it Reasonable to Believe in Miracles?

It should by now be apparent that people have disagreed about the meaning of 'miracle'.[17] But they have disagreed even more about the reasonableness of believing in the occurrence of miracles. For the most part, the disagreement has been over the occurrence of miracles in the sense of 'miracle' present in the work of authors like Aquinas, Mackie, and Swinburne. So it is now appropriate for us to consider what might be said about the reasonableness or otherwise of believing in the occurrence of miracles in this sense. The most famous and most discussed treatment of the matter is that of Hume mentioned above. So we can begin by looking at what that has to say.[18]

Hume's Account of Miracles

What is Hume seeking to show in 'Of Miracles'? His readers have often been uncertain about the precise nature of his position. And that is not surprising, for his remarks seem to pull in different directions.

Sometimes he seems to be asserting that miracles are flatly impossible. At one point, for instance, he refers to reports of miracles performed at the tomb of the Abbé Paris. Of these he observes:

And what have we to oppose to such a cloud of witnesses, but the absolute impossibility or miraculous nature of the events, which they relate? And this surely, in the eyes of all reasonable people, will alone be regarded as a sufficient refutation.[19]

At another point in his discussion Hume imagines all historians reporting that Queen Elizabeth I, having died and been buried, rose to life again. Of this possibility he says:

I should not doubt of her pretended death, and of those other public circumstances that followed it: I should only assert it to have been pretended, and that it neither was, nor possibly could be real . . . The knavery and folly of men are such common phenomena, that I should rather believe the most extraordinary events to arise from their concurrence, than admit of so signal a violation of the laws of nature.[20]

In other parts of the text, however, Hume seems to go back on this (apparently) emphatic denial that miracles are possible. Towards the end of the second part of 'Of Miracles' he writes:

I beg the limitations here made may be remarked, when I say, that a miracle can never be proved, so as to be the foundation of a system of religion. For I own, that otherwise, there may possibly be miracles, or violations of the usual course of nature, of such a kind as to admit of proof from human testimony.[21]

Elsewhere, he seems to be making a weaker claim than the one which emerges in his remarks on the Abbé Paris and Queen Elizabeth. He seems to be saying not that miracles are flatly impossible, and not that there might not be testimony which would entitle us to believe in their occurrence, but that we need to proceed with caution with reference to miracles, since there are reasons for doubting that reports of miracles are trustworthy.

Yet, though he does indeed seem to say this, he also seems to want to press a stronger conclusion, though one which is weaker than the claim that miracles are impossible. This is that we could never be justified in believing on the basis of testimony that any miracles have occurred. A key passage here occurs in Part 1 of 'Of Miracles', where Hume offers what he evidently regards as a fundamental principle. He writes:

A miracle is a violation of the laws of nature; and as a firm and unalterable experience has established these laws, the proof against a miracle, from the very nature of the fact, is as entire as any argument from experience can possibly be imagined. Why is it more than probable, that all men must die; that lead cannot, of itself, remain suspended in the air; that fire consumes wood, and is extinguished by water; unless it be, that these events are found agreeable to the laws of nature, and there is required a violation of these laws, or in other words, a miracle to prevent them?[22]

Hume allows that many witnesses may testify that a miraculous event has occurred. But, he adds,

no testimony is sufficient to establish a miracle unless the testimony be of such kind, that its falsehood would be more miraculous, than the fact, which it endeavours to establish; and even in that case there is a mutual destruction of arguments, and the superior only gives us assurance to that degree of force, which remains, after deducting the inferior.[23]

Here the suggestion seems to be that reports of miracles are intrinsically such that we *always* have more reason to reject them than to accept them. The argument seems to be like that propounded by Mackie when he observes that, when someone reports the occurrence of a miracle,

this event must, by the miracle advocate's own admission, be contrary to a genuine, not merely a supposed law of nature, and therefore maximally improbable. It is this maximal improbability that the weight of the testimony would have to overcome ... Where there is some plausible testimony about the occurrence of what would appear to be a miracle, those who accept this as a miracle have the double burden of showing both that the event took place and that it violated the laws of nature. But it will be very hard to sustain this double burden. For whatever tends to show that it would have been a violation of a natural law tends for that very reason to make it most unlikely that it actually happened.[24]

In Hume's words: 'Nothing is esteemed a miracle, if it ever happens in the common course of nature ... There must, therefore, be a uniform experience against every miraculous event, otherwise the event would not merit that appellation.'[25]

Miracles, Hume seems to be saying, are 'events' which we have overwhelming reason to believe to be impossible on the basis of experience.[26]

How Cogent are Hume's Conclusions?

Which of the conclusions noted above should actually be attributed to Hume? It may be that all of them can be attributed to him and that, as R. M. Burns suggests, 'the solution [to the apparent divergencies in 'Of Miracles'] lies in the recognition that . . . incompatible strains of argument lie in the text side by side'.[27] But warrant for attributing the above-mentioned conclusions to Hume can be found in what he writes. So let us now consider each of them in turn, starting with the conclusion that miracles are strictly impossible.

(a) *Are Miracles Impossible?*

In one sense of 'impossible' it can surely be said that miracles are not impossible. For suppose we have in mind the sense of 'impossible' as 'logically impossible', and where assertions or statements are said to be this. To say that an assertion or a statement is logically impossible is to say that it is contradictory or that it entails what is contradictory. And in this sense of 'impossible', it is hard to see that miracles are impossible. We may doubt the truth of a statement like 'Jesus gave sight to a man born blind'. But the statement does not seem logically impossible. It is hardly on a level with, for example, 'It's true that Jesus was a man, and it's not the case that Jesus was a man'.

But to say that miracles are impossible is more naturally understood as saying that, independently of questions of logical possibility, miracles just cannot happen. But why should we say this? At one point in 'Of Miracles' Hume gives the following answer:

Nothing is esteemed a miracle, if it ever happens in the common course of nature. It is no miracle that a man, seemingly in good health, should die of a sudden: because such a kind of death, though more unusual than any other, has yet been frequently observed to happen. But it is a miracle, that a dead man should come to life; because that has never been observed in any age or country. There must therefore be a uniform experience against every miraculous event, otherwise that event would not merit that appellation. And as a uniform experience amounts to a proof, there is here a direct and full *proof*, from the nature of the fact, against the existence of any miracle.[28]

Hume seems to think that the impossibility of miracles is somehow shown by the fact that their occurrence would amount to the occurrence of what has been regularly observed not to occur, or that it would amount to the occurrence of an event which experience suggests to be impossible. But that can hardly be a reason for holding that miracles cannot occur. For events may come to pass which differ from what has happened in the past and which conflict with what we think possible on the basis of experience. On the basis of previous experience, I do not expect Australian snakes to be in my study. But I would be mad to ignore someone who said there was such a snake in my study. We might say (though rather oddly) that until someone walked on the moon, people were regularly observed not to walk on the moon. But someone did walk on the moon. And people, in time, have come to do what earlier generations would rightly have taken to be impossible on the basis of their experience.[29] Hume's reasoning concerning the impossibility of miracles also has the unhappy implication that we can never revise our views concerning laws of nature in the light of observed exceptions to what we have taken to be laws. As C. D. Broad argues:

Clearly many propositions have been accounted laws of nature because of an invariable experience in their favour, then exceptions have been observed, and finally these propositions have ceased to be regarded as laws of nature. But the first reported exception was, to anyone who had not personally observed it, in precisely the same position as a story of a miracle, if Hume be right.[30]

One might, however, maintain that there is another reason for holding that miracles are impossible—a reason which gets its force from the idea that miracles are violations of natural laws. For what if there are no natural laws? Then there are no natural laws to be violated. And if a miracle is a violation of a natural law, it would seem *to be* something which *is not*, and for this reason, it would seem to be something impossible.

But if we are talking about what it is and is not reasonable to believe, such a line of argument is open to objection. Certainly, what we expect to be the case may fail to be the case; it is not, perhaps, logically absurd to suggest that the water put over a flame in an ordinary kitchen may one day turn to ice instead of heating up, and this in spite of what we have so far observed. But we would hardly be reasonable in acting on such a principle. We would normally be inclined to say, in fact, that it is the mark of a reasonable person to act otherwise. Such action certainly seems to square with reasoning that is of fundamental importance in scientific enquiry. Fundamental to such enquiry is the principle that the course of nature continues uniformly the same, and that if events of type A regularly follow events of type B in one set of circumstances, then other events of type A can be held to follow other events of type B in more or less identical circumstances unless there is some relevant difference that can itself be understood in terms of some covering law. We can express this point by saying that there is no obvious reason why we should rationally refuse to talk about laws of nature. To say that there are laws of nature is to say that reality is intelligible, in the sense that the behaviour of physical things can be predicted. Things behave in regular ways, and it is possible to frame scientific explanations and expectations. It may be held that the behaviour of many things is extremely irregular. One might appeal here to quantum physics and its talk about the random motions of fundamental particles. But at the macroscopic level it still seems that we can reasonably talk about laws; it still seems that we can talk the language of statistics and probability. We can say that when human beings suffer massive heart attacks, they can reasonably be expected to die. We can say that when you boil an egg for half an hour, you can reasonably expect to get a hard-boiled egg.

But perhaps it should now be suggested that even if there

are grounds for supposing that miracles are not impossible,
there are reasons for denying that any have occurred. And
we may now ask how we should respond to this suggestion.
Should we, for example, say that we could never be warranted
in believing reports of miracles?

(b) *Miracles and Testimony*

In addition to his suggestion (to which I shall return presently)
that the evidence against miracles having occurred must always
be held to outweigh any claim to the effect that they have
occurred, Hume makes four points designed, as he puts it, to
show that 'there never was a miraculous event established'.[31]

The first is that no reported miracle comes with the testimony of enough people who can be regarded as sufficiently
intelligent, learned, reputable, and so on to justify us in
believing the reported miracle.

There is not to be found, in all history, any miracle attested by a
sufficient number of men, of such unquestioned good-sense, education, and learning, as to secure us against all delusion in themselves;
of such undoubted integrity, as to place them beyond all suspicion of
any design to deceive others; of such credit and reputation in the eyes
of mankind, as to have a great deal to lose in case of their being
detected in any falsehood; and at the same time, attesting facts
performed in such a public manner and in so celebrated a part of the
world, as to render the detection unavoidable.[32]

The second point is that people are naturally prone to look
for marvels and wonders and that this must be taken as giving
us grounds for being sceptical of reported miracles. 'We may',
says Hume,

observe in human nature a principle which, if strictly examined, will
be found to diminish extremely the assurance, which we might, from
human testimony, have, in any kind of prodigy . . . The passion of
surprise and *wonder*, arising from miracles, being an agreeable
emotion, gives a sensible tendency towards the belief of those events,
from which it is derived. And this goes so far, that even those
who cannot enjoy this pleasure immediately, nor can believe those
miraculous events, of which they are informed, yet love to partake of
the satisfaction at second-hand or by rebound, and place a pride and
delight in exciting the admiration of others.[33]

In this connection Hume adds that religious people are particularly untrustworthy. 'A religionist', he says, 'may be an enthusiast, and imagine he sees what has no reality: he may know his narrative to be false, and yet persevere in it, with the best intentions in the world, for the sake of promoting so holy a cause.'[34] Religious people, Hume says, are subject to vanity, self-interest, and impudence.[35] He also points out that

The many instances of forged miracles, and prophecies, and supernatural events which in all ages, have either been detected by contrary evidence, or which detect themselves by their absurdity, prove sufficiently the strong propensity of mankind to the extraordinary and the marvellous, and ought reasonably to beget a suspicion against all relations of this kind.[36]

Thirdly, Hume claims that 'It forms a strong presumption against all supernatural and miraculous relations that they are observed chiefly to abound among ignorant and barbarous nations'.[37]

Hume's final point is rather more complicated. Basically he is arguing in this way. If Fred, Bill, and John testify that there is a kangaroo in the bathroom and if Mabel, Mary, and Catherine testify that there is no kangaroo in the bathroom, then the testimonies cancel each other out, and neither should be accepted. In the case of miracles, different religions report different miracles. These reports must be viewed as contradicting each other. Therefore, if any religious person testifies to the occurrence of a miracle within his or her religious tradition, the testimony can safely be ignored, since there are plenty of other reports of the occurrence of miracles within different religious traditions, and the two sets of reports cancel each other out. In Hume's own words:

To make this the better understood, let us consider that, in matters of religion, whatever is different is contrary, and that it is impossible the religions of ancient Rome, of Turkey, of Siam, and of China should, all of them, be established on any solid foundation. Every miracle, therefore, pretended to have been wrought in any of these religions (and all of them abound in miracles), as its direct scope is to establish the particular system to which it is attributed; so has it the same force, though more indirectly, to overthrow every other system. In destroying a rival system, it likewise destroys the credit of those miracles, on which that system was established.[38]

These arguments are surely very problematic, however. Hume says that history does not provide testimony to the miraculous from 'a sufficient number of men, of such un-questioned good-sense, education, and learning, as to secure us against all delusion in themselves'. But how many men constitute a sufficient number? And what counts as good sense, education, and learning? Hume does not explain. Later on in the text he accuses people of being swayed by their love of the wonderful. But he does not show that they are always so swayed or that they are always swayed in a way which would render their testimony suspect. No doubt many people are swayed by a love of the wonderful. And love of the wonderful may be the main source of many reported miracles. But is it absolutely evident that nobody who has reported the occurrence of a miracle can be deemed to have reported accurately? And is there really good evidence that religious people cannot distinguish truth from error in the case of the marvellous or that are always governed by concern to back the religious cause?

It is exceedingly difficult to answer such questions. So much depends on taking particular cases and examining them in considerable detail. I think it can be said, however, that Hume is rather premature in supposing that the observations which he makes are sufficient to justify us in concluding that we can always disregard testimony to the effect that a miracle has occurred. One should also note that in his consideration of testimony, there are things which Hume might have noted, but does not. He seems, for example, to have forgotten about the possibility of corroborating what someone claims to have occurred. But past events sometimes leave physical traces which survive into the present.[39] It may thus be urged against Hume that it is conceivable that some reported 'miraculous' events can be reasonably believed to have occurred because of what can be gleaned from some physical data in the present. Even in default of such data, unless one is determined to insist that nobody can be taken as a reliable witness to what has actually occurred, it can be said that there is no reason why the existence of laws of nature should force us to conclude that somebody who reports the violation of a natural law must be misreporting. One may grant that particular instances need to be examined very carefully indeed, and in reading Hume's discussion of miracles, one can see exactly why. But how can one rule out in advance the possibility of rationally concluding that a report of what would be a violation of a natural law is a true description of what occurred?

An objector might reply that there still remains the point about reports of miracles made from different religions. But here again Hume seems to be moving too fast. In his own day it was widely assumed that the miracles reported in the New Testament established the truth of Christianity and the absolute falsehood of all other religions. But why should we assume that if we have reports of miracles from, for example, a Christian and a Hindu, both reports cannot be accepted as reports of miracles which actually occurred? Hume seems to assume some such principle as: 'If a Christian miracle occurs, that is evidence against the truth of Hinduism. And if a Hindu miracle occurs, that is evidence against the truth of Christianity.' But this principle does not seem necessarily true. As Swinburne argues, 'Evidence for a miracle "wrought in one religion" is only evidence against the occurrence of a miracle "wrought in another religion" if the two miracles, if they occurred, would be evidence for propositions of the two religious systems incompatible with each other.'[40] We may grant that Hume has established the conclusion that 'when two religions claim mutually exclusive revelations, it is not possible for both of them to be well evidenced by the way they report their associated miracles.'[41] But to have established that conclusion is not the same as establishing that all reports of miracles are undermined by the fact that different religions report different miracles.

At this point, Hume might appeal to the argument which I said I would return to above. For let us suppose that we might well defend reporters of miracles from charges of dishonesty and the like. Let us also suppose that miracles reported from one religion might not be thought to undermine the truth of another religion. Is it not still the case that because of what a miracle is supposed to be, we have overwhelming reason for withholding assent to any reported miracle? Do we not have enormous evidence for the fact that certain laws of nature hold? And must not this evidence always outweigh any claim to the effect that, on some occasion or other, something has happened which conflicts with a law of nature? Is it not simply the case that, as Mackie puts it, miracles are 'maximally improbable' on the basis of our experience?

Those who wish to say 'Yes' to such questions have on their side the fact that experience and testimony seem strongly to suggest that laws of nature normally do operate and that events which people take to be miracles are few and far between (if they occur at all). One might also observe that, when presented with a report that such and such has happened, it often seems reasonable to assess the report in the light of what we know to have regularly happened. When it was reported in August 1991 that all sorts of dramatic changes were occurring in the Soviet Union, Western reporters and politicians were constantly cautious in believing the reports. And most people in the West agreed that they were right in being cautious. Why? Because of what they knew the Soviet Union to be and also because of what had been happening in the Soviet Union for many years previously.

On the other hand, our own regular experience does not show that we can never be reasonable in believing a report which goes clean against it. Hume and Mackie are saying that the testimony of others should not be admitted if it conflicts with what seems probable or possible to us. But that would make it unreasonable to accept testimony which we plainly would be prepared to accept. As Thomas Sherlock says, if we accept what Hume argues, we should agree that, for instance, 'a man who lives in a warm climate, and never saw ice, ought on no evidence to believe that rivers freeze and grow hard . . . for it is improbable, contrary to the usual course of nature and impossible according to his notion of things'. Yet would we be prepared to say that such a man would be unreasonable in accepting our testimony that rivers, indeed, can be solid? As Sherlock goes on to suggest, it seems wrong 'to make one man's ability in discerning, and his veracity in reporting plain facts, depend on the skill or ignorance of the hearers'.[42]

Hume might reply that it just is the case that laws of nature are never violated. He might say that our evidence always shows that a violation of a natural law is absolutely improbable on the basis of our evidence. But what are we to take as 'our evidence'? What people say is often taken as evidence, and, indeed, we believe much more on the basis of what people say than we do on the basis of what we have seen or discovered for ourselves (see Chapter 1). Also to be noted at this point is that what is contrary to a law of nature might actually be *more probable than not* with respect to our evidence. For, as Plantinga observes:

Suppose (as has been the case for various groups of people at various times in the past) we knew nothing about whales except what can be garnered by rather distant visual observation. Now it might be a law of nature that whales have some property P (mammalian construction, for example) that can be detected only by close examination; but it might also be the case that we know that most things that look and behave more or less like whales do not have this property P. Then the proposition *S is a whale and does not have P* could very well be more probable than not with respect to our evidence, even though it is contrary to a law of nature.[43]

For reasons such as these, we may take leave to doubt that Hume has shown that it is always unreasonable to accept a report that a miracle has occurred. And, to move beyond Hume's immediate concern with testimony, it is worth adding that people might be justified in supposing that a miracle has occurred on the basis of what they observe for themselves. For suppose we actually do observe an event which we have reason to suppose to be quite at odds with what can be brought about in terms of natural laws. Suppose, for example, that we witness one of the occurrences in the list given earlier: 'levitation, resurrection from the dead in full health of a man whose heart has not been beating for twenty four hours and who was dead also by other currently used criteria; water

turning into wine without the assistance of chemical apparatus
or catalysts; a man getting better from polio in a minute.' We
might seek to explain what we observe by bringing it under
some other well-established law. In default of any such known
law, we might just refuse to accept that there has been a
violation of a law of nature, and we might say that there is
some law in operation, but that we are so far ignorant of it.
But it is not inconceivable that such a way of proceeding
could land us in even greater difficulties than we would solve.
Suppose that the above-mentioned events occur and are
monitored by strict scientific methods. If we now say that they
can be explained in terms of some law of nature, we will
evidently have to show that they are further instances of some
previously noted phenomenon and that they are understand-
able on that basis. But we may not be able to do this. If we
want to deny that any natural law has been violated in this
case, we will therefore have to revise our theories about
natural laws. The trouble now is that it might be enormously
expensive (intellectually, not financially) to do so. We might
have to agree, for example, that in accordance with perfectly
natural laws it is more than conceivable that victims of polio
should recover in a minute. And such a position would play
havoc with a vast amount of scientific theory. In such circumstances it might, in fact, be more economical and more
reasonable to accept that a law of nature has been violated.
But if this is correct, it follows that a law of nature can
reasonably be said to have been violated and that it is wrong
to say that nobody can have reason for supposing that miracles
have occurred.

What do Miracles Prove?

Let us now suppose that we can be absolutely sure that violations of natural law have occurred. Let us suppose that we can
be sure that some past events are reasonably and properly
taken to be violations of natural laws. What can we conclude
on the basis of this fact? Can we, for example, conclude that

there is a God? Or can we, perhaps, conclude that some world
religion is the true religion?

As we have seen, 'miracle' has been defined so as to include
the idea that miracles are brought about by God. But can
they only be brought about by God? Much here depends on
whether or not one thinks there could be a God. But suppose
that there could be a God and that there is a God. Does it
follow that miracles must be brought about by God?

Swinburne suggests that there could well be circumstances
that made it reasonable to say that some violation of a natural
law had been brought about by something like a human agent
or agents. Let E be a violation of a natural law. Then

suppose that E occurs in ways and circumstances otherwise strongly
analogous to those in which occur events brought about intentionally
by human agents, and that other violations occur in such circumstances. We would then be justified in claiming that E and other such
violations are, like effects of human actions, brought about by agents,
but agents unlike men in not being material objects. This inference
would be justified because, if an analogy between effects is strong
enough, we are always justified in postulating slight difference in
causes to account for slight difference in effects.[44]

But would a non-material agent bringing about effects
intentionally have to be divine? Plenty of people, after all,
have thought that miracles can be brought about by 'demons',
'spirits', 'saints', and other agents who are not what many of
those who believe in God would think of as divine.

It might be argued that only God stands outside the universe
as its maker and sustainer. And if we think that a miracle is a
violation of a natural law, we might, therefore, think that only
God can bring one about. If God is no part of the universe, he
will not be subject to the constraints of natural laws. But
then one might wonder whether there might not be agents of
some kind (angels? Satan?) who, though they are not divine,
also have the power to bring about effects which can count
as violations of natural laws. We may not think that there are
any such agents. But how are we to rule them out? Perhaps
the most we can do here is appeal to a principle of economy.

One might argue along these lines: 'Given that there is a God, given that God can be the source of events called miracles, and given that we have no other reason to postulate non-divine agents as sources of such events, we should ascribe them to God.' Aquinas argues that only God can work miracles, since (1) a miracle is 'an event that happens outside the ordinary processes of the *whole* of created nature', and (2) anything other than God works according to its created nature.[45] And if we define 'miracle' as Aquinas does, his conclusion seems inescapable. But not everyone has defined 'miracle' in this way. Not even all Roman Catholics have done so. According to Pope Benedict XIV, for instance, something is a miracle if its production exceeds 'the power of visible and corporeal nature only'.[46]

What of the suggestion that miracles might prove some religion to be the true religion? That miracles do precisely this has indeed been argued. A classic statement of this view can be found in the writings of Samuel Clarke (1675–1729), according to whom, 'The Christian religion is positively and directly proved, to be actually and immediately sent to us from God, by the many infallible signs and miracles, which the author of it worked publicly as the evidence of his Divine Commission.'[47] One might also note Canon 4 of Vatican I's *Dogmatic Constitution on the Catholic Faith* in which we read:

If anyone says that all miracles are impossible, and that therefore all reports of them, even those contained in sacred scripture, are to be set aside as fables or myths; or that miracles can never be known with certainty, nor can the divine origin of the christian religion be proved from them: let him be anathema.[48]

But should it really be said that a miracle can strictly *prove* that some religion or other is the true one or (to make the question a weaker one) that some religion is true?

It is significant, perhaps, that the foundation documents of Christianity do not seem to think so (regardless of what has been argued by subsequent Christians). In St Mark's Gospel, Jesus declares that false prophets can work miracles in order to deceive.[49] And in all the synoptic gospels he refuses to work 'signs' in order to prove his divine mission.[50] One might argue, however, that miracles, if they occurred, might lend support to some religious tradition or to some religious belief. If you call on me to show that you have my support and if I do something in response to your request, others will have reason to suppose that I support you. By the same token, if, for example, people call on God to express support for the religious beliefs which they teach by effecting what is miraculous, and if some such thing is effected, it would be a very thoroughgoing sceptic who would say that no miracle can lend any credence to any religious position.

In the end, though, we are dealing here with possibilities only. It is concrete details of particular supposed miracles that are needed for matters to be usefully taken further. At this stage, therefore, it is best to move on to our final subject for discussion.

Life after Death

WE have now looked at various topics and questions. And there are many more that will have to be considered by anyone who proposes to deal seriously with the philosophy of religion. Not all of them can be considered in this book, obviously, but we ought, in conclusion, to pay some attention to the issue of life after death, for that is of fundamental importance for many religious people, and it has provoked a lot of philosophical attention. Belief in life after death has taken many forms, some of which are unique to particular religious systems, though others can be found in more than one religion. It is impossible to touch on all of them here, but two in particular have been much adhered to and much discussed by philosophers, and we will turn to them.

Two Views of Life after Death

The first has a venerable philosophical history. It can be found, for example, in Plato's *Phaedo*. Here we are presented with the figure of Socrates, who is about to drink poison because he has been condemned to death. His friends are grief-stricken, but Socrates assures them that he is perfectly capable of surviving death. Someone called Crito asks, 'But in what fashion are we to bury you?' The text continues:

'However you wish,' said he; 'provided you catch me, that is, and I don't get away from you.' And with this he laughed quietly, looked towards us and said: 'Friends, I can't persuade Crito that I am Socrates here, the one who is now conversing and arranging each of the things being discussed; but he imagines I'm that dead body he'll see in a little while, so he goes and asks how he's to bury me! But as for the great case I've been arguing all this time, that when I drink the poison, I shall no longer remain with you, but shall go off and depart for some happy state of the blessed, this, I think, I'm putting to him in vain, while comforting you and myself alike.[1]

Notice how Socrates here distinguishes between himself and his body which is soon to be lifeless. He evidently thinks of his real self as something distinct from his body. And that is how people think when they support the first of our views about life after death. For, according to this, people are not to be identified with their bodies, and they will survive their deaths in non-bodily form. As I say, this view has a long history in philosophy. Apart from Plato, a particularly famous exponent of it is Descartes:

My essence consists solely in the fact that I am a thinking thing. It is true that I may have (or, to anticipate, that I certainly have) a body that is very closely joined to me. But nevertheless, on the one hand I have a clear and distinct idea of myself, in so far as I am simply a thinking, non-extended thing; and on the other hand I have a distinct idea of body, in so far as this is simply an extended, non-thinking thing. And accordingly, it is certain that I am really distinct from my body and can exist without it.[2]

The second view of life after death is very different. The first view depends on the premiss that human beings are essentially distinct from their bodies and that life after death can be thought of in non-bodily terms. But the second view holds that life after death should be understood as bodily life. When we die, our bodies corrupt and decay, or they are destroyed (e.g. by cremation). So much seems incontestable. But according to the second view, we shall, after death, continue to live on in some kind of bodily way. Thus, for example, according to Christian orthodoxy, we may hope for the resurrection of the dead. And, for philosophical reasons, there have been philosophers who have hoped for nothing less. Peter Geach, for instance, writes: 'Apart from the *possibility* of resurrection, it seems to me a mere illusion to have any hope for life after death. I am of the mind of Judas Maccabeus: if there is no resurrection, it is superfluous and vain to pray for the dead.'[3]

Here, then, are two distinct views of life after death. According to the first, we shall survive as *disembodied selves*. According to the second, we shall live again in *bodily form*. But what are we to make of these views? Philosophers have raised two questions about them. The first can be regarded as conceptual. It basically asks whether or not either (or both) of our two views of life after death are possible, whether there *could* be what our two views say there *will* be. The second question, by contrast, abstracts from questions of possibility to focus first on actuality or grounds for belief. It asks whether it is reasonable to believe that we can look forward to disembodied survival or bodily life after death. Let us therefore consider each question in turn.

The Survival of the Disembodied Self

If human beings are not to be identified with their bodies, then, as Descartes says, there seems no obvious reason why they cannot exist without their bodies. And if human beings can exist without their bodies, then the view that they can survive death seems a plausible one. We normally think of death as the end of a person's bodily life. But if people are distinct from their bodies, then the fact that their bodies die does not entail that they die.

But is it correct to think of human beings as distinct from their bodies in such a way that it is possible for them to exist in a disembodied state? Descartes, as we have seen, thought that it is; and he certainly does not lack modern supporters. A particularly trenchant follower of Descartes is H. D. Lewis. 'My own conclusion', says Lewis, 'is that no recent discussions of the mind–body problem have succeeded in showing that we can dispense with an absolute distinction between mind and body.'[4] 'I have little doubt', he declares, 'that there are mental processes quite distinct from observable behaviour and that each individual has an access to his own experiences in having them which is not possible for the most favoured observer.'[5] Another modern advocate of a distinction between persons and their bodies is Richard Swinburne. According to him, it is

coherent to suppose that a person can exist without a body.
He writes:

A person has a body if there is one particular chunk of matter
through which he has to operate on and learn about the world. But
suppose he finds himself able to operate on and learn about the world
within some small finite region, without having to use one particular
chunk of matter for this purpose. He might find himself with knowledge of the position of objects in a room (perhaps by having visual
sensations, perhaps not), and able to move such objects just like that,
in the ways in which we know about the positions of our limbs and
can move them. But the room would not be, as it were, the person's
body; for we may suppose that simply by choosing to do so he can
gradually shift the focus of his knowledge and control, e.g., to the
next room. The person would be in no way limited to operating and
learning through one particular chunk of matter. Hence we may term
him disembodied. The supposition that a person might become
disembodied . . . seems coherent.[6]

With this point made, Swinburne then argues that if X can be
without Y, then X and Y are distinct. Since I can be without
my body, it follows, says Swinburne, that I am not my body.

   The theory of Descartes, Lewis, and Swinburne, that persons
are essentially other than their bodies, is usually referred to
as 'dualism'. So we might say that the notion of non-bodily
survival stands or falls according to whether or not a case can
be made in favour of dualism. But can such a case be made?
And are there no decisive objections to dualism?

   A number of points seem to tell in its favour. For one thing
there is the fact that we often naturally talk as if our real selves
were distinct from our bodies—as, for instance, when we say
that we *have* bodies and as when we agree that we can be the
same person over a number of years even though our bodily
make-up has drastically changed in the meantime. Another
factor to be reckoned with is the way that we seem to have a
privileged access to many of our thoughts. We can think about
something without displaying the fact by any bodily behaviour.
Even if someone were to look at our brains while we were
thinking about things, they would not see our thoughts.

   On the other hand, the fact that our language seems to

involve subscribing to a distinction between mind and body does not show that mind and body are distinct things, as the dualist takes them to be. We may speak of people as having minds and bodies. But that only shows that I am a thing distinct from my body on the assumption that talk of mind is in no way translatable into talk of body, or on the assumption that it is talk about a substance distinct from anything bodily. Yet the truth of these assumptions is just what the dualist is purporting to establish. Considered as a defence of dualism, to say that we speak of people as having minds and bodies is not to say enough. We say that a chair *has* a back, legs, and a seat. Is there, then, something besides all these that *has* them?

Then again, just what is proved by the fact that we have privileged access to many of our thoughts and feelings? Does it mean that only I can know what I am thinking? That seems patently false. You can know what I am thinking. You can actually have the same thoughts yourself. There is not a single thought which I can have which you cannot have as well. Perhaps we should say that I can always keep my thoughts secret. But that, too, seems false. Unless I spend my entire life in a permanent state of unconsciousness, in which I could never be said to think, I inevitably show what I am thinking on numerous occasions. Perhaps we should say that I can sometimes keep my thoughts secret. And that is surely true. All of us have had lots of thoughts which nobody else knew about. But this only shows that we can sometimes keep our thoughts to ourselves, not that we are things which other people cannot observe and not that thinking is always an essentially incorporeal process.

At this point, however, a defender of dualism might say that there are positive arguments in favour of dualism which are not affected by what I have just been suggesting, and that these arguments establish its truth. What might the arguments be? Here, perhaps, we might look at those offered in defence of dualism by Descartes.

One of them is that we can have a clear idea of ourselves as being non-material. I can know that I exist, says Descartes. I can also see that I am essentially a thinking thing. But might

appearances here not be deceptive? In some cases my seeming
to myself to be thus and so means that I really am thus and so.
If I seem to myself to be unhappy, then I am unhappy. On the
other hand, the fact that I seem to myself to be sober does not
necessarily mean that I am sober. Nor does it follow from the
fact that I seem to myself to be well that I am, in fact, well.

Another of Descartes's arguments is that, whereas body is
always divisible, mind is not. 'There is', he says, 'a great
difference between the mind and the body, inasmuch as the
body is by its very nature always divisible, while the mind
is utterly indivisible.'[7] But is this really such a powerful
argument? When he speaks of 'the mind', Descartes takes
himself to be speaking of himself. And he confidently asserts
that he is not divisible. But how does he know that? How does
he know that if, for example, someone takes an axe to him
(i.e. his body), he will not be divided into parts? Descartes
would say that he cannot distinguish parts in himself to be
divided. But what Descartes can or cannot distinguish is not
to the point. The question is whether or not he is really
something with parts.

But Descartes has another argument for supposing that he is
a non-bodily thing. This is an argument from doubt. I can, he
says, doubt that I have a body. But I cannot doubt that I exist.
So I am not my body. As the reader will recognize, this
argument is similar to that of Richard Swinburne noted above.
Descartes thinks that he can exist without his body and that
he and his body are therefore distinct. Swinburne thinks the
same.

The trouble with Descartes's argument, however, is that it is
invalid. Descartes is saying: 'I can doubt that I have a body,
but I cannot doubt that I exist, therefore I am not a body.'
But what if I say, 'Fred can doubt that he is a professor of
philosophy, but Fred cannot doubt that he exists, therefore
Fred is not a professor of philosophy'? Would it really follow
that Fred is not a professor of philosophy? It would not.
In fact, critics of Descartes can actually use his pattern of
reasoning against him at this point. For, as Norman Malcolm
observes:

If it were valid to argue 'I can doubt that my body exists but not that I exist, *ergo* I am not my body,' it would be equally valid to argue 'I can doubt that there exists a being whose essential nature is to think, but I cannot doubt that I exist, *ergo* I am not a being whose essential nature is to think'. Descartes is hoist with his own petard! A form of argument that he employs to help establish the doctrine *sum res cogitans* could be used, if it were valid, to refute that very doctrine.[8]

A supporter of Descartes might say that what Descartes is driving at in his argument from doubt can be cogently stated in the terms offered by Swinburne. But Swinburne's argument holds that from the fact that it is coherent (i.e. logically possible) for someone to be disembodied, it follows that someone actually can be disembodied. And this does not follow at all. It is logically possible for me to escape death by drowning. But that does not mean that I actually can escape death by drowning. Swinburne's argument also rests on the view that we really can conceive of ourselves becoming disembodied. But many will feel that they cannot do this. What, they would say, would we be conceiving of? What, for example, would Brian Davies be without physical location and the other things ascribable to him in day to day life? And how would we distinguish him from other persons on the assumption that he is incorporeal and that they might be too?

Here we need to remember that much of our understanding of 'person' involves reference to the existence and processes of bodies. Dualists have replied to this point by insisting that persons can have a very vigorous and lively 'inner' life; that they can, for example, think and have emotional experiences without showing so by any kind of overt bodily behaviour. And this is certainly true, which is why it is easy to sympathize with much of the criticism levelled by philosophers of the twentieth century against a famous attack on dualism launched by Gilbert Ryle (1900–76) in his celebrated and influential book *The Concept of Mind*.[9] Ryle sometimes spoke as if people's history is detectable simply from their bodily behaviour, which seems false, if only because one can keep certain thoughts and feelings entirely to oneself. But to be alive as a human person is also to be able to engage in all sorts of activities which would be impossible in the absence of a body.

Take, for example, thinking. We think about what we are doing, we act thoughtfully, and a proper account of thinking, therefore, seems to require a reference to behaviour and to physical context. The same applies to seeing. A full account of seeing will have to take note of such sentences as 'I can't see, it's too dark', 'Let's see if he's finished', 'I saw my friend yesterday'. In this connection we can note some pertinent remarks of Geach:

> Well, how do we eventually use such words as 'see', 'hear', 'feel', when we have got into the way of using them? We do not exercise these concepts only so as to pick out cases of seeing and the rest in our separate world of sense-experience; on the contrary, these concepts are used in association with a host of other concepts relating, e.g., to the physical characteristics of what is seen and the behaviour of those who do see. In saying this I am not putting forward a theory, but just reminding you of very familiar features in the everyday use of the verb 'to see' and related expressions; our ordinary talk about seeing would cease to be intelligible if there were cut out of it such expressions as 'I can't see, it's too far off', 'I caught his eye', 'Don't look round', etc. . . . I am not asking you to believe that 'to see' is itself a word for a kind of behaviour. But the concept of seeing can be maintained only because it has threads of connexion with these other non-psychological concepts; break enough threads and the concept of seeing collapses.[10]

Some writers who have insisted on the importance of the existence of bodies as far as the existence of persons is concerned have concluded that persons are nothing but bodies. I refer here to what has been called behaviourism and also to the so-called identity thesis, according to some versions of which thoughts, feelings, and so forth are identical with brain processes.[11] But to point to the importance of the body in our understanding of persons is not necessarily to subscribe to forms of behaviourism or the identity thesis. It is just to say that it is extremely difficult to defend a view which allows persons to be essentially distinct from their bodies, a view which allows that there can be bodiless persons recognizable as human beings.

To put it all another way, while we can easily agree that much of a person's life is private, and while we can even agree that it is possible to conceive of certain intellectual experiences occurring in a way that does not seem to depend on physical location, if we are talking about the survival of human beings, we are talking about the survival of complex entities that owe so much to being bodily that it seems impossible to say that in the absence of a body, there can really be a human person. If, then, it is said that a human person can live on as a disembodied self, the appropriate response would seem to be a puzzled scepticism.

So Descartes's arguments for dualism and Swinburne's support of Descartes seem open to challenge. And if what I have suggested in criticism of them is cogent, it would also seem that there are serious problems with the whole idea of people being immaterial things. This, at any rate, seems to be the verdict of most contemporary philosophers. And if they are right, it would also seem that there are serious problems with the view that people can survive their deaths because they are essentially incorporeal.

Survival as Bodily

Yet what of the view that people can survive death in bodily form? Perhaps its chief virtue is that it is entirely unaffected by any of the criticisms of dualism levelled above. If the argument of the preceding section is correct, it would seem that anything that could be recognized as a human existence depends on the human person being a bodily individual. And if one says that there is bodily life after death, one is at least talking about something that might, if it came about, be regarded as the life of a human person.

But one might still ask whether people can actually live after death in bodily form. I suggested earlier that from the logical possibility of people existing apart from their bodies, it does not follow that they are actually such as to be able to exist apart from their bodies. It may be logically possible for me to become a millionaire. But that does not mean that I can actually become a millionaire. And, with that truth in mind, I might wonder whether I do not also lack the power to live after my death in bodily form.

It might be said that my worries can be dispelled by recognizing that it is possible for people to live after death because replicas of their bodies can be present and because they can therefore be said to survive even if they have died. One can find this suggestion in the work of John Hick, who asks us to imagine certain extraordinary, but not logically impossible, states of affairs.

We begin with the idea of someone suddenly ceasing to exist at a certain place in this world and the next instant coming into existence at another place which is not contiguous with the first. He has not moved from A to B by making a path through the intervening space but has disappeared at A and reappeared at B. For example, at some learned gathering in London one of the company suddenly and inexplicably disappears and the next moment an exact 'replica' of him suddenly and inexplicably appears at some comparable meeting in New York. The person who appears in New York is exactly similar, as to both bodily and mental characteristics, to the person who disappears in London. There is continuity of memory, complete similarity of bodily features, including fingerprints, hair and eye coloration and stomach contents, and also of beliefs, habits and mental propensities. In fact there is everything that would lead us to identify the one who appeared with the one who disappeared, except continuous occupancy of space.[12]

According to Hick, this is a logically possible sequence of events. And the reasonable verdict on the whole sequence may just have to be that the person who appears in New York is the same as the one who disappeared in London. The person in America, says Hick, may act and behave just as we expect the person in London to. He may be as baffled by appearing in New York as anybody else. All his friends and relations may stoutly declare that he is quite definitely the person who went to the meeting in London.

But, so Hick continues, suppose now that the sequence of events is slightly different.

Let us suppose that the event in London is not a sudden and inexplicable disappearance, and indeed not a disappearance at all, but a sudden death. Only, at the moment when the individual dies a 'replica' of him as he was at the moment before his death, and complete with memory up to that instant, comes into existence in New York.[13]

Faced with the first sequence of events, it could be reasonable, Hick says, to extend our concept of 'the same person' to cover this strange new case. Faced with this second sequence, might one not be justified in doing so again? Hick argues that one might be.

Even with the corpse on our hands it would still, I suggest, be an extension of 'same person' required and warranted by the postulated facts to say that the one who died has been miraculously re-created in New York. The case would, to be sure, be even odder than the previous one because of the existence of the dead body in London contemporaneously with the living person in New York. And yet, striking though the oddness undoubtedly is, it does not amount to a logical impossibility. Once again we must imagine some of the deceased's colleagues going to New York to interview the person who has suddenly appeared there. He would perfectly remember them and their meeting, be interested in what had happened, and be as amazed and dumbfounded about it as anyone else; and he would perhaps be worried about the possible legal complications if he should return to London to claim his property and so on. Once again, I believe, they would soon find themselves thinking of him and treating him as the same person as the dead Londoner. Once again the factors inclining us to say that the one who died and the one who appeared are the same person would far outweigh the factors inclining us to say that they are different people. Once again we should have to extend our usage of 'same person' to cover the new case.[14]

But suppose we now consider another story. Suppose you give me a lethal dose of poison. This, of course, does not make me very happy. You say: 'Don't worry. I've arranged for a replica of you to appear. The replica will seem to have all your memories. He will be convinced that he is you. And he will look exactly like you. He will even have your fingerprints.' How relieved should I be?

Speaking for myself, I should not be in the slightest bit relieved. Knowing that a replica of myself will be wining and dining somewhere is not at all the same as knowing that I shall be wining and dining somewhere. For the continued existence of a person, more is required than replication. More is required than replication even when it comes to the continued existence of some physical object like a chair. You will not get much money from the lovers of art if you send them your replicas of paintings by Turner or Rembrandt. They want the original paintings. They want something which is physically continuous with what Turner or Rembrandt worked on in their studios.

It might be said, however, that I can survive the death of my body simply by coming to inhabit a different body. Something like this possibility is entertained by John Locke (1632–1704). He draws a distinction between 'man' and 'person'. A person, says Locke, is not the same as a man. A man, for Locke, is a certain sort of living organism. Men are biological entities. But persons, says Locke, are not. For Locke, a person is 'a thinking, intelligent being, that has reason and reflection, and can consider itself as itself, the same thinking thing, in different times and places; which it does only by that consciousness which is inseparable from thinking, and seems to me essential to it'. On this account we might have persons who are not men. We might have persons who exist in an entirely incorporeal world. We might also have persons who move from body to body. Or, in Locke's words:

Should the soul of a prince, carrying with it the consciousness of the prince's past life, enter and inform the body of a cobbler, as soon as deserted by his own soul, everyone sees he would be the same person with the prince, accountable only for the prince's actions . . . Had I the same consciousness that I saw the ark and Noah's flood, as that I saw an overflowing of the Thames last winter, I could no more doubt that I who write this now, that saw the Thames overflowed last winter, and that viewed the flood at the general deluge, was the same self . . . than that I who write this am the same myself now whilst I write . . . that I was yesterday.[15]

As many have pointed out, however, this position fairly bristles with difficulties. For one thing, it supposes that personal identity over time is constituted by psychological matters such as the fact that I seem to remember certain things. But, as Joseph Butler observed against Locke, memory *presupposes* personal identity, and cannot, by itself, constitute it.[16] Another problem with what Locke says is that it leads to an impossible conclusion. As Thomas Reid brings out, on Locke's view we get the curious result that

a man may be, and at the same time not be, the person that did a particular action. Suppose a brave officer to have been flogged when a boy at school for robbing an orchard, to have taken a standard from the enemy in his first campaign, and to have been made a general in advanced life; suppose, also, which must be admitted to be possible, that, when he took the standard, he was conscious of his having been flogged at school, and that, when made a general, he was conscious of his taking the standard, but had absolutely lost the consciousness of his flogging. These things being supposed, it follows . . . that he who was flogged at school is the same person who took the standard, and that he who took the standard is the same person who was made a general. Whence it follows, if there be any truth in logic, that the general is the same person with him who was flogged at school. But the general's consciousness does not reach so far back as his flogging; therefore . . . he is not the person who was flogged. Therefore the general is, and at the same time is not, the same person with him who was flogged at school.[17]

Perhaps, then, we may suggest that if I am a bodily individual, I will survive my death only by being physically continuous with what is there now. And the question is 'Can what is there now be physically continuous with what is there after my death?' In one obvious sense, of course, it can. The bodies that people bury are physically continuous with living bodies which have died. But we would not therefore say that life after death is a genuine possibility. The problem of life after death is something raised by people who know very well that the bodies that people bury are physically continuous with living bodies which have died. But do these bodies have the power of living again?

Given what we know of human beings, the answer would seem to be 'No'. But this, of course, is not to say that there is no power able to bring it about that people who have died do live again as physically continuous with people who have perished. And those who believe in God will say that there is such power. So perhaps we may suggest that if such power truly exists, then there is no conceptual barrier to supposing that people can be resurrected. But the 'if', of course, is very important.

Reasons for Believing in Life after Death

I shall be returning at the end of this chapter to some further conceivability questions about life after death. But for the moment we can now move on to the question of whether it is reasonable to hold that on either of the above views of life after death there is such a thing.

One reason that has been offered for saying that it is reasonable to hold such a view can be dealt with very briefly. This is not because the reason is trivial or silly or not worth investigating at length. It is just that it cannot be properly assessed in this book. It takes the form of an experimental argument for life after death, and is entirely based on psychical research. A great deal of effort has been directed to this research, and many consider that its results make it reasonable to believe in life after death. But psychical research presents a vast amount of data on which there is considerable disagreement among those who have studied it, and, since this book is not an examination of such research, its results cannot be adequately commented on here. We can, however, note that there are philosophers who have thought that it may prove significant. Thus, for example, Hick suggests that 'even if we discount the entire range of psychical phenomena, it remains true that the best cases of trance utterance are impressive and puzzling, and taken at face value are indicative of survival and communication after death'.[18]

But if it is not possible for us to engage with the experimental argument for life after death, we might yet make some effort to consider the philosophical arguments that have been advanced. They take various forms, but two of the most popular argue from the nature of the self and from morality. And there is a particularly famous, though different, pair of arguments for life after death to be found in Plato's *Phaedo*.[19]

Plato's defence of belief in life after death begins with the question 'Does a man's soul exist when he has died?' Socrates argues with Cebes that opposites come from opposites in the case of things which have an opposite. Thus the beautiful and the ugly, the just and the unjust, the larger and the smaller, the stronger and the weaker, the faster and the slower, the better and the worse. So, says Socrates, a thing comes to be alive from being dead. For the opposite of living is being dead.

> 'You say, don't you, that being dead is opposite to living?'
> 'I do.'
> 'And that they come to be from each other?'
> 'Yes.'
> 'Then what is it that comes to be from that which is living?'
> 'That which is dead.'
> 'And what comes to be from that which is dead?'
> 'I must admit that it's that which is living.'
> 'Then it's from those that are dead, Cebes, that living things and living people are born.'
> 'Apparently.'
> 'Then our souls do exist in Hades.'[20]

To this is added the argument that if everything which came to be dead remained dead, then everything would end up dead. If everyone who went to sleep did not awake, then all would be asleep. If everyone who died did not come to life from death, all would be dead. So 'there really is such a thing as coming to life again, living people *are* born from the dead, and the souls of the dead exist'.[21]

Ingenious though these arguments may seem, however, they are surely misguided. Things may have opposites, but it does not follow that if something comes to be, there is something which is its opposite from which it comes. Nor does it follow that if something ceases to be, something comes to be which is opposite to something existing earlier. As one commentator on Plato puts it:

Life and existence, it may reasonably be held, both begin for a living thing at birth or conception. Yet [Plato's first argument for survival after death] treats the predicate 'alive' as if it stood for an attribute capable of being acquired by an antecedently existing subject, and 'birth' as if it were something undergone by such a subject, rather than the coming into being of something that did not previously exist . . . If 'death' consists in a living thing's ceasing to exist, then when someone passes from being alive to being dead, he will not, in the latter state, enjoy discarnate existence, but will have ceased to exist altogether.[22]

As for Plato's second argument, this does not work because it mistakenly assumes that if all who have lived come to be dead, it follows that everyone has come to be dead. It is true that if everyone who has gone to sleep has not awoken, then everyone who has gone to sleep has not awoken. But it does not follow that nobody is awake. And though it is true that all who have died have died and (maybe) do not exist, it does not follow that everyone has died and is dead or non-existent. Those who have died may constitute a given number which is added to as people come to be born and die. And there need be no limit to the number involved.[23]

What, though, of the argument for life after death based on the notion of the self? This runs roughly as follows. How is it that things pass out of existence? The answer is by means of a dissolution of parts which usually comes about because of the action of some exterior force. Thus a human body can perish because something harms it, thereby causing it to break up in some sense. The human person, on the other hand, is not to be identified with a body. The human self is really a non-material, unextended entity. But if this is the case, then it cannot pass out of existence by means of a dissolution of parts. And since it is not a material thing, it is hard to see how something can exert any force on it so as to bring about its destruction. The human person is therefore immortal.

But this argument is surely a very weak one. For one thing it evidently presupposes that a person could be said to live as a disembodied self, and we have already seen reasons to question that view. But even allowing that the view is correct, there are difficulties with the argument. Perhaps things generally do pass out of existence because some kind of physical deterioration takes place in them, and perhaps we can speak here about a dissolution of parts. Perhaps too we can normally explain the destruction of things by referring to something that is acting upon them physically in some way. But none of this entitles us to claim any certainty that things can only cease to exist because they have parts that can dissolve. Nor does it entitle us to claim that something can only cease to exist because something physical has acted on it.

A famous version of the moral argument for life after death can be found in Kant. Earlier on we saw that Kant holds that it is possible to move from the fact of moral obligation to the existence of God. But he also holds that moral obligation has implications for life after death:

The realization of the *Highest Good* in the world is the necessary object of a will determinable by the moral law. But in this will the *perfect accordance* of the mind with the moral law is the supreme condition of the *Highest Good*. This then must be possible, as well as its object, since it is contained in the command to promote the latter. Now the perfect accordance of the will with the moral law is *holiness*, a perfection of which no rational being of the sensible world is capable at any moment of his existence. Since, nevertheless, it is required as practically necessary, it can only be found in a progress *in infinitum* towards that perfect accordance, and on the principles of pure practical reason it is necessary to assume such a practical progress as the real object of the will. Now, this endless progress is only possible on the supposition of an *endless* duration of the *existence* and personality of the same rational being (which is called the immortality of the soul). The *Highest Good*, then, practically is only possible on the supposition of the immortality of the soul; consequently this immortality, being inseparably connected with the moral law, is a postulate of pure practical reason (by which I mean a *theoretical* proposition, not demonstrable as such, but which is an inseparable result of an unconditional *a priori practical* law).[24]

But this line of argument also fails to provide very good reason for believing in life after death. Some people, of course, would dismiss it at once, because, as we have seen, they would reject any notion of a moral law over and against them. They would say, for example, that moral judgements are grounded on something like subjective feeling. But even if such people are wrong, it is implausible to argue that there are moral obligations that cannot be cancelled by death. I may say that I ought to do certain things, and I may regret that I cannot do them this side of the grave. But if I really cannot do them, then it is wrong to say that I ought to do them. Kant, of course, will reply that I can actually do what I ought, even though I cannot do so in this life. For, according to Kant, the existence of God is a guarantee that the Highest Good will finally be realized. But, as I argued in Chapter 9, Kant's argument for God as ensuring the realization of the Highest Good is itself a weak one. If one could rely on there being a God to provide a context in which the Highest Good can be realized, then it might be reasonable to hold that human beings will survive their deaths as part of the grand realization. But Kant's case for saying that there is such a God is not convincing.

Can it be restated so as to seem so? Some would argue that it can. It has been urged that morality is really pointless if there is no life after death. For this reason, it is sometimes said, the basic thrust of Kant's argument is correct. In the words of Joseph Prabhu:

The seriousness of our endeavour to shape our lives according to ideals of truth, wisdom, love and compassion, and all that they entail in terms of the development of virtue, together with the sense of inadequacy in our actual achievement, warrant the presumption that a single life cannot be all that we are destined to have. To grant that would make a mockery of our moral experience.[25]

Others have maintained that if God exists, he can be expected to give people life after death, for he is powerful and benevolent and would surely not leave us with nothing but the prospect of extinction. This argument is often supplemented by appeal to God's justice. God, it is said, is just, and justice requires that evil people should be punished and good ones rewarded. Therefore God will punish evil people and reward good ones, and, since he cannot do so until they have reached the end of their lives, he will do so when they die, in which case there is life after death.

But these arguments are also very weak. Why say that morality is pointless if there is no life after death? If there is any point in being moral in this life, then morality *ipso facto* has a point without reference to life after death. And for many people, of course, morality makes perfectly good sense in thoroughly worldly terms—think back to the position of Geach touched on in Chapter 9. As for the view that the existence of God guarantees the inevitability of life after death, that too is open to question. Let us suppose that God exists. Can we then be sure that he will bring it about that people survive death? A lot here depends on one's view of God. If one thinks of God as a just moral agent who has the power to make people survive their deaths, one might plausibly conclude that he will ensure that people survive death. For that is what a just moral agent with the necessary power would be likely to do. But, as I argued in Chapter 3, we do not have to think of God as a moral agent at all. And if this view is accepted, then nothing can be inferred about the likelihood of his behaving as such. If God is not a moral agent, one cannot argue about him on the contrary assumption; that would be like predicting the behaviour of dogs on the basis of our knowledge of elephants.

Must we, then, conclude that it is not reasonable to believe in life after death? No, for there may be excellent arguments for life after death that I have not considered. But we have now examined some classical philosophical arguments for life after death, and these are not convincing. So perhaps we can here conclude on an agnostic note. Life after death is possible, but we have seen no decisive philosophical reason for believing in it. Many religious believers would say that there are other reasons for belief in life after death. According to them, we can be sure that people survive death because survival after death is an item of faith.[26] But this view involves theological considerations that cannot be properly entered into here. In assessing it, we would obviously have to consider the whole question of religious faith. This, in turn, would lead us to other questions, particularly questions about revelation and (in the technical theological sense) religious 'doctrine'.

The Desirability of Life after Death

So far I have suggested that life after death is possible. I have also suggested that certain arguments in favour of it are open to question. In conclusion, I would like to say something about a problem concerning belief in life after death which is rarely considered, but which evidently interests some people. Suppose it could be shown that there is reason to believe in life after death. Would that be good news? Should it be cause for rejoicing? Would it mean that human beings have something to look forward to?

It may seem strange to wonder whether the knowledge that we shall survive death would count as good news. Is life not intrinsically desirable? Who would choose to pass out of existence? Is not the prospect of extinction a terrible one? But lots of people wish for death while also believing that it will be the end of them. And it is far from obvious that the prospect of continuing to exist is a desirable one. Suppose I am frozen and continue to exist for centuries in a state of unconscious suspended animation. Would that be an attractive end for me? Some writers have held that any kind of life is better than extinction. A good example is Miguel de Unamuno (1864–1936). 'For myself', he confesses, 'I can say that as a youth, and even as a child, I remained unmoved when shown the most moving pictures of hell, for even then nothing appeared to me quite so horrible as nothingness itself.'[27] Elsewhere he declares: 'I do not want to die—no; I neither want to die nor do I want to want to die; I want to live for ever and ever and ever. I want this "I" to live—this poor "I" that I am and that I feel myself to be here and now, and therefore the problem of the duration of my soul, of my own soul, tortures me.'[28] But not everyone would speak in such terms. They would say that survival after death is only to be rejoiced in if it brings with it a life worth living.

People who believe in life after death have, of course, rarely spoken of it as nothing but the alternative to extinction. They have presented it as something to look forward to, as something desirable. But can it be presented in such terms? Can it be shown that life after death is worth having?

It seems to me extremely difficult to show the desirability of life after death on one view of survival. This is the view that a person can survive death in non-bodily form. Even if we accept it, even if we waive the objections to it raised earlier, the prospect it holds out for us is surely bleak indeed. This point is well made by Bernard Williams in dialogue with H. D. Lewis. According to Lewis, we can believe in a non-bodily life after death if we think of it either as involving experiences like those we have when dreaming or as a state of living in 'a world of thoughts alone'.

If my body were whisked away while I dream and I nonetheless continued to have a coherent dream experience, this could be an excellent model of one sort of after life we may envisage . . . The same principles apply in essentials, but obviously in ways we find harder to anticipate, if we think of the remaining alternative . . . We may approach it if we think of ourselves so deeply absorbed in some intellectual activity that we become almost oblivious of our bodies and our surroundings and suppose that our bodies were then whisked away and we continued with our train of thought.[29]

Williams replies to all this by referring to Lewis's first alternative. This, he says,

makes the whole of future life into a kind of delusion. It is very like perceiving . . . but it obviously is not perceiving, in just the same way that dreaming is not perceiving and it seems to me that one thing I do not want to do is to spend the rest of eternity in a delusive simulacrum of perceptual activity. That just seems to me a rather lowering prospect. Why should a future of error be of interest to me?

Talking of Lewis's 'world of thoughts alone', Williams continues:

The alternative was the slightly higher-minded alternative, that [life after death] might consist of purely intellectual activity, which of course many philosophers have seen as the ideal future. I can see why *they* might be particularly interested in it; others might be less so . . .

I mean, suppose that the prospects of Heaven or the future life are those of intellectual contemplation, and I am a jolly, good-hearted fun-loving sensual character from the seaside.[30]

So if life after death is something to look forward to, it might have to involve more than is possible on the picture provided by a theory of a disembodied future. But it would also have to involve more than bodily resurrection, if that is understood as nothing but the continuation of our present mode of life. For some people's lives are not all that desirable. Some people are beautiful, healthy, intelligènt, and happy. Others are ugly, sick, stupid, and miserable.

This does not mean that people whose lives are now a burden cannot become transformed. Suppose we continue with the notion of life after death as conceived in terms of resurrection. That would mean continuing with the model of life after death as a continued physical life for the people who have died. Now many people suffer from various disadvantages in this life. But it is surely possible that these disadvantages could be removed without the people who suffer from them ceasing to be human beings. For as long as we are dealing with a human being, we are dealing with something that could, logically speaking, be relieved of its disadvantages without ceasing to be a human being. Take, for example, an extreme disadvantage such as that which might follow from severe brain damage. Let us suppose that people suffer such damage but continue to live. We may say that their lives are not worth living, that they have become human vegetables. But we would hesitate, I think, to say that they have ceased to be human beings. Certainly they are very different from healthy people. But they are not things of a different kind. Becoming a human vegetable is not the same as becoming a real vegetable. And if human vegetables were somehow relieved of their disadvantages, then it would make sense to say that human beings have been restored to full human life.

In this way, I think, it is possible to suggest that life after death, conceived of in terms of resurrection, could be attractive. For while it is not desirable for human beings to continue to exist after death in just the way that many of them do now, it would surely be desirable for them to continue to exist after death without the various currently prevailing impediments to an enjoyable life. And the desirability of their doing so would be increased if there were reason to believe that, after death, human beings have available to them sources of enjoyment or happiness that are presently unknown. If, then, the notion of resurrection is not a conceptually impossible one, resurrection could well be an attractive prospect.

And there, perhaps, we can leave things, for the development of such reflection would involve more space than is available here. If readers wish to follow up things for themselves, they will find relevant material in the Bibliography. But just to round off the present chapter, we can, on the basis of what has been argued, suggest that an attractive form of life after death is not to be dismissed as impossible, though we have seen no compelling reason to believe in life after death in any form. Many religious writers say a good deal more than this, but their suggestions raise a whole host of questions the consideration of which would take me further afield than I can now travel.

Notes

Chapter 1. Philosophy and Religious Belief

1. Cf. Michael Peterson, William Hasker, Bruce Reichenbach, and David Basinger, *Reason and Religious Belief* (Oxford and New York, 1991), 8, 'Philosophy of religion is the attempt to analyze and critically evaluate religious beliefs.'

2. David Hume, *An Enquiry concerning Human Understanding*, ed. L. A. Selby-Bigge (3rd edn., Oxford, 1975), 165. Readers of Hume might reasonably suggest that, on his own admission, his *Enquiry* should have been burned. For it hardly meets his requirements for a book to escape the flames.

3. Friedrich Waismann, 'Logische Analyse des Wahrscheinlich-keitsbegriffs', *Erkenntnis*, 1 (1930–1).

4. A. J. Ayer (ed.), *Logical Positivism* (Glencoe, Ill., 1959), 63.

5. A. J. Ayer, *Language, Truth and Logic* (2nd edn., London, 1946), 115. 1st edn., 1936. References here are to the 2nd edn.

6. Antony Flew, 'Theology and Falsification', reprinted in Basil Mitchell (ed.), *The Philosophy of Religion* (London, 1971).

7. Flew's 'parable' derives from John Wisdom's 'Gods', to be found in John Wisdom, *Logic and Language*, vol. 1 (Oxford, 1951), and *idem*, *Philosophy and Psychoanalysis* (Oxford, 1953).

8. Mitchell (ed.), *Philosophy of Religion*, 13.

9. Ibid. 21.

10. Moritz Schlick, 'Meaning and Verification', reprinted in Herbert Feigl and Wilfrid Sellars (eds.), *Readings in Philosophical Analysis* (New York, 1949).

11. Richard Swinburne, *The Coherence of Theism* (Oxford, 1977), 27.

12. Ibid. 28.

13. For Church's discussion, see Alonzo Church, review of Ayer, *Language, Truth and Logic* (2nd edn.), *Journal of Symbolic Logic*, 14 (1949), 52 ff. For Ayer's admission, see his *The Central Questions of Philosophy* (London, 1973).

14. Karl Barth, *Church Dogmatics* (Edinburgh, 1960), vol. 1, pt. 1, 448 ff.

15. For the statement of a view similar to that of Phillips, see D. C.

Barrett, 'Faith and Rationality', in A. Phillips Griffiths (ed.), *Key Themes in Philosophy* (Cambridge, 1989).

16. Ludwig Wittgenstein, *Philosophical Investigations*, trans. G. E. M. Anscombe (Oxford, 1968), paras. 123–4.

17. Ibid., para. 664.

18. D. Z. Phillips, *The Concept of Prayer* (London, 1965), 1 ff.

19. Ibid. 67 ff.

20. Ibid. 81.

21. D. Z. Phillips, *Religion without Explanation* (Oxford, 1976), 174.

22. Ibid. 181.

23. Antony Flew, *The Presumption of Atheism* (London, 1976), ch. 1. For a similar viewpoint, see W. K. Clifford, 'The Ethics of Belief', in W. K. Clifford, *Lectures and Essays* (London, 1879), and J. L. Mackie, *The Miracle of Theism* (Oxford, 1982), 4.

24. Isaiah 46: 5. All quotations of Scripture are taken from the RSV.

25. Psalms 50: 21.

26. Cf. Thomas Aquinas, *Summa Theologiae*, Ia, 2, 3. This way of talking can also be found in writers such as St Augustine (345–430) and Anselm. In the twentieth century it has been much employed by Paul Tillich. Cf. also Gareth Moore, *Believing in God* (Edinburgh, 1989).

27. Elizabeth Anscombe, 'What is it to Believe Someone?', in C. F. Delaney (ed.), *Rationality and Religious Belief* (Notre Dame, Ind., and London, 1979).

28. Cf. Ludwig Wittgenstein, *On Certainty*, ed. G. E. M. Anscombe and G. H. von Wright, trans. Denis Paul and G. E. M. Anscombe (Oxford, 1974), paras. 160–7. See also Norman Malcolm, 'The Groundlessness of Belief', in Stuart C. Brown (ed.), *Reason and Religion* (Ithaca, NY, and London, 1977).

29. These defensive moves are actually made by Plantinga. See Alvin Plantinga, 'Reason and Belief in God', in Alvin Plantinga and Nicholas Wolterstorff, *Faith and Rationality* (Notre Dame, Ind., 1985). See also *idem*, 'Is Belief in God Rational?', in Delaney (ed.), *Rationality and Religious Belief*.

30. Phillips has been especially badly served by critics, for his position (what he actually wants to say) has been much misrepresented in the literature. For an attempt by Phillips to clarify matters, see the Appendix to 'Belief, Change, and Forms of Life: The Confusions of Externalism and Internalism', in Frederick J. Crosson (ed.), *The Autonomy of Religious Belief* (Notre Dame, Ind., and London, 1981), 85 ff.

31. Romans 1: 19–21.
32. Vatican I, *Dogmatic Constitution on the Catholic Faith*, ch. 2. See Norman P. Tanner, SJ (ed.), *Decrees of the Ecumenical Councils* (London and Washington, 1990), ii. 806.
33. Aquinas, *Summa Theologiae*, Ia2ae, 67, 3.
34. Cf. Plantinga, 'Is Belief in God Rational', 78 ff.

Chapter 2. Talking about God

1. Moses Maimonides, *The Guide for the Perplexed*, trans. M. Friedlander (London, 1936), 86 ff. Other famous exponents of speaking of God by means of negation include Dionysius the Areopagite (*c.* 5th century AD) and John Scotus Eriugena (AD *c.*810–*c.*877). For Dionysius see *Pseudo-Dionysius: The Complete Works*, trans. Colm Luibheid and Paul Rorem (London and Mahwah, NJ, 1987). For Eriugena see *Periphyseon (De Divisione Naturae)*, ed. I. P. Sheldon Williams (Dublin, 1978).
2. Aquinas, *Summa Theologiae*, Ia, 13, 5.
3. Ibid.
4. See David Hume, *A Treatise of Human Nature*, ed. L. A. Selby-Bigge (2nd edn., Oxford, 1978), and *idem, Enquiry*.
5. See Appendix 2 to Volume 3 of the Blackfriars edition of the *Summa Theologiae*, ed. Herbert McCabe, OP (London, 1964), 102.
6. Notice that Aquinas's distinction between univocal, equivocal, and analogical is a distinction between *literal* modes of discourse. To say that we speak of God analogically is not, for Aquinas, to say that we speak of him figuratively.
7. Aquinas, *Summa Theologiae*, Ia, 13, 5.
8. Ibid., Ia, 13, 2.
9. Wittgenstein, *Philosophical Investigations*, para. 66.
10. Patrick Sherry, 'Analogy Today', *Philosophy*, 51 (1976), 445.
11. Peter Geach, *Reason and Argument* (Oxford, 1976), 39.

Chapter 3. God and Evil

1. H. J. McClosky, 'God and Evil', *Philosophical Quarterly*, 10 (1960), 97.
2. Mary Baker Eddy, *Science and Health with Key to the Scriptures* (Boston, 1971), 257.

3. Richard Swinburne, *The Existence of God* (Oxford, 1979; rev. edn., 1991), 210 ff.

4. Ibid. For development of this position by Swinburne see his 'Knowledge from Experience, and the Problem of Evil', in William J. Abraham and Steven W. Holtzer (eds.), *The Rationality of Religious Belief* (Oxford, 1987).

5. John Hick, *Evil and the God of Love* (2nd edn., London, 1977), 372 ff.

6. See Augustine, *The City of God*, book 2.

7. C. S. Lewis, *The Problem of Pain* (London, 1940), 122 ff.

8. Alvin Plantinga, *God, Freedom and Evil* (London, 1975), 58. In speaking of non-human agency as he does, Plantinga is not asking us to believe that there are non-human agents responsible for evil. He is asking us to note a possible explanation for certain kinds of evil. As Plantinga puts it, he is concerned to offer a 'defence' rather than a 'theodicy'. See ibid. 28.

9. Peter Geach, *Logic Matters* (Oxford, 1972), 305.

10. Job 9: 22–3; Luke 13: 2–3; John 9: 3.

11. Phillips, *Concept of Prayer*, 93.

12. Dostoevsky, *The Brothers Karamazov*, trans. Constance Garnett (London, 1950), vol. 1, pt. 2, book 5, ch. 4, 250.

13. A similar line is pressed by Kenneth Surin in *Theology and the Problem of Evil* (Oxford, 1986), 80 ff.

14. Wittgenstein, 'A Lecture on Ethics', *Philosophical Review*, 74 (1965).

15. In Brown (ed.), *Reason and Religion*, 115.

16. Herbert McCabe, O.P., *God Matters* (London, 1987), 31. Cf. Aquinas, *Summa Theologiae*, Ia, 22, 2.

17. William L. Rowe, 'The Problem of Evil and Some Varieties of Atheism', *American Philosophical Quarterly*, 16 (1979), reprinted in Marilyn McCord Adams and Robert Merrihew Adams (eds.), *The Problem of Evil* (Oxford, 1990).

18. Cf. Stephen J. Wykstra, 'The Humean Obstacle to Evidential Arguments from Suffering: On Avoiding the Evils of "Appearance"', *International Journal for Philosophy of Religion*, 16 (1979), reprinted in Adams and Adams (eds.), *Problem of Evil*.

19. J. L. Mackie, 'Evil and Omnipotence', *Mind*, 64 (1955), reprinted in Adams and Adams (eds.), *Problem of Evil*, 33.

20. Flew, *Presumption of Atheism*, 88.

21. John Lucas, *The Future* (Oxford, 1989), 229.

22. Aquinas, *Summa contra Gentiles*, III, 67.

23. McCabe, *God Matters*, 14.
24. Ibid. 15. For the same view, see James F. Ross, 'Creation II', in Alfred J. Freddoso (ed.), *The Existence and Nature of God* (Notre Dame, Ind., and London, 1983), and Germain Grisez, *Beyond the New Theism* (Notre Dame, Ind., and London, 1975), ch. 18.
25. McCabe, *God Matters*, 36.
26. C. J. F. Williams, 'Knowing Good and Evil', *Philosophy*, 66 (1991), 238.
27. Cf. Swinburne, *Coherence of Theism*, ch. 11.
28. Cf. Walter Eichrodt, *Theology of the Old Testament*, vol. 1 (London, 1961), 240.

Chapter 4. The Ontological Argument

1. Echoes of Anselm's definition can be found in St Augustine (cf. *De Doctrina Christiana* I, vii). But the nearest verbal parallel to Anselm's formula comes in Seneca, who says that God's 'magnitude is that than which nothing greater can be thought'. Cf. *L. Annaei Senecae Naturalium Questionum libri viii*, ed. Alfred Gercke (Stuttgart, 1907), 5. In the *Proslogion* and elsewhere Anselm speaks not only of *aliquid quo nihil maius cogitari possit* but of *id quo maius cogitari nequit/non potest/non possit*, *aliquid quo maius cogitari non valet/potest/possit*, and *id quo maius cogitari non potest*. But the variations can hardly be significant.
2. Cf. R. W. Southern, *Saint Anselm: A Portrait in a Landscape* (Cambridge, 1991), 130: 'If this argument [sc. *Proslogion* 2] is sound, we can go a step further. The argument has forced an intelligent listener to agree that God exists both in the mind and outside the mind. But many other things exist both in the mind and outside the mind: for instance, the pen I am holding exists both in my mind and outside my mind. It exists *in re* and *in mente*; but it does not *necessarily* exist *in re* because it exists *in mente*.'
3. That different purposes underlie *Proslogion* 2 and *Proslogion* 3 is argued by D. P. Henry, *Medieval Logic and Metaphysics* (London, 1972), 105 ff.
4. René Descartes, *Meditations on First Philosophy*, trans. John Cottingham (Cambridge, 1986), 46 ff.
5. Norman Malcolm, 'Anselm's Ontological Arguments', *Phil-*

osophical Review, 69 (1960), reprinted in John Hick (ed.), *The Existence of God* (London and New York, 1964).

6. Hick (ed.), *Existence of God*, 56.

7. See Robert C. Stalnaker, 'Possible Worlds', in Ted Honderich and Myles Burnyeat (eds.), *Philosophy as it Is* (London, 1979).

8. Alvin Plantinga, *The Nature of Necessity* (Oxford, 1974), 213.

9. Ibid. 214.

10. Gaunilo's reply is entitled *Quid Ad Haec Respondeat Quidam Pro Insipiente*.

11. *St Anselm's Proslogion*, trans. M. J. Charlesworth (Oxford, 1965; Notre Dame, Ind., 1979), 163 ff.

12. Indeed, Anselm himself offers the reply in a response to Gaunilo called *Quid Ad Haec Respondeat Editor Ipsius Libelli*.

13. Plantinga, *God, Freedom and Evil*, 91.

14. Immanuel Kant, *Critique of Pure Reason*, trans. Norman Kemp Smith (London, 1964), 502 ff.

15. Ibid. 504 ff.

16. W. V. O. Quine speaks in this connection of the 'tangled doctrine [which] might be nicknamed *Plato's Beard*' ('On What There Is', in W. V. O. Quine, *From a Logical Point of View* (Cambridge, Mass., and London; 2nd edn., 1961), 2).

17. 'Faithful husbands exist' might be thought to state that there are several faithful husbands, whereas 'Someone is a faithful husband' does not. To avoid this difficulty we can say that 'A faithful husband exists' is equivalent to 'Someone is a faithful husband' or that 'Faithful husbands exist' is equivalent to 'Some people are faithful husbands'. My point is just that the work done by 'exist' in 'Faithful husbands exist' is work done by 'Some' in either 'Someone is a faithful husband' or 'Some persons are faithful husbands'.

18. Cf. Bertrand Russell, *Logic and Knowledge* (London and New York, 1956), 234: 'You sometimes know the truth of an existence-proposition without knowing any instance of it. You know that there are people in Timbuctoo, but I doubt if any of you could give me an instance of one. Therefore you clearly can know existence-propositions without knowing any individual that makes them true. Existence-propositions do not say anything about the actual individual but only about the class or function.'

19. Gottlob Frege, *The Foundations of Arithmetic*, trans. J. L. Austin (Oxford, 1980), 59.

20. Ibid. 65.

21. C. J. F. Williams, *What is Existence?* (Oxford, 1981), 54 ff.

22. John Hick, 'A Critique of the "Second Argument"', in John Hick and Arthur McGill (eds.), *The Many Faced Argument* (London, 1967), 353 ff.

23. Aquinas, *Summa Theologiae*, Ia, 2, 1.

24. For a critical discussion of Plantinga's argument see Peter van Inwagen, 'Ontological Arguments', *Nous*, 11 (1977).

Chapter 5. The Cosmological Argument

1. William Lane Craig, *The Kalām Cosmological Argument* (London, 1979), 149 ff.

2. *Thomas Reid's Inquiry and Essays*, ed. Ronald E. Beanblossom and Keith Lehrer (Indianapolis, 1983), 330.

3. Hume, *A Treatise*, 79 ff.

4. F. C. Copleston, *A History of Philosophy*, vol. 5 (London, 1959), 287.

5. Elizabeth Anscombe, '"Whatever has a Beginning of Existence must have a Cause": Hume's Argument Exposed', *Analysis*, 34 (1974), 150. This paper is reprinted in G. E. M. Anscombe, *Collected Philosophical Papers* (Oxford, 1981), vol. 1.

6. Anscombe, *Collected Philosophical Papers*, ii. 62.

7. *The Letters of David Hume*, ed. J. Y. T. Greig (Oxford, 1932), i. 187; emphasis original.

8. C. D. Broad, 'Kant's Mathematical Antinomies', *Proceedings of the Aristotelian Society*, 40 (1955), 10.

9. Richard Swinburne, *Space and Time* (2nd edn., London, 1981), 258. Cf. Mackie, *Miracle of Theism*, 93.

10. Classical authors famous for maintaining that there are good philosophical arguments for the view that the universe had a beginning include Al-Ghazali (b. 1058/9), the sixth-century writer John Philoponus, and St Bonaventure (c.1217–74). A philosophically lively discussion of ancient and medieval authors on the beginning of the world can be found in Richard Sorabji, *Time, Creation and the Continuum* (London, 1983), chs. 13–17.

11. For an expression of this argument, see William Charlton, *Philosophy and Christian Belief* (London, 1988), ch. 2. For recent defence of the argument, see William Lane Craig, 'Time and Infinity', *International Philosophical Quarterly*, 31 (1991).

12. See Aquinas, *Summa Theologiae*, Ia, 46, 1, and *idem*, *De Aeternitate Mundi*.

13. G. W. Leibniz, *On the Ultimate Origination of Things*, in G. H. R. Parkinson (ed.), *Leibniz: Philosophical Writings* (London and Toronto, 1973), 137.

14. Aristotle presents an argument like that of Aquinas in *Physics*, VII. Aquinas acknowledges his debt to Aristotle's argument in his *Summa contra Gentiles*, where he offers a longer version of what appears in the *Summa Theologiae* as the First Way.

15. In Aquinas's Latin, the subject of the First Way is *motus*. This is sometimes translated 'movement' or 'motion'. But 'change' is perhaps the best English equivalent. For, as Aquinas understands it, *motus* covers what we should normally call change of quality, change of quantity, and change of place.

16. Aquinas calls the First Way 'the most obvious' (*manifestior*) proof. That, I presume, is chiefly because what he calls *motus* is something which impinges on us all the time. Maimonides and Averroës (1126–98) are two other medieval authors who thought that the truth of the reasoning which surfaces in the First Way is particularly evident. Cf. Maimonides, *Guide for the Perplexed*, 149 ff. and Averroës, *Epitome of Metaphysics*, IV.

17. Cf. Patterson Brown, 'St Thomas' Doctrine of Necessary Being', in Anthony Kenny (ed.), *Aquinas: A Collection of Critical Essays* (London and Melbourne, 1969).

18. There is a textual problem concerning the Third Way which my brief account of it bypasses. For a discussion of the issues and for a treatment of different interpretations of the Third Way see Fernand Van Steenberghen, *Le Problème de l'existence de Dieu dans les Ecrits de S. Thomas d'Aquin* (Louvain-La-Neuve, 1980), 188–201, and William Lane Craig, *The Cosmological Argument from Plato to Leibniz* (London, 1980), 182–94.

19. Anthony Kenny, *The Five Ways* (London, 1969), 28.

20. Ibid. 21.

21. Ibid. 22 ff.

22. Ibid. 43 ff.

23. 'A Debate on the Existence of God', reprinted in Hick (ed.), *Existence of God*, 167–91.

24. John Hick, *Philosophy of Religion* (2nd edn., Englewood Cliffs, NJ, 1973), 21.

25. Cf. P. T. Geach, review of Kenny, *The Five Ways*, *Philosophical Quarterly*, 20 (1970), 311–12.

26. See Aquinas, *Summa Theologiae*, Ia, 3, 1.

27. Christopher Martin (ed.), *The Philosophy of Thomas Aquinas* (London and New York, 1988), 61.

28. Norman Kemp Smith (ed.), *Hume's Dialogues concerning Natural Religion* (London, 1947), 190 ff.

29. Kai Neilsen, *Reason and Practice* (New York, 1971), 171. Cf. Paul Edwards, 'The Cosmological Argument', in Paul Angeles (ed.), *Critiques of God* (Buffalo, 1976), 48 ff.

30. James Sadowsky, 'The Cosmological Argument and the Endless Regress', *International Philosophical Quarterly*, 20 (1980), 465 ff. For a classical philosopher making the same point neatly, see Leibniz, *Ultimate Origination*.

31. Sadowsky's example about asking for permission reminds me of a story I recently read in a newspaper. A Somerset farmer who kept ferrets found that all his ferrets had vanished. He concluded that they must have eaten each other.

32. Hume, *Enquiry*, 63.

33. G. E. M. Anscombe and P. T. Geach, *Three Philosophers* (Oxford, 1961), 112.

34. David Braine, *The Reality of Time and the Existence of God* (Oxford, 1988), 10.

Chapter 6. The Argument from Design

1. Cicero, *The Nature of the Gods*, trans. Horace C. P. McGregor (Harmondsworth, 1972), 124.

2. *The Works of William Paley*, vol. 4: *Natural Theology* (Oxford, 1838), 1.

3. Ibid. 2.

4. Swinburne, *Existence of God*, 136.

5. Ibid. 138 ff.

6. Thomas McPherson, *The Argument from Design* (London, 1972), 20.

7. Hume, *Enquiry concerning Human Understanding*, 136.

8. Smith (ed.), *Hume's Dialogues*, 149.

9. Ibid. 149 ff.

10. Ibid. 160.

11. Ibid. 161 ff.

12. Ibid. 164.

13. Ibid. 168.

14. Ibid. 167.

15. Ibid. 163.

16. Richard Swinburne, 'The Argument from Design', *Philosophy*, 43 (1968), 205.

17. Ibid. 209.

18. Smith (ed.), *Hume's Dialogues*, 168.
19. Swinburne, 'Argument from Design', 211.
20. Cf. Robert Hambourger, 'The Argument from Design', in Cora Diamond and Jenny Teichman (eds.), *Intention and Intentionality* (Brighton, 1979), 112.
21. For a neat anticipation of Darwin's theory of natural selection, see Aquinas's commentary on Book 2 of Aristotle's *Physics*, §243.
22. Kenny, *Five Ways*, 118.
23. Peter Geach, 'An Irrelevance of Omnipotence', *Philosophy*, 48 (1973), 330.
24. Anthony Kenny, *Reason and Religion* (Oxford, 1987), 82.
25. Not everyone has believed this, of course. The Aztecs thought that every so often a crisis came and that thereafter the unexpected was to be expected—hence the impact on them of the arrival of the Spaniards with their weapons.
26. Cf. Swinburne, *Existence of God*, 136 and 138.
27. Ralph Walker, *Kant* (London, 1978), 171.
28. Swinburne, *Existence of God*, 138.
29. Ibid.
30. Peter Geach, *Providence and Evil* (Cambridge, 1977), 74.

Chapter 7. Experience and God

1. Bertrand Russell, *Religion and Science* (London, 1935), 188.
2. H. D. Lewis, *The Philosophy of Religion* (London, 1965), 144; cf. H. D. Lewis, *Our Experience of God* (London, 1970), 193 ff.
3. Lewis, *Our Experience of God*, 45.
4. Lewis, *Philosophy of Religion*, 144.
5. H. P. Owen, *The Christian Knowledge of God* (London, 1969), 307.
6. Aquinas, *Summa Theologiae*, Ia, 12, 1.
7. A. E. Peers (ed.), *The Complete Works of Saint John of the Cross* (London, 1943), 96.
8. Ibid. 74.
9. Wittgenstein, *Philosophical Investigations*, 193 ff.
10. John Hick, 'Religious Faith as Experience-As', in G. N. A. Vesey (ed.), *Talk of God* (London, 1969), 22 ff.
11. Ibid. 23, 26, 27.

Chapter 8. Eternity

1. Boethius, *The Consolation of Philosophy*, V, 6.
2. Anselm, *Proslogion*, ch. 19.
3. Swinburne, *Coherence of Theism*, 221.
4. In traditional theological language, Swinburne's view is that God is *sempiternal*. But I shall not employ this term here because it is not much used now, and because those who believe that God is sempiternal regularly express themselves by saying that God is eternal.
5. J. R. Lucas, *A Treatise on Space and Time* (London, 1973), 200.
6. Grace Jantzen, in Alan Richardson and John Bowden (eds.), *A New Dictionary of Christian Theology* (London, 1983), 573.
7. Swinburne, *Coherence of Theism*, 221.
8. Nelson Pike, *God and Timelessness* (London, 1970), 106.
9. Ibid. 107.
10. Cf. Aquinas, *Summa Theologiae*, Ia, 18, 3.
11. My language suggests otherwise, but readers should not suppose that I am taking times to be a species of object, things which one can single out and ascribe properties to.
12. Jon Sobrino, *Christianity at the Crossroads* (London, 1978), 197. Sobrino is quoting from Jürgen Moltmann, *The Crucified God* (London, 1974).
13. Aquinas, *Summa Theologiae*, Ia, 20, 2.
14. Ibid., Ia, 19, 3 ad 1.
15. Lucas, *The Future*, 214.
16. Ibid. 215.
17. Swinburne, *Coherence of Theism*, 214 ff.
18. John L. McKenzie, *Dictionary of the Bible* (London, 1975), 247 ff.
19. G. Kittel (ed.), *Theological Dictionary of the New Testament* (Grand Rapids, Mich., 1965), 202.
20. Aquinas, *Summa contra Gentiles*, III, 96.
21. For St Thomas on Scripture and the interpretation of it see Thomas Gilby, OP, 'The Summa and the Bible', Appendix 11 to Volume 1 of the Blackfriars edition of *Summa Theologiae* (London, 1964).
22. Anthony Kenny, *The God of the Philosophers* (Oxford, 1979), 38 ff. The same argument is used by Kenny in 'Divine Foreknowledge and Human Freedom', in Kenny (ed.), *Aquinas: A Collection of Critical Essays*.

23. Aquinas, *Commentary on Aristotle's Peri Hermeneias*, book 1, lectio 14.
24. Paul Helm, *Eternal God* (Oxford, 1988), 27.
25. Ibid.
26. Cf. P. T. Geach, 'Some Problems about Time', in *Logic Matters*, 311 ff.
27. Cf. P. T. Geach, 'What Actually Exists', in *God and the Soul* (London, 1969), 66 ff.
28. Cf. P. T. Geach, 'God's Relation to the World', in *Logic Matters*, 322.
29. Swinburne, *Coherence of Theism*, 211.
30. Ibid.
31. Cf. C. J. F. Williams, *Being, Identity and Truth* (Oxford, 1992), chs. 6 and 8; also Geach, *Logic Matters*, 308 ff.
32. Helm, *Eternal God*, 37 ff.
33. Cf. Brian Leftow, *Time and Eternity* (Ithaca, NY, and London), 267 ff.
34. I should stress that 'unchangeable' here means 'unchangeable in himself'. One might say that a thing has changed if, for example, someone starts thinking of it (one might say 'It used not to be thought of and it has come to be thought of'). But this is not a change in the thing itself, and those who hold that God is unchangeable are saying that God can undergo no change in himself.
35. See Sorabji, *Time, Creation and the Continuum*, 83.
36. Newton, *Principia Mathematica* (1686), scholium to Definition 8.
37. Aristotle, *Physics*, 218b21 ff.
38. Ibid. 218b9–20. I quote from *Aristotle's Physics, Books III and IV*, trans. with notes by Edward Hussey (Oxford, 1983), 42–4.
39. Swinburne, *Space and Time*, 172.
40. Ibid. 174.
41. e.g. Helm, *Eternal God*, 36.
42. Versions of this argument are offered by Leftow, *Time and Eternity*, 270 and 278 ff.
43. Sorabji, *Time, Creation and the Continuum*, 255.
44. William Lane Craig, *The Only Wise God* (Grand Rapids, Mich., 1987), 70 ff. Cf. Craig's review of Sorabji, *Time, Creation and the Continuum*, *International Philosophical Quarterly*, 25 (1985), 319–26.
45. Boethius, *Consolation of Philosophy*, book 5. Cf. Aquinas, *Commentary on Aristotle's Peri Hermeneias*, book 1, lectio 14.

Chapter 9. Morality and Religion

1. Kant, *Critique of Practical Reason*, trans. Thomas Kingsmill Abbott (London, New York, and Toronto, 1909), 34.
2. Ibid. 115.
3. Ibid. 129 ff.
4. H. P. Owen, *The Moral Argument for Christian Theism* (London, 1965), 49 ff.
5. J. H. Newman, *A Grammar of Assent*, ed. C. F. Harold (London and New York, 1947), 83.
6. See Dom Illtyd Trethowan, *Absolute Value* (London, 1970), and *idem*, *Mysticism and Theology* (London, 1974).
7. Trethowan, *Absolute Value*, 84 ff.; emphasis original.
8. Ibid. 89.
9. James Rachels, 'God and Human Attitudes', *Religious Studies*, 7 (1971), 334.
10. Such a line is advanced by Rousseau (1712–78) in *The Social Contract* (1762).
11. Lucretius, *De Rerum Natura*, I, 101.
12. Bertrand Russell, *Why I am not a Christian* (London, 1927), 37.
13. Søren Kierkegaard, *Fear and Trembling*, trans. Robert Payne (London, New York, and Toronto, 1939), 84 ff.
14. D. Z. Phillips, 'God and Ought', in Ian Ramsey (ed.), *Christian Ethics and Contemporary Philosophy* (London, 1966), 137 ff.
15. Cf. Elizabeth Anscombe, 'Modern Moral Philosophy', *Philosophy*, 33 (1958). Here Anscombe suggests that a law conception of ethics derives from Jewish and Christian views about God as the giver of law.
16. Illtyd Trethowan, *The Basis of Belief* (London, 1960), 117.
17. Peter Geach, 'The Moral Law and the Law of God', in Geach, *God and the Soul*, 121.
18. If God is creator and sustainer of the universe, however, it is by virtue of his will that all sorts of vicious actions happen. For this reason, we might decline to say that God always wills what is morally obligatory.
19. Kant, *Foundations of the Metaphysics of Morals*, trans. Lewis White Beck, ed. Robert Paul Wolff (Indianapolis, 1969), 19.
20. Peter Geach, *The Virtues* (Cambridge, 1977), 151 ff.
21. For a classical attempt to show how moral judgements can be defended without reference to theism see Aristotle's *Ethics*. For recent attempts see Philippa Foot, *Virtues and Vices* (Oxford,

1978); Alasdair MacIntyre, *After Virtue* (2nd edn., Notre Dame, Ind., 1984); and *idem*, *Whose Justice? Which Rationality?* (London, 1988).

22. Philip L. Quinn, *Divine Commands and Moral Requirements* (Oxford, 1978), 6 ff.

23. Rachels, 'God and Human Attitudes', 334.

24. Ninian Smart, *The Phenomenon of Religion* (London and Oxford, 1978), 10.

25. William P. Alston, 'Religion', in Paul Edwards (ed.), *The Encyclopedia of Philosophy*, vol. 7 (New York and London, 1967).

26. Mary Midgley, *Wickedness* (London, 1984), 6.

27. Ibid.

Chapter 10. Miracle

1. Hume, *Enquiry*, p. 115.

2. Richard Swinburne, 'Miracles', *Philosophical Quarterly*, 18 (1968), reprinted in William L. Rowe and William J. Wainwright (eds.), *Philosophy of Religion: Selected Readings* (2nd edn., New York and London, 1973).

3. Mackie, *Miracle of Theism*, 19 ff.

4. *Summa contra Gentiles*, III, 101, 2–4.

5. Cf. Isaiah 38: 7 ff. and Joshua 10: 12–14.

6. R. F. Holland, 'The Miraculous', in D. Z. Phillips (ed.), *Religion and Understanding* (Oxford, 1967), reprinted in Richard Swinburne (ed.), *Miracles* (New York and London, 1989).

7. Swinburne (ed.), *Miracles*, 53 ff.

8. Holland is evidently thinking of the mother in the story as viewing the deliverance of her child as something consonant with the Christian belief that God can deliver people in difficulty. So my comments might not apply to his notion of miracle as coincidence.

9. Swinburne (ed.), *Miracles*, 6.

10. See R. M. Burns, *The Great Debate on Miracles: From Joseph Glanville to David Hume* (London and Toronto, 1981), 70 ff.

11. Alvin Plantinga, 'Is Theism Really a Miracle?', *Faith and Philosophy*, 3 (1986), 111.

12. One might prefer to speak in this connection of 'exceptions' rather than 'violations'; for to call miracles 'violations' of natural law might be taken to imply that when a miracle occurs, some

natural law ceases to operate throughout the world. Cf. Richard
L. Purtill, 'Miracles: What if they Happened?', in Swinburne
(ed.), *Miracles*, 194 ff.

13. Samuel M. Thompson, *A Modern Philosophy of Religion*
(Chicago, 1955), 454 ff.

14. R. H. Fuller, *Interpreting the Miracles* (London, 1966), 8 ff.

15. Swinburne (ed.), *Miracles*, 84.

16. John 9: 32 ff.

17. J. C. A. Gaskin, *The Quest for Eternity* (Harmondsworth, 1984),
137, offers a nice definition of 'miracle' which seems to take
account of much of the diversity to which I have referred:
'*Miracle*: an event of religious significance, brought about by God
or a god or by some other visible or invisible rational agent with
sufficient power, *either* in violation of the laws of nature (the
'violation concept') *or* as a striking coincidence within the laws of
nature (the "coincidence concept").'

18. Notice, however, that all the points about miracles argued by
Hume can be found in the work of writers working before the
publication of 'Of Miracles'. This fact is ably demonstrated by
Burns, *Great Debate*.

19. Hume, *Enquiry*, 125.

20. Ibid. 128.

21. Ibid. 127.

22. Ibid. 114 ff.

23. Ibid. 115 ff.

24. Mackie, *Miracle of Theism*, 25 ff.

25. Hume, *Enquiry*, 115.

26. For an earlier statement of this argument, see Thomas Sherlock,
The Trial of the Witnesses of the Resurrection (1st edn., 1729, 8th
edn., London, 1736), 58.

27. Burns, *Great Debate*, 143.

28. Hume, *Enquiry*, 115.

29. Cf. J. C. A. Gaskin, *Hume's Philosophy of Religion* (2nd edn.,
London, 1988), 163 ff.

30. C. D. Broad, 'Hume's Theory of the Credibility of Miracles',
Proceedings of the Aristotelian Society, 17 (1916–17), 77–94.

31. Hume, *Enquiry*, 116.

32. Ibid. 116 ff.

33. Ibid. 117.

34. Ibid. 117 ff.

35. Ibid. 118.

36. Ibid.
37. Ibid. 119.
38. Ibid. 121 ff.
39. Cf. Swinburne (ed.), *Miracles*, 134 ff.
40. Richard Swinburne, *The Concept of Miracle* (London, 1970), 60.
41. Gaskin, *Hume's Philosophy of Religion*, 142.
42. Sherlock, *Trial of the Witnesses*, 58 ff.
43. Plantinga, 'Is Theism Really a Miracle?', 112 ff.
44. Swinburne, *Concept of Miracle*, 57.
45. Aquinas, *Summa Theologiae*, Ia, 110, 4.
46. Pope Benedict XIV, *De Servorum Dei Beatificatione et Beatorum Canonizatione, iv: de Miraculis* (1738).
47. Samuel Clarke, *1705 Boyle Lectures* (7th edn., London, 1727), i. 383.
48. Tanner (ed.), *Decrees of the Ecumenical Councils*, ii. 810. I am told, however, that 'proved' in this text need mean no more than 'supported by reason'. From *his* use of 'proved', Clarke too seems to be saying that the miracles of Christianity are less than one might expect. See *1705 Boyle Lectures*, i. 156.
49. Mark 13: 22 ff.
50. Matthew 4: 6; 12: 38–41; Mark 8: 11–13; 15: 31–2; Luke 4: 23.

Chapter 11. Life after Death

1. David Gallop (ed.), *Plato's Phaedo* (Oxford, 1975), 69 ff.
2. Descartes, *Meditation* VI, 54.
3. Geach, *God and the Soul*, 29.
4. Lewis, *Philosophy of Religion*, 286.
5. Ibid. 282. Cf. H. D. Lewis, *The Self and Immortality* (London, 1973), 62 and 68.
6. Sydney Shoemaker and Richard Swinburne, *Personal Identity* (Oxford, 1984), 23 ff.
7. Descartes, *Meditation* VI, 59.
8. Norman Malcolm, 'Descartes's Proof that his Essence is Thinking', in Willis Doney (ed.), *Descartes* (London and Melbourne, 1968), 329.
9. Gilbert Ryle, *The Concept of Mind* (London, 1949).
10. Geach, *God and the Soul*, 29.
11. Cf. C. V. Borst (ed.), *The Mind/Brain Identity Thesis* (London, 1970).
12. John Hick, *Death and Eternal Life* (London, 1979), 280.

13. Ibid. 284.

14. Ibid.

15. John Locke, *An Essay concerning Human Understanding*, ed. Peter H. Nidditch (Oxford, 1975), book 2, ch. 27.

16. Joseph Butler, 'Of Personal Identity', Appendix to *The Analogy of Religion* (Oxford, 1897).

17. Thomas Reid, *Essays on the Intellectual Powers of Man* (Edinburgh, 1785), essay 6, ch. 5.

18. Hick, *Philosophy of Religion*, 128.

19. *Phaedo* 69e6–72e1. Translation and commentary in Gallop (ed.), *Plato's Phaedo*.

20. Gallop (ed.), *Plato's Phaedo*, 17 ff.

21. Ibid. 19.

22. Ibid. 105 ff.

23. For more detailed discussion of Plato's arguments see David Bostock, *Plato's Phaedo* (Oxford, 1986), 42 ff.

24. Kant, *Critique of Practical Reason*, 218 ff.

25. Joseph Prabhu, 'The Idea of Reincarnation', in Steven T. Davis (ed.), *Death and Afterlife* (London, 1989), 66.

26. Christians sometimes say that belief in human immortality is an item of faith. But this is debatable. To call something immortal is to say that it is intrinsically beyond death. In the New Testament, however, it is said that God alone possesses immortality (1 Timothy 6: 16). In 1 Corinthians 15: 53–4 it is said that people get clothed in immortality. But there is no suggestion that there is anything in people which is innately immortal.

27. Miguel de Unamuno, *The Tragic Sense of Life* (London, 1962), 28.

28. Ibid. 60.

29. H. D. Lewis, *Persons and Life After Death* (London, 1978), 53 ff.

30. Ibid. 69 and 72.

Bibliography

Many of the works referred to in the notes to this book provide important reading matter for anyone interested in pursuing the philosophy of religion. This bibliography is mainly confined to useful material not so far mentioned.

Beginners in the philosophy of religion will benefit from introductory works on philosophy and/or the history of philosophy. Particularly helpful are A. J. Ayer, *The Central Questions of Philosophy* (London, 1973); William Charlton, *The Analytic Ambition* (Oxford, 1991); F. C. Copleston, *A History of Philosophy* (9 vols., London, 1946–74); John Hospers, *An Introduction to Philosophical Analysis* (3rd edn., London, 1990); D. J. O'Connor (ed.), *A Critical History of Western Philosophy* (London, 1964); Anthony O'Hear, *What Philosophy Is* (Harmondsworth, 1985); Bertrand Russell, *The Problems of Philosophy* (Oxford, 1967); Jenny Teichman and Katherine C. Evans, *Philosophy: A Beginner's Guide* (Oxford, 1991). A good introduction to the writers commonly considered historically important for the philosophy of religion is M. J. Charlesworth, *Philosophy of Religion: The Historic Approaches* (London, 1972).

Helpful general introductions to the philosophy of religion are William Abraham, *An Introduction to the Philosophy of Religion* (Englewood Cliffs, NJ, 1985); J. C. A. Gaskin, *The Quest for Eternity* (Harmondsworth, 1984); John Hick, *The Philosophy of Religion* (4th edn., Englewood Cliffs, NJ, 1990); H. D. Lewis, *The Philosophy of Religion* (London, 1965); Anthony O'Hear, *Experience, Explanation and Faith* (London, 1984); Michael Peterson, William Hasker, Bruce Reichenbach, and David Basinger, *Reason and Religious Belief: An Introduction to the Philosophy of Religion* (Oxford and New York, 1991); William L. Rowe, *Philosophy of Religion* (Encino and Belmont, Calif., 1978).

Useful readers in the philosophy of religion are Steven M. Cahn and David Shatz (eds.), *Contemporary Philosophy of Religion* (Oxford, 1982); Basil Mitchell (ed.), *The Philosophy of Religion* (Oxford, 1971); Thomas V. Morris (ed.), *The Concept of God* (Oxford, 1987); Louis P. Pojman (ed.), *Philosophy of Religion: An Anthology* (Belmont, Calif., 1987); William L. Rowe and William

J. Wainwright (eds.), *Philosophy of Religion: Selected Readings* (2nd edn., New York and London, 1973); Patrick Sherry (ed.), *Philosophers on Religion* (London, 1987).

For an introductory discussion of verificationism, falsificationism, and religious belief see Frederick Ferré, *Language, Logic and God* (London and Glasgow, 1970). For a more technical discussion see R. S. Heimbeck, *Theology and Meaning* (London, 1969). For an introduction to logical positivism see Oswald Hanfling, *Logical Positivism* (Oxford, 1981) and Oswald Hanfling (ed.), *Essential Readings in Logical Positivism* (Oxford, 1981). For a trenchant defence of an empirical critique of belief in God see Kai Neilsen, *Scepticism* (London, 1973) and *An Introduction to the Philosophy of Religion* (London, 1982). For subtle criticism of certain verificationist assumptions see W. V. Quine, 'Two Dogmas of Empiricism', in W. V. Quine, *From a Logical Point of View* (Cambridge, Mass., and London, 1953; 2nd edn., 1961). For an introduction to Karl Barth see John Bowden, *Karl Barth* (London, 1971); Alasdair Heron, *A Century of Protestant Theology* (Guildford and London, 1980); S. W. Sykes (ed.), *Karl Barth—Studies of his Theological Method* (Oxford, 1979). Writings by D. Z. Phillips not mentioned in the text include *Faith and Philosophical Enquiry* (London, 1970); *Faith after Foundationalism* (London and New York, 1988); *From Fantasy to Faith* (London, 1991). Writings by Alvin Plantinga not mentioned in the text include 'The Reformed Objection to Natural Theology', *Christian Scholar's Review*, 11 (1982) and 'Is Belief in God Properly Basic?', *Nous*, 15 (1981). For an authoritative account of Wittgenstein's views on religion see Cyril Barrett, *Wittgenstein on Ethics and Religious Belief* (Oxford, 1991).

For informative material on analogy and related matters see William P. Alston, *Divine Nature and Human Language* (Ithaca, NY, and London, 1989); David B. Burrell, *Aquinas, God and Action* (London and Henley, 1979); E. L. Mascall, *Existence and Analogy* (London, 1966); Humphrey Palmer, *Analogy* (London, 1973); Patrick Sherry, *Religion, Truth and Language-Games* (London, 1977). A complex modern treatment of analogy is J. F. Ross, *Portraying Analogy* (Cambridge, 1981). A good discussion of analogy in the context of helpful discussion of metaphor can be found in Janet Martin Soskice, *Metaphor and Religious Language* (Oxford, 1985).

A good selection of readings on the problem of evil can be found in Nelson Pike (ed.), *God and Evil: Readings on the Theological Problem of Evil* (London, 1971) and Marilyn McCord Adams and Robert Merrihew Adams (eds.), *The Problem of Evil* (Oxford, 1990).

254 *Bibliography*

Other works worth consulting are M. B. Ahern, *The Problem of Evil* (London, 1971); A. Farrer, *Love Almighty and Ills Unlimited* (London, 1961); Barry L. Whitney, *What are they Saying about God and Evil?* (New York and Mahwah, NJ, 1989). For a splendid account of one great thinker's attempts to deal with the problem of evil see G. R. Evans, *Augustine on Evil* (Cambridge, 1982).

For good surveys and discussions of the question of God's existence see Richard M. Gale, *On the Nature and Existence of God* (Cambridge, 1991); Hans Küng, *Does God Exist?* (London, 1980); J. L. Mackie, *The Miracle of Theism* (Oxford, 1982); Richard Swinburne, *The Existence of God* (Oxford, 1979; rev. edn., 1991). See also Herbert McCabe, *God Matters* (London, 1987) and Thomas V. Morris, *Our Idea of God* (Notre Dame and London, 1991). Swinburne has produced a short summary of his book in *Evidence for God* (Oxford, 1986) and 'Arguments for the Existence of God', in A. Phillips Griffiths (ed.), *Key Themes in Philosophy* (Cambridge, 1989).

For the ontological argument in Anselm see G. E. M. Anscombe, 'Why Anselm's Proof in the *Proslogion* is Not an Ontological Argument', *Thoreau Quarterly*, 17 (1985); G. R. Evans, *Anselm* (London, 1989); R. W. Southern, *Saint Anselm: A Portrait in a Landscape* (Cambridge, 1991). For a modern logical treatment of the argument see Jonathan Barnes, *The Ontological Argument* (London, 1972). An excellent reader on the ontological argument is John Hick and Arthur McGill (eds.), *The Many Faced Argument* (London, 1967). The notion of existence is crucial to the ontological argument. The most impressive modern treatment of the notion is C. J. F. Williams, *What is Existence?* (Oxford, 1981). See also C. J. F. Williams, *Being, Identity and Truth* (Oxford, 1992).

A good survey of the history of the cosmological argument is William Lane Craig, *The Cosmological Argument from Plato to Leibniz* (London, 1980). For discussion of some famous versions of the argument see William Rowe, *The Cosmological Argument* (Princeton, NJ, and London, 1975). Historically influential statements of the argument can be found in Plato, *Laws*, book 10; Aquinas, *Summa Theologiae*, Ia, 2; Descartes, *Meditations on First Philosophy*, Meditation III; John Locke, *An Essay concerning Human Understanding*, book 4, ch. 10. For medieval versions of the argument see Herbert A. Davidson, *Proofs for Eternity, Creation and the Existence of God in Medieval Islamic and Jewish Philosophy* (Oxford, 1987). For Aquinas on the argument and its implications see Brian Davies, *The Thought of Thomas Aquinas* (Oxford, 1992). For modern attempts to advance a version of the cosmological argument see

David Braine, *The Reality of Time and the Existence of God* (Oxford, 1988); Germain Grisez, *Beyond the New Theism* (Notre Dame, Ind., and London, 1975); Barry Miller, *From Existence to God* (London and New York, 1992); John J. Shepherd, *Experience, Inference and God* (London, 1975). For a research bibliography on the cosmological argument, see Clement Dore, *Theism* (Dordrecht, Boston, and Lancaster, 1984), 166–70.

A good general work on the argument from design is Thomas McPherson, *The Argument from Design* (London, 1972). See also R. H. Hurlbutt, *Hume, Newton and the Design Argument* (Lincoln, Nebr., 1965); J. C. A. Gaskin, *Hume's Philosophy of Religion* (2nd edn., London, 1988), ch. 2; Robert Hambourger, 'The Argument from Design', in Cora Diamond and Jenny Teichman (eds.), *Intention and Intentionality* (Brighton, 1979). Writings by Richard Swinburne defending the argument from design include the following: 'The Argument from Design', *Philosophy*, 43 (1968); 'The Argument from Design—A Defence', *Religious Studies*, 8 (1972); *The Existence of God* (rev. edn.), ch. 8 and Appendices A and B.

The claim to experience God is often discussed under the heading 'Religious Experience' or 'Mysticism'. Works that purport to deal with these topics may therefore be usefully considered with reference to experience of God. One might begin by looking at Peter Donovan, *Interpreting Religious Experience* (London, 1979); S. Hook (ed.), *Religious Experience and Truth* (New York, 1961); H. J. N. Horsburgh, 'The Claims of Religious Experience', *Australasian Journal of Philosophy*, 35 (1957), reprinted in J. Houston (ed.), *Is it Reasonable to Believe in God?* (Edinburgh, London, and Melbourne, 1984); Steven T. Katz (ed.), *Mysticism and Philosophical Analysis* (London, 1978). See also Caroline Franks Davis, *The Evidential Force of Religious Experience* (Oxford, 1989) and William P. Alston, *Perceiving God* (Ithaca and London, 1991).

A concise and reliable introduction to recent discussions of God's attributes is Ronald H. Nash, *The Concept of God* (Grand Rapids, Mich., 1983). For modern philosophical study of eternity and time-lessness, each arguing for different conclusions, see Paul Helm, *Eternal God* (Oxford, 1988); Brian Leftow, *Time and Eternity* (Ithaca, NY, and London, 1991); Nelson Pike, *God and Timelessness* (London, 1970); John C. Yates, *The Timelessness of God* (Lanham, Md., New York, and London, 1990). For a discussion of classical texts on eternity see F. H. Brabant, *Time and Eternity in Christian Thought* (London, 1937); Richard Sorabji, *Time, Creation and the Continuum* (London, 1983); Michael J. Dodds, *The Unchanging God of Love: A Study of the Teaching of St Thomas Aquinas on Divine*

Immutability in View of Certain Contemporary Criticism of this Doctrine (Fribourg, 1986). For an introduction to process theologians see John B. Cobb and David Ray Griffin, *Process Theology: An Introductory Exposition* (Belfast, 1976). For an introduction to process theologians, with a critique, see David Basinger, *Divine Power in Process Theism* (New York, 1988).

On issues relevant to the relationship between morality and religion see Paul Helm (ed.), *Divine Commands and Morality* (Oxford, 1981). Students approaching the topic of morality and religion would benefit from some work on contemporary moral philosophy. Good introductions are W. D. Hudson, *A Century of Moral Philosophy* (Guildford and London, 1980); D. D. Raphael, *Moral Philosophy* (Oxford, 1981); J. G. Warnock, *Contemporary Moral Philosophy* (London, 1967). For a general account of Kant on religion, including an analysis of his moral argument for God's existence, see Bernard M. G. Reardon, *Kant as Philosophical Theologian* (London, 1988).

For a reader including important texts on miracles see Richard Swinburne (ed.), *Miracles* (New York and London, 1989). For Hume on miracles and for the background to Hume on miracles see R. M. Burns, *The Great Debate on Miracles: From Joseph Glanville to David Hume* (London and Toronto, 1981). A collection of essays relevant to Descartes on mind and body can be found in Willis Doney (ed.), *Descartes* (London and Melbourne, 1968). See also Bernard Williams, *Descartes: The Project of Pure Enquiry* (Harmondsworth, 1978). John Hick's *Death and Eternal Life* and H. D. Lewis's *The Self and Immortality* both contain extremely good bibliographies on matters relating to the topic of life after death.

For an excellent reader on life after death see Paul Edwards (ed.), *Immortality* (New York, 1992). For a selection of different views on life after death see Stephen T. Davis (ed.), *Death and Afterlife* (London, 1989). For recent philosophical essays on mind and body consult Anthony Kenny, *The Metaphysics of Mind* (Oxford, 1989); Colin McGinn, *The Character of Mind* (Oxford, 1982); Sydney Shoemaker and Richard Swinburne, *Personal Identity* (Oxford, 1984); Richard Swinburne, *The Evolution of the Soul* (Oxford, 1986). An excellent philosophical and theological critique of Cartesian views on persons is Fergus Kerr, *Theology after Wittgenstein* (Oxford, 1986). For an important discussion of personal identity produced in the context of a full-scale treatment of identity see C. J. F. Williams, *What is Identity?* (Oxford, 1989). For a discussion of the desirability of life after death see Thomas Nagel, 'Death', in *Mortal Questions* (Cambridge, 1979).

Index

OXFORD

MORE OXFORD PAPERBACKS

This book is just one of nearly 1000 Oxford Paperbacks currently in print. If you would like details of other Oxford Paperbacks, including titles in the World's Classics, Oxford Reference, Oxford Books, OPUS, Past Masters, Oxford Authors, and Oxford Shakespeare series, please write to:

UK and Europe: Oxford Paperbacks Publicity Manager, Arts and Reference Publicity Department, Oxford University Press, Walton Street, Oxford OX2 6DP.

Customers in UK and Europe will find Oxford Paperbacks available in all good bookshops. But in case of difficulty please send orders to the Cash-with-Order Department, Oxford University Press Distribution Services, Saxon Way West, Corby, Northants NN18 9ES. Tel: 0536 741519; Fax: 0536 746337. Please send a cheque for the total cost of the books, plus £1.75 postage and packing for orders under £20; £2.75 for orders over £20. Customers outside the UK should add 10% of the cost of the books for postage and packing.

USA: Oxford Paperbacks Marketing Manager, Oxford University Press, Inc., 200 Madison Avenue, New York, N.Y. 10016.

Canada: Trade Department, Oxford University Press, 70 Wynford Drive, Don Mills, Ontario M3C 1J9.

Australia: Trade Marketing Manager, Oxford University Press, G.P.O. Box 2784Y, Melbourne 3001, Victoria.

South Africa: Oxford University Press, P.O. Box 1141, Cape Town 8000.

PHILOSOPHY IN OXFORD PAPERBACKS
THE GREAT PHILOSOPHERS
Bryan Magee

Beginning with the death of Socrates in 399, and following the story through the centuries to recent figures such as Bertrand Russell and Wittgenstein, Bryan Magee and fifteen contemporary writers and philosophers provide an accessible and exciting introduction to Western philosophy and its greatest thinkers.

Bryan Magee in conversation with:

A. J. Ayer

Michael Ayers

Miles Burnyeat

Frederick Copleston

Hubert Dreyfus

Anthony Kenny

Sidney Morgenbesser

Martha Nussbaum

John Passmore

Anthony Quinton

John Searle

Peter Singer

J. P. Stern

Geoffrey Warnock

Bernard Williams

'Magee is to be congratulated . . . anyone who sees the programmes or reads the book will be left in no danger of believing philosophical thinking is unpractical and uninteresting.' Ronald Hayman, *Times Educational Supplement*

'one of the liveliest, fast-paced introductions to philosophy, ancient and modern that one could wish for' *Universe*